Lizbet & Daughters

COUNTRY COOKING

© Copyright April 2009 | Elizabeth Troyer

All rights reserved. No portion of this book may be reproduced by any means, electronic or mechanical, including photocopying, recording, or by any information storage retrieval system, without written permission of the copyright owner, except for the inclusion of brief quotations for a review.

First Printing	April 2007	2.5 m
Second Printing	May 2009	2.5 m
Third Printing	December 2013	2 m

For additional books, contact:

Elizabeth Troyer

2531 State Route 93, Sugarcreek, Ohio 44681

ph: 330.852.1354

Carlisle Printing
OF WALNUT CREEK Ltd.

2673 TR 421
Sugarcreek, OH 44681

Introduction

FOR ME, A DREAM has come true. It has been in the back of my mind for a long time to get our family recipes all in one book, especially so since the granddaughters are getting married and need recipes. Our daughters so kindly helped me or I'd never have gotten it accomplished. A special thank-you to my daughters and granddaughters for their encouragement and help in handing in their favorite recipes.

My dear husband Delbert also deserves credit. With six daughters to teach how to cook and bake, all mothers know there are plenty of flops! All six worked at factories and at times served as a *maud*. They all liked to try new recipes, so many recipes were tried out. Some were not to our liking and were made only once! Delbert was so very patient and encouraging through the girls' learning years. Thanks to his mother for teaching him to be thankful for the food that's prepared and not be a complaining, picky eater.

One tradition that my family remembers is that Saturday dinners without freshly baked custard pie, made by using my mother's recipe, were very few. Some of these recipes were ones our mothers, Mrs. Roman (Mattie) Troyer and Mrs. Noah (Lovina) Miller, used. We have many fond memories of eating at their table. We hope this cookbook can be enjoyed and will prove useful to others.

— *Lizbet*

Delbert	born 03-10-1928	Died Apr. 30, 2010
Elizabeth	born 02-14-1930	
married	12-07-1950	

Lizbet and Daughters—Country Cooking

Contributors

MARTHA, born 12-14-1951, married to Merle D. Miller, born 03-01-1952. Address: 4994 SR 557, Millersburg, Ohio.

Children:

Marion	born 09-12-1975
Marnita	born 03-04-1977, married Daniel H. Miller
Merle Ray	born 03-26-1982, married Cheryl Miller
Maynard	born 05-31-1986, married Laura V. Miller
Mary Elizabeth	stillborn 05-25-1989

RUBY, born 09-19-1954, married Vernon R. Miller, born 06-23-1953. Address: 824 Pleasant Valley Road SW, Sugarcreek, Ohio.

Children:

Regina	born 06-08-1976, died 06-12-1976
Kristine	born 05-05-1978, married Paul Hershberger, Jr.
Linda	born 09-07-1979, married Andrew S. Yoder
Mandy	born 04-06-1981, married James J. Troyer
Nora	born 04-30-1983, married Leon R. Hochstetler
Mark	born 06-20-1985
Arlen	born 12-01-1987, married Ruth Ann V. Miller

Christ is the head of the home
The unseen guest at every meal
The silent listener to every conversation.

Lizbet and Daughters—Country Cooking

contributors, cont.

INA, born 06-07-1956, married Abe H. Mast, born 04-12-1955. Address: 2058 SR 93, Baltic, Ohio.
Children:

Anna Lisa	born 09-17-1980, married Orin J. Mast
Rachel	born 07-12-1982, married Merle J. Troyer
Aaron	born 11-25-1983, married Marlene W. Miller
Carrie	born 09-19-1986, married Henry Hershberger
Naomi	born 07-12-1988, married Steven Hershberger
Leah	born 10-12-1992

NAOMI, born 06-15-1958, married Aden H. Beachy, born 08-25-1956. Address: 5908 TR 355, Millersburg, Ohio.
Children:

Matthew	born 05-01-1982, married Regina P. Kauffman
Ruby	born 05-21-1985, married Alvin A. Schlabach
Rebekah	born 11-02-1987, married Marion Troyer

LINDA, born 06-07-1961, married John A. Miller, born 04-20-1960. Address: 2541 SR 93, Sugarcreek, Ohio.
Children:

Nathan	born 05-14-1987
Laina	born 07-19-1988, married Emanuel R. Troyer
Andrew	born 12-11-1990
David	born 10-17-1994
Eva	born 12-21-1997

contributors, cont.

DOROTHY, born 11-12-1966, married Andrew Beachy, Jr., born 04-13-1963. Address: 7119 SR 515, Dundee, Ohio.

Children:
Emily	born 06-10-1989, married Joe E. Troyer
Ian	born 11-19-1991, married Susan A. Miller
Joey	born 10-13-1993
Matthew	born 03-24-1997
Michael	born 04-09-1999
Caleb	born 06-27-2002, died 07-17-2002
Luke	born 10-13-2004

MAYNARD, born 04-27-1969, married Marietta Mast, born 07-02-1970. Address: 129 SR 7, Columbiana, Ohio.

Children:
Diana	born 05-19-1992
Laurie	born 06-23-1993
Hannah	born 11-07-1997
Sara	stillborn 02-15-1999
Samantha	born 05-14-2000
Benjamin	born 07-08-2003

Lizbet and Daughters—Country Cooking

Memories

Family ties are precious things,
    Woven through the years
Of memories of togetherness—
    Of laughter, love and tears.

Family ties are cherished things,
    Forged in childhood days
By love of parents, deep and true,
    And sweet familiar ways.

Family ties are treasured things,
    And far though we may roam,
The tender bands with those we love
    Still pull our hearts toward home.

—*Virginia Blanck Moore*

Lizbet and Daughters—Country Cooking

Memories of Mother XIII

Appetizers, Beverages and Dips 1

Breads, Rolls, Muffins and Cereals 17

Breakfast 37

Soups, Salads and Salad Dressings 49

Meats and Main Dishes.................... 77

Cookies and Bars 123

Cakes and Frostings...................... 163

Desserts 197

Pies..................................... 231

Candies and Snacks...................... 259

Large Quantity Recipes................... 275

Canning and Freezing.................... 287

Miscellaneous........................... 307

Index 321

Lizbet and Daughters—Country Cooking

Memories of Mother

*Following are recipes that Mother used,
and are in her own handwriting.*

Oatmeal Cake
1½ cup quick Oatmeal
1 ¾ " Boiling water
1. ½ cup flour
¾ cup Butter
¼ " white Sugar
1 ½ " Brown sugar
3 eggs,
1 ½ teaspoon Cinnamon
1 ½ " " Soda
pinch Salt,
Soak the oatmeal in
Boiling water
while Creaming the

Butter & Sugar
together. Add
eggs + Beat well.
sift flour, Soda
and Cinnamon, Sift
together. add
alternately with
the oatmeal
mixture. Bake
in 9 x 12 greased Pan
for a about 30 min.
Remove from Oven
to spread with topping
and return to oven
for about 5 min.
for Topping

1 Cup Cocoanut
½ " Butter
1 teaspoon Vanilla
1 Cup Brown Sugar
1 " nuts
¼ " Cream

XIII

Lizbet and Daughters—Country Cooking

Very good Ginger Bread

1 cup Gran. Sugar
1/2 " Butter or Lard
2 eggs
1 cup Dark molasses
2 level teaspoon Soda
1/4 teaspoon Cloves
1/2 " " Cinnamon
1 large " Ginger
2 1/2 cup flour
1 cup hot (rst. Boil) water - last

Waffles

6 eggs
6 T. flour
3 teaspoon Baking P.
1/3 teaspoon salt
1 cup sweet milk

Makes 8 — 7 inch Waffles

Glazed Doughnuts

1 cup Sugar
1 " Shortening
1 qt Scalding milk & cooled to Lukewarm
1 cup mashed potatoes
6 eggs. 2 teaspoon Salt
3 pk yeast. 13 cup sifted flour

Blend shortening in lukewarm milk, & Sugar, then add beaten eggs, Salt & yeast which had been soaked in 1/2 cup warm water, add flour & let stand 1 hr. then make in Doughnuts & let rise again.
Bake & Glaze, from the miller Cousin Circle letter, guess it was from Ale's Lizzie in Geauga

Appetizers, Beverages & Dips

Home is where the heart is,

The soul's bright guiding star.

Home is where real love is,

Where our own dear ones are.

Home means someone waiting,

To give a welcome smile.

Home means peace and joy and rest

And everything worthwhile.

—*Author Unknown*

Ice Slush

2 (3 oz.) pkg. Jell-O, cherry, orange, lemon or lime
2 c. sugar
1 qt. boiling water
2 c. cold water
46 oz. pineapple juice
12 oz. frozen orange juice
7-Up

Dissolve Jell-O and sugar in boiling water, then add cold water, pineapple juice and orange juice. Freeze. Fill glass ¾ full with slush. Fill it up with 7-Up. Refreshing in warm weather. To fill a 5 gallon cooler, mix 2 batches and add 1 liter 7-Up.

Sherbet Punch

½ gal. sherbet, any flavor
2 liters 7-Up

Mix all together and enjoy. Very refreshing.

Apple Punch

3 cans frozen apple juice
4 liters Sprite
4 liters ginger ale

Mix well and serve.

Orange Slush Drink

6 bananas
12 oz. orange juice
2 (48 oz.) cans pineapple juice
3 c. water
1 c. sugar
2 qt. (+) 7-Up, chilled

Mash bananas in blender. Add remaining ingredients, except 7-Up. Freeze at least 24 hours or longer. Remove from freezer 1 hour before serving; add 7-Up.

Lizbet and Daughters—Country Cooking

Golden Punch

7 pkg. orange Kool-Aid
48 oz. frozen orange juice

10 liters Sprite or 7-Up

Prepare Kool-Aid according to package directions. Mix all together. Makes 5 gallons. Delicious.

Purple Cow

1 c. grape juice, chilled
2-3 Tbsp. sugar, optional

3-5 Tbsp. milk
2 lg. scoops vanilla ice cream

Combine grape juice, sugar and milk in shaker. Shake well and add ice cream. Shake again until blended. Pour into cold glasses and serve with a smile.

Slushy Drink

3 pkg. Jell-O, any flavor
9 c. hot water
4 c. white sugar

4 c. water
2 (46 oz.) cans pineapple juice
2 liters 7-Up

Mix Jell-O and hot water. Cook sugar and water. Add to Jell-O mixture. Add pineapple juice. Freeze. Stir in 7-Up while it thaws.

Wedding Punch

20 pkg. watermelon cherry Kool-Aid
12 c. white sugar

6 qt. water
10 liters 7-Up
4 qt. crushed ice

Mix Kool-Aid and sugar with water. Put 7-Up and crushed ice in after everything is mixed.

Quick Root Beer

2 c. white sugar
1 gal. water
4 tsp. root beer extract
1 tsp. yeast

Mix really well. Pour into jars and seal. Set in sun for 4 hours.

Tea Concentrate

4 c. water
¾ c. sugar
4 c. lightly packed tea leaves

Boil water and sugar together for 5 minutes. Add tea leaves. Cover and let set for 6-7 hours or overnight. I like to make a large batch and freeze in 2-cup containers. (2 c. concentrate + 2 qt. water.)

Rhubarb Punch

2 qt. rhubarb
2½ c. white sugar
2 Tbsp. strawberry Jell-O or Kool-Aid
2 c. hot water
2 c. pineapple juice
½ c. lemon juice
2 liters 7-Up

Dice rhubarb and add water to cover. Boil for 10 minutes. Drain in colander for 1 hour. If there isn't enough juice, add water to make 2 qt. Combine sugar and Jell-O with hot water. Add the rest of the juices. Cold pack for 14 minutes or freeze. Add 7-Up when ready to serve. Very refreshing.

Eggnog

1 egg
¼ c. sugar
2 c. milk
⅛ tsp. salt
½ tsp. vanilla
½ tsp. nutmeg

Beat egg with egg beater until fluffy. Add sugar, milk, salt and vanilla. Beat mixture again. Sprinkle nutmeg on top.

Lizbet and Daughters—Country Cooking

Chocolate Syrup

4 c. brown sugar
4 c. white sugar
2 c. cocoa

4 c. water, divided
½ c. corn syrup
¼ c. vanilla

Mix sugars, cocoa and 2 c. water into 6 qt. pan until blended. Add remaining 2 c. water and stir again. Bring to a boil for 5 minutes on low heat. Add corn syrup and vanilla. To can syrup, put in jars and put lids on. It will seal. Approximately 3 qt. This is good to make chocolate milk.

Cappuccino

16 oz. French vanilla Coffee Mate
1½ c. hot chocolate mix
1 c. dry milk

½ c. instant coffee
1 c. powdered sugar
½ c. white sugar

Mix all together. Store in airtight container. Put ¼ c. mix into a mug; add 1 c. hot water. Enjoy.

Hot Chocolate Mix

5 c. dry milk
6 oz. dry coffee creamer

1 c. powdered sugar
2 c. chocolate drink mix

Mix all ingredients. Store in airtight container. Use ⅓ c. mix to 1 c. hot water.

Maple Hot Chocolate

¼ c. white sugar
1 Tbsp. cocoa
½ tsp. salt
¼ c. hot water
1 Tbsp. butter

4 c. milk
1 tsp. maple flavoring
1 tsp. vanilla flavoring
12 lg. marshmallows

In large saucepan combine sugar, cocoa and salt. Stir in hot water and butter. Bring to a boil. Add milk, maple flavoring, vanilla and marshmallows.

Kraft Cheese

2 lb. white American cheese
1½ c. milk, divided

Put ½ c. milk in top of double boiler with cheese slices. Put warm water in bottom of double boiler. Keep hot, but do not boil. Heat until cheese is soft and creamy. Stir and mix in rest of milk. Stir often. When creamy and melted, heat for another 10 minutes. Pour into a container that has a cover to keep a skin from forming on top.

Fresh Salsa

3 med. tomatoes
1 med. onion
½ c. green peppers +
  a little hot pepper
½ tsp. salt
¼ tsp. black pepper
½ tsp. sugar
1 Tbsp. vinegar

Place all ingredients in chopper and chop until chunky. Delicious served with tortilla chips.

Cream Cheese Salsa Dip

8 oz. cream cheese
16 oz. sour cream
1 pkg. taco seasoning
1 (12 oz.) jar salsa
8 oz. cheddar cheese, shredded

Mix cream cheese, sour cream and taco seasoning together. Spread in a Tupperware container. Layer salsa on top. Add a layer of cheddar cheese. Serve with tortilla chips.

Cream Cheese and Salsa Dip

8 oz. cream cheese
1 pt. salsa

Soften cream cheese, then add salsa. Serve with tortilla chips.

Lizbet and Daughters—Country Cooking

Warm Taco Dip

2 lb. hamburger
1 lb. Velveeta cheese
1 can tomato soup
1 can cream of mushroom soup
1 tsp. chili powder
1 tsp. Worcestershire sauce
1 tsp. onion powder
1 tsp. garlic salt
green peppers
onions

Fry hamburger; add spices and soups, then add Velveeta cheese. Serve with taco chips.

Cheesy Chicken Dip

1 c. fried chicken breast pieces
1 c. salsa
½ c. sour cream
1 lb. Velveeta cheese

Melt cheese and salsa over low heat. When melted add chicken and sour cream. Serve with assorted crackers or chips.

Sausage Dip

2 lb. sausage
1 (2 lb.) box Velveeta cheese
1 pt. salsa

Brown sausage. Add cheese and melt over low heat. Add salsa. Eat warm with chips.

Cheesy Hamburger Chip Dip

2 lb. Velveeta cheese
1 jar nacho cheese spread
milk to desired thickness
1 pt. salsa
1½ lb. hamburger, fried and drained

An easy way to melt cheese is to put it into the oven in a bowl. Add milk and salsa. Add hamburger. Keep warm in crockpot. Serve with chips.

Bacon Dip

1 c. sour cream
1 c. mayonnaise
½ c. bacon bits
1 Tbsp. parsley
1 Tbsp. onion
1 tsp. dill weed

Mix all ingredients; cover. Refrigerate several hours or overnight. Makes 20 servings.

Layered Taco Delight

8 oz. cream cheese
1 c. sour cream
2 c. salsa
1 lb. hamburger, browned
1 pkg. taco seasoning
shredded lettuce
chopped onions
chopped tomatoes
chopped green peppers
1½ c. shredded cheddar cheese

Mix cream cheese and sour cream. Spread on a large round tray or in a Tupperware pan. Spread salsa on top. Mix hamburger and taco seasoning. Spread on top of salsa. Layer remaining ingredients in order given. Serve with tortilla chips.

Cheesy Dip

1 can cheddar cheese soup
1 can Fiesta nacho cheese soup
16 oz. sour cream
1 lb. Mexican Velveeta cheese

Mix all together and heat until cheese is melted. This is good with nacho or tortilla chips.

Lizbet and Daughters—Country Cooking

Community Dip

2 c. sour cream
½ c. salad dressing
4 oz. cream cheese
1½ tsp. Worcestershire sauce
½ pkg. onion soup mix

1 tsp. sugar
2 tsp. lemon juice
1 Tbsp. ketchup
bacon bits
salt and pepper to taste

Mix everything together and serve with vegetables.

Dill Vegetable Dip

1 c. sour cream
1 tsp. dill weed
1 tsp. onion flakes

1 c. Hellman's mayonnaise
1 tsp. seasoned salt
1 Tbsp. parsley flakes

Mix together. Do not substitute for mayonnaise.

Quick and Easy Tortilla Roll-Ups

8 flour tortillas
Ranch dressing

chip-chopped ham
shredded cheddar cheese

Pour a thin layer of Ranch dressing on tortillas. Layer ham slices on tortillas then shredded cheddar cheese. Roll up and wrap separately in plastic wrap. A treat for lunch boxes.

Church members are like automobiles.
They start missing before they quit.

Tortilla Pinwheels

16 oz. sour cream
4 oz. cream cheese
1 pkg. Ranch dressing mix
8 flour tortillas
broccoli
cauliflower
onions
grated cheddar cheese
crumbled bacon

Mix sour cream, cream cheese and Ranch mix. Spread over tortillas. Top with remaining ingredients. Salsa Master works great to chop broccoli and cauliflower. Roll up and chill overnight. Slice ½" thick.

Appetizer Roll-Ups

5 slices med. sliced ham
8 oz. cream cheese
2 Tbsp. butter
1 c. shredded cheddar cheese
3 Tbsp. chopped green peppers, optional

Mix cream cheese, butter, cheese and peppers together. Spread on ham. Roll up and refrigerate. Slice when ready to serve.

Fruit Dip

2 c. pineapple juice
2 Tbsp. clear jel
8-9 oz. Cool Whip
½ c. white sugar
8 oz. cream cheese
fruit

Cook juice, sugar and clear jel until thick. Let cool. Add cream cheese. When cold add Cool Whip. Favorite fruits are bananas, apples and strawberries.

Lizbet and Daughters—Country Cooking

Fruit Dip

8 oz. cream cheese
½ c. sour cream
¼ c. white sugar
¼ c. packed brown sugar
1-2 Tbsp. maple syrup

Mix all together and serve with fruit.

Fruit Dip

8 oz. cream cheese
8 oz. marshmallow créme
12 oz. Cool Whip

Mix all ingredients together. Serve with fresh fruit.

Caramel Dip for Apples

sweetened condensed milk

Remove labels from cans. Set 4 cans in a 4-quart stainless steel kettle. Fill with cold water. Turn on medium-high heat until it cooks. Turn down to medium. Keep adding warm water. Do not let the water evaporate or cans will explode. Boil for 2 hours. Cool. Delicious dip for Golden Delicious apples.

Cheez Whiz

2 lb. Velveeta cheese
1 can evaporated milk
1 c. milk
3 Tbsp. butter

Melt together in double boiler.

Pineapple Cheese Ball

16 oz. cream cheese
¼ c. chopped green pepper
1 Tbsp. seasoned salt
2 Tbsp. chopped onion
18½ oz. crushed pineapple, drained
2 c. chopped nuts

Mix everything together except nuts. Chill and shape into ball. Roll into nuts. Refrigerate until ready to serve. Can be frozen.

Cheese Ball

16 oz. cream cheese
16 oz. Velveeta cheese
8 oz. cheddar cheese
1 tsp. onion salt
1 Tbsp. finely chopped onion
1 Tbsp. Worcestershire sauce

Mix together. Serve with crackers.

Cheese Ball

16 oz. cream cheese
1 sm. pkg. shredded cheddar cheese
1 Tbsp. chopped onions, optional
1 tsp. lemon juice
2 tsp. Worcestershire sauce
1 Tbsp. parsley flakes
seasoned salt

Mix all together except seasoned salt. Chill until firm. Form into ball and roll in seasoned salt.

Chocolate Chip Cheese Ball

8 oz. cream cheese, softened
½ c. butter
¾ c. powdered sugar
¼ tsp. vanilla
2 Tbsp. brown sugar
½ c. mini chocolate chips

Mix butter, cream cheese and vanilla. Add sugars then chocolate chips. Serve with graham crackers. Keep refrigerated.

Lizbet and Daughters—Country Cooking

Fudgesicles

1 pkg. instant chocolate pudding
2 c. milk
1 c. evaporated milk
¼ c. sugar

Add milk to pudding and stir thoroughly. Add sugar and evaporated milk and let set for 5 minutes. Pour into containers and freeze.

Popsicles

1 pkg. Jell-O
1 pkg. soft drink mix, unsweetened
2 c. cold water
2 c. boiling water
1 c. sugar

Add boiling water to Jell-O, sugar and drink mix. Stir until dissolved. Add cold water and pour into individual containers. Freeze.

Pinwheel Finger Jell-O

3 oz. Jell-O
¾ c. boiling water
2 c. mini marshmallows

Dissolve ingredients together and pour in an 8" pan. When set, roll up and slice.

Finger Jell-O

3 pkg. Jell-O, any flavor
4 c. boiling water
4 pkg. Knox gelatin
1 c. cold water

Dissolve gelatin in cold water. Mix Jell-O with boiling water. When dissolved, add gelatin. Put in cookie sheets and cool. Cut in squares.

Finger Jell-O

2 Tbsp. gelatin
3 (3 oz.) pkg. any flavor Jell-O
3 c. boiling water
1 c. whipping cream

Place first 3 ingredients in bowl and stir until dissolved. Add cream and pour in pan. Will separate as it cools.

Eagle Brand Finger Jell-O

4 pkg. Jell-O, divided
1⅓ c. water, divided
4 pkg. gelatin, divided
4 c. boiling water, divided

White Layer –
4 pkg. gelatin
1 can sweetened condensed milk
¾ c. cold water
2 c. boiling water

Use 4 different flavors Jell-O. Add 1 pkg. gelatin dissolved in ⅓ c. cold water to each box of Jell-O with 1 c. boiling water. White Layer: Dissolve gelatin in cold water. Combine boiling water and sweetened condensed milk. Add to dissolved gelatin. Layer 1 flavor of Jell-O in 9" x 13" pan. Chill until set, then cover with 1⅓ c. white layer and chill again. Repeat until you have 7 layers, ending with Jell-O. Sometimes the white layer sets before last layers are finished. Set in dish of hot water until it is thin again. A good Christmas snack, using red and green Jell-O alternately.

Patty Shells

2 eggs
1 c. milk
1 c. flour
1 tsp. white sugar
1 tsp. baking powder
pinch of salt

Beat eggs. Add milk. Mix dry ingredients and slowly add egg mixture. Use a patty iron and dip into mixture, then deep fry. Roll into powdered sugar.

Some people eat to live, others live to eat.

Lizbet and Daughters—Country Cooking

Breads, Rolls, Muffins & Cereals

Give us this day our daily bread.

. . . . . .

Man shall not live by bread alone,

Our Lord and Master said,

But by the living Word of God

Our souls must needs be fed.

—*Selected*

. . . . .

Let us not forget to be more grateful

to the giver of our food

than to the one who prepared it.

Recipe for Life

1 c. good thoughts
3 c. forgiveness
1 c. kind deeds

2 c. well-beaten faults
1 c. consideration for others

Mix thoroughly and add tears of joy, sorrow and sympathy for others. Fold in 4 c. prayer and faith to lighten other ingredients and raise the texture to new heights of Christian living. After pouring all of this into your daily life, bake well with the heat of human kindness. Serve with a smile.

Tips for Breadmaking

Beat liquid and first few cups of flour vigorously with wire whisk for fine textured bread. Let dough set for 30 minutes before kneading. Spray pans with cooking spray for easy removal from pans. You do not need to butter the tops when you take the loaves out of the oven if you put them in plastic bags while still hot. The bags will gather moisture, but it will be reabsorbed by the bread and make it nice and soft. Oven does not need to be preheated. Turn oven to 350° and bake for 30 minutes. If oven is preheated, bake for 25 minutes.

Honey Bread

2 c. scalded milk
2 c. water
1 c. honey
4 eggs, beaten
1 c. vegetable oil

½ c. sugar
8 tsp. yeast
4 tsp. salt
1 c. whole wheat flour
bread flour as needed

Dissolve yeast in water and add liquids, sugar, salt and whole wheat flour. Add enough bread flour to make a stiff dough. Let set for 30 minutes; add flour as needed to knead. Let rise until double in bulk, punch down and let rise again. Bake at 350° for 30 minutes. Makes 7 loaves.

Lizbet and Daughters—Country Cooking

Bread

¾ c. sugar
¾ c. bread flour
1 Tbsp. salt
¼ c. instant potato flakes

3½ c. warm water
2 Tbsp. yeast
¾ c. vegetable oil
8 c. bread flour

Mix all ingredients together except for 8 c. flour. Beat well by hand or with mixer. Let set for 10 minutes, then add rest of flour. Let rise until double in size. Work out in 4 pans. Let rise again. Bake at 300° for 30 minutes.

Bread

4 c. warm water
8 tsp. yeast
1 c. sugar
1 c. oil

4 tsp. salt
2 c. whole wheat flour
10 c. bread flour

Dissolve sugar and yeast in warm water. Add oil, salt and whole wheat flour and beat vigorously with a whisk. Add rest of flour as needed to make a stiff dough. Let set for 30 minutes before kneading. Let rise. Work down and let rise again. Makes 5 loaves.

Bread

1¾ c. flour
¾ c. sugar (half brown, half white)
1 Tbsp. salt
1 c. boiling water
2 c. cold water

2 Tbsp. yeast
¾ c. vegetable oil
1 c. whole wheat flour
3 Tbsp. vinegar
5-6 c. bread flour

Mix first 9 ingredients with a mixer or egg beater for 2-3 minutes. Let set for 15 minutes. Add the bread flour and knead. Let rise until double in size. Shape into 4 loaves and place in pans to rise again until nearly double. Bake at 350° for 25 minutes.

Zucchini Pizza Bread

12 c. bread flour
4 c. grated zucchini, unpeeled
1½ c. milk
3 Tbsp. salt
3 eggs, beaten
2 Tbsp. yeast
⅔ c. butter

4 Tbsp. sugar
2 Tbsp. oregano
3 Tbsp. onion
2 c. cubed Swiss cheese
2 c. cubed Colby cheese
½ c. warm water
pepperoni, cut in small pieces

Scald milk. Add butter, sugar and salt. Add zucchini, oregano and onion. Dissolve yeast in warm water and add to milk mixture. Add beaten eggs and last add cheeses and pepperoni. Knead in flour well. Let rise until double; knead down and let rise again. Form loaves and let rise again. Bake at 350° for 35-40 minutes or until done.

Bread Sticks

bread dough
butter, melted
Parmesan cheese

garlic salt
pizza sauce

Use regular bread or dinner roll dough. Let rise and shape into ½" x 7" rectangles. Bake. When finished dip in butter, then sprinkle with Parmesan cheese and garlic salt. Serve with warm pizza sauce. Delicious.

I mixed up a Johnny cake and forgot to add the "rais'ins" and since I didn't put it in, it baked without the "rais'ins." It ended up very flat – results from missing "rais'ins." If fluffy cake is your desire, add full the proper "rais'ins."

P.S. "Rais'ins" are baking powder or soda.

Lizbet and Daughters—Country Cooking

Cheesy Onion Burger Buns

5¾-6¾ c. flour, divided
3 Tbsp. sugar
1½ tsp. salt
2 Tbsp. yeast

2 Tbsp. butter, melted
2 c. hot water
1½ c. shredded cheddar cheese
¼ c. minced onion

In a large bowl combine 2 c. water, sugar, salt, yeast and butter. Let set until yeast is dissolved. Add 3 c. flour and mix really well. Stir in cheese, onion and enough of the remaining flour to form a soft dough. Turn out onto floured surface. Knead until smooth and elastic, about 6-8 minutes. Place dough in a warm place and let rise until double, about 1 hour. Punch dough down onto a lightly floured surface. Divide dough into 20 equal pieces, shape in balls and put on a greased baking sheet. Let rise until double. Bake at 350° for 15-20 minutes. These are delicious with barbecued burgers.

Family Reunion Buns

⅔ c. milk
⅔ c. sugar
⅓ c. butter
1 tsp. salt

⅔ c. warm water
2 pkg. (2 Tbsp.) yeast
3 eggs, beaten
6¾ c. bread flour

Scald milk; add sugar, salt and butter. Cool to lukewarm. Add yeast to warm water. Add eggs and yeast mixture to lukewarm milk mixture. Add flour; knead until smooth and elastic. Place in greased bowl. Brush top with oil. Let rise until doubled, about 1 hour. Punch down and make 24 buns, place about 2" apart on cookie sheet and let rise until doubled. Bake at 400° for about 20 minutes.

2008: Americans are getting stronger. Twenty years ago, it took 2 people to carry $10.00 worth of groceries. Today a 5 year old can do it.

Grandma Miller's Cinnamon Rolls

⅔ c. milk, scalded
½ c. white sugar
1 tsp. salt
6 Tbsp. shortening, melted
⅔ c. warm water
2 pkg. (2 Tbsp.) yeast
2 Tbsp. white sugar
3 eggs, well beaten
4 c. bread flour
butter
brown sugar
cinnamon

Combine first 4 ingredients. Cool to lukewarm. Measure water, yeast and sugar into bowl. Let set until dissolved. Add milk mixture and eggs. Stir in bread flour. Let rise for 2 hours. Roll out dough. Spread with butter and sprinkle with brown sugar and cinnamon. Roll together and cut in slices. Put in pans and let rise until almost double. Bake at 350° until done. Cool and frost with brown sugar frosting.

Cinnamon Rolls in a Snap

4½ c. biscuit/baking mix
1⅓ c. milk
¼ c. sugar
1 tsp. cinnamon

Icing –
2 c. powdered sugar
2 Tbsp. milk
2 Tbsp. butter, melted
1 tsp. vanilla

In a bowl combine biscuit mix and milk. Turn onto a floured surface; knead 8-10 times. Roll the dough into a 12" x 10" rectangle. Spread with butter. Sprinkle with cinnamon and sugar mixture. Roll up from long side. Cut into 12 slices. Put into greased baking pan. Bake at 450° for 10-12 minutes. Frost while still warm. A very quick and easy roll.

If you don't want the fruits of sin,
stay out of the orchard.

Lizbet and Daughters—Country Cooking

Refrigerator Rolls

½ c. sugar
1 Tbsp. salt
3 Tbsp. cooking oil
¾ c. hot water
1 egg, beaten

2 Tbsp. yeast
1 c. warm water
½ tsp. sugar
5¼ c. bread flour

Mix first 4 ingredients. Let cool to lukewarm. Mix egg and yeast and sugar dissolved in warm water and then add egg and yeast mixture. Now add enough bread flour so it can be worked with the hands. When ready to use, let rise once. Work down and let rise again. Form 2 walnut-sized balls for each muffin cup. Let rise and bake at 350° for 20 minutes.

Sour Cream Rolls

1 Tbsp. yeast
¼ c. warm water
¼ c. sugar
6 Tbsp. butter

1 tsp. salt
½ c. sour cream
2 eggs, beaten
2¼ c. flour

Glaze-
¼ c. butter
½ c. sour cream

¾ c. brown sugar

Knead like bread dough. Cover and let rise for 2 hours. Knead dough and divide into 2 parts. Roll each part into a 12" circle. Brush with melted butter. Top with a mixture of 1 c. brown sugar, 1 tsp. cinnamon and nuts. Cut into 12 wedges. Roll from wide end to point. Put 24 rolls into a cake pan. Let rise. Bake at 350° for 25-30 minutes. For glaze, bring ingredients to a slow boil. Pour over rolls as soon as they are out of oven.

Doughnuts from Scratch

10 c. scalded milk
⅔ c. yeast
13 c. all-purpose flour
10 eggs, beaten

2½ c. white sugar
14 c. all-purpose flour
2½ c. vegetable oil
3 Tbsp. salt

Beat the first 3 ingredients and let set for 20 minutes. Add remaining ingredients. You may have to use your hands to get it all mixed. Let rise for 1 hour. Fry.

Easy Cake Mix Rolls

2 Tbsp. yeast
1 yellow cake mix

4½ c. flour
2½ c. warm water

Soak yeast in warm water. Add cake mix and flour to this. Let rise. Roll out dough and spread with butter, cinnamon and brown sugar. Roll up and cut off pieces. Let rise. Bake at 350° until done.

Sweet Rolls

1 Tbsp. yeast
½ c. warm water
1 c. mashed potatoes
¾ c. butter, melted
½ c. sugar

1 Tbsp. salt
1½ c. warm water
2 eggs, beaten
6 c. flour (approximately)

Soak yeast in warm water. Add remaining ingredients, adding flour to right consistency.

Cinnamon Rolls

½ c. warm water
2 pkg. dry yeast
2 Tbsp. sugar
1 pkg. vanilla instant pudding
½ c. + 2 Tbsp. butter, melted, divided

2 eggs, beaten
1 tsp. salt
6 c. flour
½ c. brown sugar
cinnamon

Combine water, sugar and yeast. Stir until dissolved; set aside. Mix pudding as directed. Add ½ c. butter, eggs and salt. Add yeast mixture. Add flour; knead until smooth. Cover and let rise. Punch down and let rise again. Roll out and brush with melted butter and spread brown sugar and cinnamon on top. Roll like jelly roll and cut. Bake at 350° for 15-20 minutes. Frost with your favorite icing.

Refrigerated Crescent Rolls

1 c. warm water
1 Tbsp. yeast
1 tsp. sugar
3 eggs, beaten

1 tsp. salt
½ c. sugar
½ c. butter, softened
5 c. flour

Beat together first 4 ingredients and let set for 10 minutes. Add remaining ingredients. Knead until smooth. Place in large covered container and refrigerate overnight or up to one week. Makes 2 crusts. This is good to use for vegetable pizza.

Butterhorns

1 Tbsp. yeast
½ c. sugar, divided
3 eggs, beaten
4½-5 c. bread flour

1 c. lukewarm water
½ c. butter, melted
1 tsp. salt

Blend yeast with 1 Tbsp. sugar. Add beaten eggs and rest of sugar. Add the rest of ingredients, adding flour last. Refrigerate overnight. Roll out like pie dough. Cut in pie shaped wedges and roll up. After rolled up, dip in melted butter. Let rise for 3 hours and bake at 325° for 15-20 minutes. If you leave in refrigerator for a while, punch down each day.

Pluckets

1 c. scalded milk
⅓ c. sugar
½ tsp. salt
1 Tbsp. yeast

¼ c. lukewarm water
⅓ c. butter, melted
3 eggs, well beaten
3¾ c. flour

Dissolve yeast in water. Add sugar, butter and salt to scalded milk. When lukewarm, add dissolved yeast, eggs and enough flour to make a stiff batter. Cover and let rise until mixture is doubled in size. Knead and let rise again. Roll into small balls, about the size of walnuts, and dip in melted butter. Roll each ball in mixture of ¾ c. sugar, ½ c. ground nuts and 3 tsp. cinnamon. Pile balls loosely in an ungreased angel food cake pan and let rise again for 30 minutes. Bake about 40 minutes, beginning with 400° and decreasing heat after 10 minutes. Bake until brown. Invert immediately. Serve warm.

Lizbet and Daughters—Country Cooking

Sweet Potato Butterhorns

1 c. water
2 pkg. yeast
2 c. cooked, mashed sweet potatoes
½ c. sugar
½ c. shortening

1 egg, beaten
1½ tsp. salt
5-5½ c. bread flour
¼ c. butter

Dissolve yeast in water; let set for 5 minutes. Beat in sweet potatoes, sugar, shortening, egg, salt and 3 c. flour. Add enough remaining flour to form a stiff dough. Turn onto floured surface. Knead until smooth and elastic. Place in greased bowl. Cover and let rise. Divide into 3 parts. Roll each portion in a 12" circle. Brush with melted butter. Sprinkle with cinnamon and sugar. Cut into 12 pieces. Roll up with pointed end down. Cover and let rise until doubled. Bake at 350° for 15 minutes or until done. Brush with butter. Serve warm with honey butter.

Cheddar Garlic Biscuits

2 c. Bisquick
¾ c. milk
½ c. shredded cheddar cheese

2 Tbsp. butter, melted
½ tsp. garlic powder

Heat oven to 450°. Stir Bisquick, milk and cheese until soft dough forms. Drop by spoonful onto ungreased cookie sheet. Bake for 8-10 minutes or until golden brown. Stir together butter and garlic powder and brush over warm biscuits. Makes 9-10 biscuits.

Southern Biscuits

2 c. flour
¼ c. shortening
¾ tsp. salt

3 tsp. baking powder
1 c. buttermilk
1 tsp. soda

Cut shortening into the dry mixture until it resembles small crumbs. Add milk all at once and stir just until dough pulls away from bowl. Roll out to ½" thick. Cut with biscuit cutter. Place on ungreased cookie sheet. Bake at 450° for 10-12 minutes.

Biscuits Supreme

2 c. flour
2 tsp. sugar
½ tsp. salt
½ c. shortening

4 tsp. baking powder
½ tsp. cream of tartar
⅔ c. milk

Sift dry ingredients together. Cut in shortening until mixture resembles coarse crumbs. Add milk all at once and stir. Roll ½" thick. Cut with biscuit cutter. Place on ungreased cookie sheet. Bake at 425° for 10-12 minutes.

Doughnuts from Mix

2 c. lukewarm water
1 pkg. (1 Tbsp.) yeast

2½ lb. doughnut mix

Glaze–
1 lb. powdered sugar
1 Tbsp. cornstarch

1 tsp. vanilla
water to desired consistency

Dissolve yeast in water. Add mix until dough is formed. Let rise in a warm place. Roll out and cut with doughnut cutter. Fry. Makes 3 dozen doughnuts.

Garlic Toast

bread
butter

garlic salt
oregano

Spread one side of bread with butter. Sprinkle with garlic salt and oregano. Toast on griddle. Can also use hot dog buns. Very good to eat with spaghetti or Spanish rice. Can also be heated in oven at 350°.

Lizbet and Daughters—Country Cooking

Mini Garlic Bread

4-5 Tbsp. butter, softened
½ tsp. dill weed
½ tsp. garlic powder
4 hot dog buns, sliced

In a bowl combine butter, dill weed and garlic powder, stirring well to blend. Spread on cut side of each hot dog bun. Place on baking sheet. Broil until golden brown.

Pumpkin Bread

3 c. sugar
1 c. vegetable oil
2 c. cooked, mashed pumpkin
1 c. water
4 eggs
1 tsp. baking powder
2 tsp. soda
1½ tsp. salt
1 tsp. cinnamon
½ tsp. nutmeg
4 tsp. pumpkin pie spice
3½ c. flour

Mix well and bake in 3 small loaves at 350° for 1 hour.

Soft Pretzels

2½ c. lukewarm water
3 Tbsp. yeast
¾ c. brown sugar
1 tsp. salt
7-8 c. bread flour

Dissolve yeast in water; let set for 5 minutes, then add sugar, salt and flour. Pull apart in about 15 pieces. Roll with hands to a thin, long rope-like string. Shape like pretzels. Dissolve 1½ tsp. soda in 1 c. hot water. Dip pretzels in this solution. Let rise about 15 minutes. Bake at 400° until brown. Brush with butter; sprinkle with pretzel salt *before* baking.

Corn Bread or Muffins

1 c. cornmeal
½ c. sugar
1 c. flour
1 tsp. salt
½ c. corn oil
2 eggs
1 c. sour milk or buttermilk
1 tsp. soda

Mix all ingredients together and bake at 400° for 15 minutes in a well greased pan or muffin pan.

Pumpkin Cream Cheese Muffins

Cream Cheese Filling–
8 oz. cream cheese
1 egg
1 tsp. vanilla
3 Tbsp. brown sugar

Streusel Topping–
4½ Tbsp. all-purpose flour
5 Tbsp. white sugar
¾ tsp. cinnamon
3 Tbsp. butter
3 Tbsp. chopped nuts

Muffin Batter–
2½ c. all-purpose flour
2 c. white sugar
2 tsp. baking powder
2 tsp. cinnamon
½ tsp. salt
2 eggs
1⅓ c. canned pumpkin
⅓ c. olive oil
2 tsp. vanilla

Cream cheese filling: In a medium bowl beat cream cheese until soft. Add egg, vanilla and brown sugar. Beat until smooth. Set aside. Streusel topping: Mix flour, sugar, cinnamon and nuts. Cut in butter with a fork until crumbly. Muffin batter: Mix flour, sugar, baking powder, cinnamon and salt. Add eggs, pumpkin, oil and vanilla. Beat together until smooth. Fill muffin cups half full. Add 1 Tbsp. cream cheese filling in the middle of batter. Sprinkle streusel topping over top. Bake at 375° for 20-25 minutes. Makes 18 muffins.

Lizbet and Daughters—Country Cooking

Blueberry Sour Cream Streusel Muffins

2 c. sifted all-purpose flour
2 tsp. baking powder
½ tsp. baking soda
½ tsp. salt
3 Tbsp. sugar
1 egg, well beaten
1 c. sour cream

⅓ c. milk
¼ c. vegetable oil
1½ c. blueberries
½ c. light brown sugar, packed
¼ c. all-purpose flour
1 tsp. ground cinnamon
butter

Sift 2 c. flour with baking powder, soda, salt and sugar. Beat egg with sour cream and milk. Stir in oil. Add liquid all at once to dry ingredients. Stir until just blended. Carefully fold in blueberries. Spoon mixture into greased muffin pans. Mix brown sugar with ¼ c. flour and cinnamon. Cut butter into mixture until crumbly. Sprinkle crumbs over top of muffins. Bake at 425° for 15-20 minutes or until topping is deep brown. Remove muffins and cool on a rack. Serve warm or cold. Serves 10-12 people.

Zucchini Muffins

1½ c. all-purpose flour
¾ c. sugar
½ c. brown sugar
1 tsp. soda
1 tsp. cinnamon
½ tsp. salt
1 egg, slightly beaten

½ c. vegetable oil
¼ c. milk
1 Tbsp. lemon juice
1 tsp. vanilla
1 c. shredded zucchini
¼ c. mini chocolate chips
½ c. chopped walnuts

Combine flour, sugars, soda, cinnamon and salt. Combine egg, oil, milk, lemon juice and vanilla. Mix well and stir into dry mixture, just until moistened. Fold in zucchini, chips and nuts. Bake at 350° for 20-25 minutes.

Cappuccino Muffins with Espresso Spread

½ c. butter, melted
¾ c. sugar
1 egg, beaten
1 tsp. cinnamon
2 c. flour
2½ tsp. baking powder

1 tsp. vanilla
½ tsp. salt
1 c. milk
2 Tbsp. instant coffee granules
¾ c. mini chocolate chips

Espresso Spread–
4 oz. cream cheese
1 Tbsp. sugar
½ tsp. instant coffee granules

½ tsp. vanilla
¼ c. mini chocolate chips

Dissolve coffee granules in milk. Mix and bake at 375° for 17-20 minutes. Makes 14 muffins. Store spread in refrigerator.

Cinnamon Apple Muffins

2 c. flour
1 tsp. salt
1 tsp. cinnamon
¾ c. milk
1 c. grated, peeled apples

⅓ c. sugar
1 Tbsp. baking powder
1 egg, beaten
3 Tbsp. shortening, melted

Cinnamon/Sugar Mixture–
1 tsp. cinnamon
⅔ c. white sugar

⅔ c. brown sugar

Sift dry ingredients together. Mix egg, milk, shortening and apples. Add to dry ingredients all at once. Stir only until flour is moistened. Fill muffin pan ⅔ full. Bake at 350° for 25-30 minutes. Dip in melted butter then roll in cinnamon/sugar mixture.

A child grows best in a climate of love, acceptance, joy and peace.

Lizbet and Daughters—Country Cooking

Lollipops

2 c. brown sugar
2 c. water
3 Tbsp. clear jel

Mix brown sugar and clear jel. Add water and cook until thick. In a 9" x 13" pan put 8 small round balls of bread dough. Pour sauce over top. Let rise until almost double. Bake at 350° for 25 minutes. Serve warm with milk.

Apple Fritters

1 c. flour
2 Tbsp. sugar
½ c. milk
1½ tsp. baking powder
½ tsp. salt
1 egg
5-6 apples

Core and peel apples. Slice and put in batter. Drop by spoonful in 1" of fat or oil in frying pan. Drain on paper towel or in colander. Sprinkle with powdered sugar or eat with syrup. Prick with fork when frying to test if apples are soft. Makes about 4 skillets full of fritters.

Grapenuts

8 c. whole wheat flour
4 c. brown sugar
2 Tbsp. salt
3⅓ c. sour milk or buttermilk
½ c. butter, melted
½ tsp. maple flavoring
1 Tbsp. vanilla
1 Tbsp. soda

Mix dry ingredients together. Mix soda in milk; add to dry ingredients. Add butter and flavorings. Mix well. Spread in 2 greased 9" x 13" pans. Bake at 350° until done. Cool; cut into strips and put through Salad Master (shoestrings). Toast at 300° in shallow pans, stirring often.

Chocolate Chip Granola Cereal

6 c. quick oatmeal
2 c. brown sugar
2 tsp. salt
4 c. whole wheat flour

1 c. coconut, optional
1½ tsp. baking soda
1 c. chocolate chips
1½ c. butter, melted

Mix all dry ingredients except chips. Add melted butter. Mix well with hands. Place in two 9" x 13" cake pans and bake at 400° for 30 minutes. Stir often to keep from getting lumpy. Add chocolate chips after cereal is cooled. Very delicious and nutritious.

Many people have tried to be Christians, but they have found it difficult because they did not have enough courage to be different from the world.

Lizbet and Daughters—Country Cooking

Breakfast

Lord, this humble house we'd keep

Sweet with play and calm with sleep.

Help us so that we may give

Beauty to the lives we live.

Let thy love and let thy grace

Shine upon our dwelling place.

—Edgar Guest

. . . . .

A home is made of love,

Warm as the golden hearthfire on the floor.

—Author Unknown

Notes

Breakfast Pockets

2 pkg. active dry yeast
½ c. warm water
¾ c. milk
½ c. vegetable oil

¼ c. sugar
1 egg
1 tsp. salt
3-4 c. bread flour

Filling–
1 lb. sausage
2½ c. shredded potatoes
7 eggs, beaten
1 c. milk

1 Tbsp. flour
1 tsp. salt
2½ c. shredded cheddar or mozzarella cheese

In mixing bowl, dissolve yeast in water. Add milk, oil, sugar, egg, salt and 2 c. flour; beat until smooth. Add enough remaining flour to form a soft dough. Do not knead. Cover and let rise in warm place until doubled, about 1 hour. Meanwhile, cook sausage and fry potatoes until soft. Mix sausage, potatoes, eggs, milk, flour and salt. Cook and stir until eggs are completely set. Sprinkle with cheese. Divide dough into 14 equal pieces. Roll out dough into a 7" circle. Top each with about ⅓ c. filling. Fold dough over and pinch edges to seal. Place on greased cookie sheets. Bake at 350° for 15-20 minutes.

Ham and Cheese Oven Omelet

8 eggs
1 c. milk
½ tsp. seasoned salt
3 oz. shredded ham, sausage or bacon

1 c. shredded cheddar, Swiss or mozzarella cheese
3 Tbsp. chopped onion

Beat eggs. Add rest of ingredients. Bake at 325° for 40-45 minutes.

Lizbet and Daughters—Country Cooking

Sunrise Burritos

1 lb. bulk sausage
chopped onions
chopped peppers
mushrooms

8 eggs
4 Tbsp. water
8 (10") flour tortillas
cheese of your choice

Brown sausage, onions and peppers. Add mushrooms. Scramble eggs and add water. Add sausage mixture. Do not overcook. Eggs should be soft with no liquid remaining. Melt cheese on top. Heat tortillas on warm pan then fill with scrambled egg mixture and roll up.

Smokies in a Blanket

1 tube refrigerated biscuits or crescent rolls

1 pkg. little smokies

Cut biscuits in fourths. Wrap one piece around a smokie and put on cookie sheet. Bake at 350° until lightly browned.

Cranberry Meatballs and Sausage

1 egg, beaten
1 sm. onion, chopped
¾ c. dry bread crumbs
1 Tbsp. parsley flakes
1 Tbsp. Worcestershire sauce
¼ tsp. salt

1 lb. bulk pork sausage
16 oz. jellied cranberry sauce
3 Tbsp. cider vinegar
2 Tbsp. brown sugar
1 Tbsp. prepared mustard
1 lb. smokies

In a large bowl combine the first 6 ingredients. Crumble bulk sausage over the mixture and mix well. Shape into 1" balls. In a large skillet cook meatballs over medium heat until browned. Drain. In a large saucepan, combine the cranberry sauce, vinegar, brown sugar and mustard. Cook and stir over medium heat until cranberry sauce is melted. Add the meatballs and smokies. Bring to a boil. Reduce heat and simmer uncovered for 10-15 minutes or until meatballs are no longer pink and sauce is slightly thickened.

Campfire Breakfast

2 lb. bacon
2 lb. hash browns
12 eggs, scrambled
Velveeta cheese

On a grate over an open fire, heat an iron skillet. Fry bacon; remove bacon and put in a Dutch oven. Fry hash browns and layer these on top of bacon. Put a layer of Velveeta slices on top. Fry scrambled eggs with bacon grease and put on top of hash browns. Put another layer of cheese slices on top. When ready to eat take a large spoon and stir everything together. Season with salt and pepper. Delicious served with toast made over the fire and jelly.

Sausage Gravy

2 lb. sausage
¼ c. butter
1¼ c. flour
2 qt. milk
salt
pepper
seasoned salt

Fry sausage in butter until browned. Add flour and stir well. Gradually add milk. Continue to heat and keep stirred. It will thicken as it cooks. Add more milk if too thick. Add seasonings according to your taste.

Bacon Roll-Ups

12 slices bread
1 can cream of mushroom soup
12 slices bacon

Spread cream of mushroom soup on bread. Roll up bread across corner. Wrap one slice of bacon around each slice of bread. A toothpick may be used to hold bread in place. Place on cookie sheet and bake at 375° for 35-45 minutes or until bacon is crisp. Delicious and simple for breakfast.

Lizbet and Daughters—Country Cooking

Breakfast Pizza

2 rolls biscuits
home fries
scrambled eggs
sausage gravy
Velveeta cheese
crumbled bacon

Layer in pizza pan in order given. Bake at 350° for 20 minutes or until biscuits are done. For a large amount, layer everything in a large roaster until full. Save biscuits to put on top 20 minutes before it's done baking. A Lifetime roaster needs 3 hours to heat if it is made the day before and refrigerated.

Breakfast Pizza

2 tubes crescent rolls
12 eggs, scrambled
Velveeta cheese
2 cans mushroom soup
1 c. sour cream
sausage or ham
1 (2 lb.) pkg. hash browns
cheddar cheese

Layer crescent rolls on cookie sheet. Bake lightly. Layer with remaining ingredients. Bake at 350°. Delicious.

Baked Oatmeal

½ c. butter, melted
1 c. brown sugar
2 eggs, beaten
1 tsp. salt
1 c. milk
2 tsp. baking powder
3 c. quick oats

Mix together and bake at 350° for 30 minutes. Serve warm with milk. This can be mixed the evening before. Two batches fill a 9" x 13" pan.

Nutty Baked French Toast

1 loaf white bread, sliced
8 eggs
2 c. milk
2 c. half and half

2 tsp. vanilla
½ tsp. nutmeg
½ tsp. cinnamon

Nut Topping–
¾ c. butter, softened
1⅓ c. brown sugar

3 Tbsp. dark corn syrup
1⅓ c. coarsely chopped nuts

Grease a 9" x 13" baking pan. Fill pan with bread slices to within ½" of top. Blend together eggs, milk, half and half, vanilla, nutmeg and cinnamon. Pour over bread slices. Cover and refrigerate overnight. Combine topping and set aside until time to bake toast. Spread topping over toast. Bake at 350° for 50 minutes, until puffed and golden. If top browns too quickly, cover with foil.

French Toast

1 Tbsp. flour
2 eggs

½ c. milk
pinch salt

Beat eggs, milk, flour and salt. Dip bread (homemade is best) in egg mixture. Fry in butter for 2-3 minutes per side. Serve with syrup.

Some people grow up and spread sunshine;
others just spread.

Blueberry French Toast

12 slices bread, cubed
16 oz. cream cheese, cubed
12 eggs

Sauce-
1 c. water
1 c. white sugar
2 Tbsp. cornstarch

½ c. pancake syrup
1 c. milk
1 c. blueberries

1 c. blueberries
1 Tbsp. butter

Put bread cubes in baking dish. Put cream cheese and blueberries over bread. Beat together eggs, pancake syrup and milk and pour over bread cubes. Cover and bake at 350° for 30 minutes. Uncover and bake for another 30 minutes. Cook water, sugar and cornstarch for 3 minutes and add blueberries and butter. Cook for another 8-10 minutes. Serve with French toast.

Caramelized French Toast

½ c. butter
½ c. brown sugar
¼ c. maple syrup
12 slices bread
4 oz. cream cheese

1 tsp. vanilla
cinnamon
6 eggs
1⅔ c. milk

Combine sugar, butter and syrup. Cook until sugar is melted. Spread bread slices with cream cheese. Sprinkle cinnamon over top. Layer bread in baking dish. Pour syrup mixture over top. Make 2 layers. Now beat eggs, add milk and vanilla and pour over all. Cover and set in fridge. The next morning uncover and bake in 350° oven for 30-40 minutes.

Favorite Pancakes

1 egg	1 c. buttermilk
2 Tbsp. butter, melted	1 Tbsp. sugar
1 c. all-purpose flour	1 tsp. baking powder
½ tsp. baking soda	½ tsp. salt

Beat egg and add remaining ingredients in order listed and beat until smooth. Pour batter from pitcher onto hot greased griddle. Turn pancakes as soon as they are puffed and full of bubbles. Bake on other side until golden brown.

Waffles

2 c. flour	6 Tbsp. butter, melted
1 tsp. salt	2 eggs, separated
2 Tbsp. sugar	1½ c. milk
4 tsp. baking powder	

Mix dry ingredients in large bowl. Beat egg yolks and add milk. Combine with flour mixture. Add melted butter. Last fold in stiffly beaten egg whites. Pour 1 c. on hot griddle. Makes 6 large waffles.

Pancake Syrup

2 c. water	1 tsp. maple flavoring
3½ c. brown sugar	

Bring water to a rapid boil. Turn off heat and stir in brown sugar. Add maple flavoring; stir well. Let set for 24 hours to blend flavors before using. This makes 1 qt. of delicious syrup.

Lizbet and Daughters — Country Cooking

Cheese Flitzes

8 oz. cream cheese
¼ c. sugar
1 egg yolk
½ c. butter

1 c. white sugar
1 tsp. cinnamon
1 loaf sandwich bread

Cream together cream cheese, ¼ c. sugar and egg yolk. Melt butter. Mix 1 c. sugar and cinnamon. Trim crust from bread. Roll slices thin with a rolling pin. Spread with cream cheese mixture. Roll up. Dip in butter then in sugar mixture. Bake at 350° for 15 minutes.

Caramel Breakfast Ring

16 frozen dinner rolls
3 oz. cook and serve vanilla or butterscotch pudding
¾ c. brown sugar

½ c. butter, melted
½ c. chopped pecans or walnuts
cinnamon

Prepare the night before serving. Spray Bundt pan or angel food cake pan with cooking spray. Put in a layer of nuts then put in frozen rolls. Mix brown sugar and pudding together and sprinkle over rolls. Sprinkle cinnamon over pudding. Melt butter and pour over rolls. Add another layer of nuts. Cover with cloth and put in oven overnight. Do not turn oven on. In the morning, remove pan from oven. Preheat oven to 325°. Bake for 30 minutes. Turn upside down on platter to serve.

Mice

2 cans biscuits

Filling-
8 oz. cream cheese   1 c. powdered sugar

Sauce-
½ c. brown sugar   ¼ c. butter

For sauce, heat butter and brown sugar until completely dissolved. Roll or pat biscuits to make a 3-4" circle. Put 1 Tbsp. filling on one half of biscuit. Fold over and press edge together. Put in baking pan and pour sauce over all. Bake at 350° until light brown.

Easy Caramel Rolls

2 tubes buttermilk biscuits   cinnamon

Icing-
6 Tbsp. butter   ¾ c. brown sugar
½ c. sour cream

Cut each biscuit into 4 pieces with scissors. Sprinkle cinnamon over cut biscuits and bake. Brown butter, then add sour cream and brown sugar. Heat to boiling point. Let set awhile to thicken before pouring over rolls.

Quick Rolls

½ c. butter   2 cans biscuits
½ c. light Karo   ½ c. nuts
¾ c. brown sugar

Melt and heat first 3 ingredients; add nuts. Pour half in a Bundt pan. Set the biscuits in sideways and pour rest of mixture over all. Bake at 350° for 20 minutes.

Lizbet and Daughters—Country Cooking

Frozen Fruit Slush

3 med. firm bananas
½ c. lemonade concentrate
6 med. ripe peaches, sliced
3 c. water
1 can crushed pineapples, undrained
2 c. sugar
1⅓ c. seedless red grapes, halved
1 c. orange juice concentrate

In a large bowl stir the bananas and lemonade concentrate until coated. Stir in the remaining ingredients. Cover and freeze for 8 hours or until firm. Remove from the freezer 1-1¼ hours before serving so mixture becomes slushy.

Barbecue Smokies

1 pkg. smokies
1 c. ketchup
2 tsp. mustard
2 Tbsp. vinegar
¼ c. brown sugar

Mix and put in casserole dish. Bake at 350° for 45 minutes or until hot.

Egg in a Hole

1 piece bread
1 egg

Use a glass and press in center of bread to take out a 2" hole. Melt butter in skillet and add bread slice. Break egg into hole. Stir up egg with fork. When bread is toasted add more butter and turn bread and egg over. Ready when egg is set. Also toast the circle of bread to eat.

Six active gifts to give your child—

time, touching and talking,

listening, laughing and loving

Soups, Salads, Salad Dressings & Jell-O Salads

Buhne Supp un Lattwarick Brod,
Die Deitsche ihre Freed,
Es is nix es besser nunner geht
Un macht der Bauch so braid.
Deel Leit gehn fa Lewwerwasht,
Mosch un Seideschpeck,
Awwer Buhne Supp un Lattwarick Brod
Legt alles in der Dreck.

Bean soup and apple butter bread,
The joy of the Dutch,
There is nothing that goes down better
And makes the belly so wide.
Some folks go for liverwurst,
Corn mush and bacon,
But bean soup and apple butter bread
Leaves all else in the dirt.

Notes

Chicken Chowder

2 c. celery
2 c. carrots
2 c. potatoes
½ c. butter, melted
8-10 Tbsp. flour

2 c. milk
4 c. chicken broth
3-4 c. chicken pieces
½ lb. Velveeta cheese

Dice celery, carrots and potatoes. Cook until soft. Melt butter; add flour to thicken. Add milk, broth, chicken and cheese. Stir in vegetables. Do not boil after adding Velveeta cheese.

Baked Potato Soup

⅔ c. butter
⅔ c. all-purpose flour
7 c. milk
4 lg. baking potatoes, baked, cooled, peeled, cubed
4 green onions

1¼ c. shredded cheddar cheese
1 c. sour cream
¾ tsp. salt
½ tsp. pepper
12 strips bacon, fried, crumbled

Melt butter; stir in flour. Heat and stir until smooth. Gradually add milk, stirring until thick and smooth. Add potatoes and onions and bring to a boil, stirring constantly. Simmer for 10 minutes. Add rest of ingredients. Stir until cheese is melted. Serve immediately. Serves 8-10 people.

Slim Soup Mix

2 c. instant non-fat dry milk
1 c. cornstarch

2 Tbsp. dried minced onion
¼ tsp. pepper

Mix together and store in airtight container. To equal 1 can soup, combine ⅓ c. dry milk mixture and 1¼ c. water or milk in a small pan. Bring to boil and stir until thickened. For mushroom soup: Add 1 (4 oz.) can mushrooms, chopped and drained. For vegetable soup: Add ½ c. diced, cooked vegetables. For chicken soup: Add ½ c. cooked, diced chicken and chicken base.

Lizbet and Daughters — Country Cooking

Just-Like-Campbell's Tomato Soup

1½ c. butter
¼ c. chopped onion
2¼ c. flour
¾ c. sugar

6-7 qt. tomato juice
¼ c. salt
1½ tsp. pepper

Sauté onion in butter. Stir in flour, sugar, salt and pepper. Cook until smooth and bubbly. Remove from heat. Gradually stir in tomato juice. Bring to a boil, stirring constantly. Boil for 1 minute. Fill jars and process at 10 pounds for 10 minutes. To serve, gradually stir hot tomato mixture into about an equal amount of cold milk. Heat to serving temperature.

Chili Soup

8 lb. hamburger
26 oz. tomato soup
1 pt. ketchup
1½ c. white sugar
1½ Tbsp. dry mustard
1½ Tbsp. chili powder
5 qt. tomato juice

7 oz. tomato paste
1½ qt. kidney beans
1 onion, chopped
1½ c. brown sugar
4 Tbsp. clear jel
4 pkg. chili seasoning

Brown hamburger; season with onion, seasoned salt, salt and pepper. Combine all ingredients, adding hamburger and kidney beans last. Makes approximately 16 qt. Cold pack for 2 hours.

Chili Soup

1 (15 oz.) tomato puree
26 oz. tomato soup
1 pt. ketchup
6 lb. hamburger
1½ c. white sugar
1½ Tbsp. dry mustard
1½ Tbsp. chili powder

5 qt. tomato juice
7 oz. tomato paste
1½ qt. kidney beans
1 onion, chopped
1½ c. brown sugar
4 Tbsp. flour
½ tsp. ketchup spice

Brown hamburger; add onions. Season with seasoned salt, salt and pepper. Combine all other ingredients, adding hamburger and kidney beans last. Bring to a boil and simmer for 10 minutes to let flavor go through. Yield: 16 qt.

Bean with Bacon Soup

2 lb. dry navy beans
6 qt. water
2 lb. bacon
4 c. diced potatoes
8 tsp. salt
¾ tsp. pepper

4 c. diced celery
2 c. diced carrots
3 c. chopped onions
3 qt. tomato juice
½ c. brown sugar

Combine beans and water in large kettle. Bring to boil, and boil for 2 minutes. Remove from heat; cover and let set for 1 hour. Fry bacon until crisp. Add to beans. Cook onions in bacon drippings until soft and brown. Add to soup along with drippings. Bring beans, bacon and onions to a boil and simmer covered for 1 hour or until beans are tender. Add remaining ingredients. Simmer until vegetables are tender. Cold pack for 1½ hours. Pressure cook 1 hour at 10 pounds pressure. Makes 10 qt.

Lizbet and Daughters — Country Cooking

Chicken Noodle Soup

10 lb. chicken tidbits
2 qt. celery
2 qt. carrots
2 qt. potatoes
5 (8 oz.) pkg. Kluski noodles

Cook chicken until tender; pick off meat. Use broth to cook noodles in. Season with chicken base seasoning to your taste. Be careful not to overcook. Cook each vegetable separately in salt water. Do not cook too soft. Mix noodles and vegetables together in canner. Add enough water to make it as soupy as you like. Season to your taste. Put in jars and pressure cook for 20 minutes at 10 pounds pressure or cold pack for 1½ hours.

Chunky Vegetable Soup

2½ gal. water
2 lg. cans beef broth
1¼ c. beef soup mix
¼ c. salt
4 qt. tomato juice
½ c. butter
1 c. sugar
2 lg. onions, cut finely
4 qt. carrots
4 qt. potatoes
3 qt. peas
2 qt. green beans
2 qt. flour
water
5 lb. hamburger
salt and pepper to taste

Heat water, broth, soup mix, salt, tomato juice, butter and sugar to boiling, then add vegetables which have been cooked and salted separately. Add enough water to flour to make a paste to thicken soup. Season hamburger with salt and pepper and fry until brown. Add to soup, also adding drippings. Cold pack for 3 hours. Pressure can for 45 minutes at 10 pounds pressure. Makes 27-30 qt.

Vegetable Soup

2-3 qt. beef chunks, cooked
1 qt. diced celery
1 qt. corn
1 qt. peas
1 qt. yellow beans
1 qt. diced potatoes
1 qt. diced carrots
1 qt. green beans
1 pt. (1 lg.) chopped onion

1 lg. can soup beans
6 qt. tomato juice
1 sm. can tomato puree
2 qt. beef broth
3 c. white sugar
1 tsp. chili powder
2-3 Tbsp. salt
1 c. ABC macaroni

Cook beef. Cook vegetables until tender. Do not drain juice. Add remaining ingredients, including broth from meat, and cook until heated through. Put in canning jars. Pressure cook for 20 minutes at 10 pounds pressure. You may use 2 gallons mixed vegetables or any combination of your choice. Makes approximately 36 pt.

Broccoli Cheese Soup with Noodles

3 Tbsp. butter
¾ c. chopped onion
6 c. water
3 Tbsp. chicken base
1 tsp. salt
8 oz. fine noodles

20 oz. frozen, chopped broccoli, or
   1½ lb. fresh broccoli, chopped
¼ tsp. garlic powder
dash of pepper
6 c. milk
½-1 lb. Velveeta cheese

Sauté onion in butter. Add water, chicken base, salt and noodles and bring to a boil. Add broccoli, garlic powder and pepper. Cook for 4-5 minutes. Add milk and cheese, stirring until cheese melts.

Lizbet and Daughters—Country Cooking

Coffee Soup

4 c. hot coffee
4 slices bread

brown sugar to taste
cream to taste

Break each slice bread into 1" pieces and place in 4 small serving bowls. Add brown sugar and cream to your taste. Pour 1 c. hot coffee in each bowl. Serve hot. Soda crackers can also be used.

Cheesy Ham Chowder

2 c. water
2 c. diced potatoes
½ c. diced carrots
½ tsp. salt
pepper

2 c. diced ham
¼ c. butter
¼ c. flour
2 c. milk
1 c. cheddar cheese

Cook vegetables until soft. Do not drain off water. While vegetables are cooking, make white sauce. Melt butter, add flour and stir until smooth. Add milk and cheese; heat until thickened, stirring constantly. Add cheese sauce to vegetables and ham. Mix well and serve.

Cheesy Bacon Potato Soup

1 c. butter
1 c. flour
8 c. milk
6 lg. potatoes, diced
1 med. onion, chopped
1 lb. bacon, fried, crumbled

1½ c. shredded cheddar or
    Velveeta cheese
1 c. sour cream
1 tsp. salt
½ tsp. pepper

Cook potatoes and onion in salt water until tender. Drain. In large soup kettle melt the butter. Stir in flour until smooth. Gradually add milk and stir until thickened. Add potatoes and onion. Bring to a boil, stirring constantly. Reduce heat; simmer for 10 minutes. Add bacon, cheese, sour cream, salt and pepper. Stir until cheese is melted.

Split Pea Soup

16 oz. split peas
3 qt. water
1 sm. ham shank
1 lg. onion
1 bay leaf
2 Tbsp. chicken soup base

½ tsp. garlic powder
½ tsp. oregano
¼ - ½ tsp. pepper
1½ c. shredded carrots
1 c. diced celery

In a large pot combine peas, water, ham shank, onion, soup base and seasonings. Simmer for 1½ hours. Remove ham shank from pot and debone meat; return meat to soup. Stir in carrots and celery. Simmer for 2 hours longer or until soup reaches desired thickness. Makes 9 cups.

Amish Bean Soup

6 Tbsp. butter
1 c. navy beans
3 qt. milk

salt and pepper to taste
2 qt. bread cubes

Brown butter in a saucepan. Add beans. Bring to a boil then add milk, salt and pepper. Bring to a boil and remove from stove. Add enough bread cubes to thicken. Cover and let set for 20-25 minutes before serving.

Cheeseburger Soup

½ lb. hamburger
¾ c. chopped onions
¾ c. carrots
¾ c. celery
1 tsp. parsley flakes
4 Tbsp. butter
3 c. chicken broth

4 c. diced potatoes
¼ c. flour
1 c. shredded cheese
1½ c. milk
¾ tsp. salt
¼ tsp. pepper

Brown beef; sauté onions, carrots, celery and parsley with 1 Tbsp. butter for 10 minutes. Add broth, potatoes and beef. Simmer for 10-12 minutes. Melt rest of butter; add flour and cook for 4 minutes. Add to soup. Add milk and cheese when ready to serve.

Lizbet and Daughters—Country Cooking

Taco Soup

1 lb. ground beef
15 oz. chili beans
1 sm. onion, chopped
1 pkg. taco seasoning mix

1½ qt. tomato juice
1 pt. corn
⅓ c. sugar

Brown ground beef and onion. Add tomato juice, corn, beans, sugar and taco seasoning. Bring to a boil, then simmer for 15-20 minutes. Serve over crushed Doritos. Sprinkle with shredded cheese and top with sour cream.

Geauga Soup

hamburger
cream of mushroom soup

milk

Brown hamburger. Add 1 Tbsp. flour. Add soup, amount of milk needed for your family and salt and pepper to taste.

Rivel Soup

1 c. flour
1½ tsp. salt

1 egg
1 qt. milk

Mix salt with flour then toss egg lightly through flour with fork until small crumbs form. Stir into scalding milk. Bring to boil. Serve at once.

Little by little, day by day—
Friends and flowers grow that way.

Broccoli Soup

1 sm. can chicken broth
2 bouillon cubes
10 oz. broccoli
¼ c. chopped onion
4 Tbsp. flour

3 Tbsp. butter
½ tsp. salt and pepper
2¼ c. milk
1 c. Velveeta cheese
1 c. mashed potatoes

Simmer broth, bouillon cubes and broccoli until tender. Use as much broccoli as desired. Simmer onions, flour, butter, salt and pepper in large pan. Stir until thick. Add milk and Velveeta cheese. Add broth and broccoli to mixture then mashed potatoes.

Chili Corn Bread Salad

1 (8 or 12 oz.) pkg. corn bread muffin mix
1 can chopped green chilies, undrained
⅛ tsp. dried oregano
1 c. mayonnaise
1 c. sour cream
1 pkg. Ranch dressing mix
2 cans pinto beans, rinsed, drained

2 cans corn, drained
3 med. tomatoes
1 c. chopped peppers
1 c. chopped onions
10 strips bacon
2 c. cheddar cheese

Prepare corn bread batter according to package instructions. Stir in chilies and oregano and spread in greased 8" square pan. Bake at 400° for 20-25 minutes. Cool. Mix together mayonnaise, sour cream and Ranch dressing. Layer in 9" x 13" pan as follows—half of corn bread, half of beans, half of mayonnaise mixture, half of corn, half of tomatoes, half of peppers, onions, bacon and cheese. Repeat layers. Dish will be very full. Should set for 2 hours before serving.

Lizbet and Daughters—Country Cooking

Pasta Salad

1½ lb. pasta, cooked and drained
8 oz. ham, diced
cheddar cheese
½ c. chopped celery

2 tomatoes, chopped
1 onion, chopped
1 green pepper, chopped
1 can ripe olives, chopped

Dressing-
3 c. salad dressing
¼ c. mustard
¾ c. oil
½ Tbsp. salt

¼ c. vinegar
1 Tbsp. onion salt
½ Tbsp. celery seed
½ c. sugar

Mix well. Can make it a day before. If dressing is too thick, add a little milk.

Ramen Noodle Salad

2 heads broccoli, cut fine
1 red pepper, diced, or
   baby carrots, sliced thin
1 onion, chopped

1 c. roasted sunflower seeds or
   chopped walnuts
2 pkg. Ramen noodles

Dressing-
2 pkg. seasoning from noodles
1 c. oil
1 c. white sugar

⅓ c. red wine vinegar or
   apple cider vinegar

Mix all ingredients together except for noodles. Mix together dressing ingredients and pour over broccoli mixture. Add the broken up Ramen noodles and mix into salad really well just before serving.

A good exercise for the heart is bending down to help people.

Loaded Baked Potato Salad

5 lb. sm. unpeeled red potatoes, cubed
1 tsp. salt
½ tsp. pepper
8 hard-boiled eggs, chopped
1 lb. bacon, cooked, crumbled
2 c. shredded cheddar cheese
1 med. onion, chopped
3 dill pickles, chopped
1½ c. sour cream
1 c. mayonnaise
2 tsp. prepared mustard

Bake potatoes until tender. Cool. In a large bowl, combine potatoes, salt, pepper, eggs, bacon, cheese, onion and pickles. In a small bowl, combine sour cream, mayonnaise and mustard. Pour over the potato mixture and toss to coat. Serve immediately.

Taco Salad

1 med. head lettuce, chopped
1 lb. hamburger, fried, drained
8 oz. cheddar cheese
1 sm. can kidney beans, drained
1 lg. onion, chopped
4 med. tomatoes, diced
1 pkg. Doritos, crushed
1 pkg. taco seasoning

Dressing–
1 Tbsp. taco seasoning
⅓ c. sugar
8 oz. Thousand Island dressing
1 Tbsp. taco sauce

Brown hamburger. Add taco seasoning, reserving 1 Tbsp. seasoning for dressing. Combine cooled hamburger with all the rest of ingredients except Doritos. Dressing: Mix all together. Toss salad with dressing and Doritos just before serving.

Lizbet and Daughters—Country Cooking

Broccoli Salad

2 bunches broccoli, cut fine
1 head cauliflower, cut fine
1 lb. bacon, fried, crumbled

2 c. shredded cheese
1 sm. onion, chopped, optional

Sauce—
1½ c. sour cream
1 c. white sugar

1½ c. mayonnaise
½ tsp. salt

Combine sauce ingredients and mix well. Pour over broccoli mixture. Can be made a day ahead.

Broccoli Salad

1 head broccoli
1 head cauliflower

grape tomatoes
Italian dressing

Cut broccoli and cauliflower into bite-sized pieces. Add tomatoes. Add dressing and serve.

Potato Salad

12 c. potatoes
12 eggs

1 sm. onion
1 c. diced celery

Dressing-
3 c. salad dressing
2 c. sugar
3 tsp. mustard

2 tsp. salt
¼ c. vinegar

Cook potatoes; cool and peel. Cook eggs. Put potatoes and eggs through Salad Master while still warm. Add the rest of ingredients.

What we are is God's gift to us.
What we become is our gift to God.

7-Layer Salad

1 lg. head lettuce
1 lb. bacon
1½ c. frozen peas
2 c. shredded cheese
8 hard-boiled eggs
2 c. salad dressing
2 Tbsp. sugar
1 tsp. salt

Layer first 5 ingredients in 9" x 13" pan or on a glass plate in order given. Combine salad dressing, sugar and salt to make dressing. Pour over salad, sealing edges. Sprinkle a little bacon and cheese over top.

Vegetable Pizza

2 pkg. crescent rolls
1 head cauliflower
2 bunches broccoli
1 onion
8 oz. cream cheese
16 oz. sour cream
1-2 pkg. Ranch dressing mix
1½ c. Miracle Whip
tomatoes
peppers
shredded cheese

Put crescent rolls on large cookie sheet. Bake at 350° for 11 minutes. Don't overbake. Cool. Meanwhile, cut up cauliflower, broccoli and onion. Mix cream cheese, sour cream, Miracle Whip and Ranch dressing mix. Spread over crust. Top with your choice of vegetables and cheese. Very good.

Taco Seasoning Mix

1 tsp. chili powder
1 tsp. paprika
1½ tsp. cumin
1 tsp. parsley flakes
1 tsp. onion powder
½ tsp. garlic salt
½ tsp. oregano

This is equal to one package store-bought taco seasoning.

Lizbet and Daughters—Country Cooking

Coleslaw

1 med. head cabbage
½ c. vinegar
1 c. chopped celery
2 c. sugar

1 tsp. mustard seed
½ c. chopped green peppers
1 tsp. celery seed

Grate cabbage and add all other ingredients. May be eaten right away or frozen.

Cucumber Salad

3 c. thinly sliced cucumbers
1 c. thinly sliced onions, optional
1 c. mayonnaise
1 c. sour cream

½ c. sugar
1 tsp. salt
1 tsp. celery seed, optional
2 Tbsp. lemon juice

Mix all ingredients together, except cucumbers and onions. Let set until sugar is melted, then pour over cucumbers and onions. This is good to put on top of cooked salt water potatoes.

Coleslaw Dressing

¾ c. Miracle Whip
½ c. sugar
8 oz. sour cream

¼ tsp. salt
⅛ tsp. pepper

Mix all together.

Sweet and Sour Dressing

1 c. white sugar
1 c. salad dressing

1 c. Wesson oil
celery seed to taste

Stir white sugar and salad dressing together. Slowly beat Wesson oil into this mixture. If you don't beat enough, oil will separate. If too thick I stir in a little water. Mix in celery seed.

Sweet and Sour Dressing

¾ c. vegetable oil
¾ c. white vinegar
½ onion, chopped
1 tsp. salt
2 Tbsp. mustard

½ tsp. garlic salt
2¼ c. white sugar
2 c. Miracle Whip
¾ tsp. celery seed

Blend onions with oil and vinegar. Add rest of ingredients until it's not gritty. Add celery seed last.

Ranch Dressing

2 c. mayonnaise or salad dressing
½ tsp. garlic salt
2 c. buttermilk or sour cream

1 tsp. parsley flakes
½ tsp. onion salt
½ tsp. celery salt

Mix all ingredients and shake in a jar. Do not use blender. Use only 1 c. buttermilk if using for a vegetable dip. This is good used on vegetable pizza.

Thousand Island Dressing

1 qt. mayonnaise
½ c. ketchup

½ c. relish
⅔ c. white sugar

Mix all together.

Like Hartville Sweet and Sour

1½ c. sugar
2 tsp. dry mustard
1 tsp. salt
1 tsp. celery seed

½ c. vinegar
1 med. onion
2 c. salad oil

Add oil last. Blend into rest of ingredients very slowly.

Lizbet and Daughters—Country Cooking

Russian Dressing

1½ c. white sugar
1½ c. oil
2 c. ketchup

1 Tbsp. vinegar
1 tsp. salt
1 lg. onion

Beat with mixer at low speed. Makes 1 qt. and keeps well in refrigerator.

Cooked Salad Dressing

¼ c. vinegar
1¼ c. water
1 Tbsp. butter
½ c. white sugar

½ tsp. salt
2 Tbsp. flour
1 tsp. prepared mustard
1 egg

Bring vinegar, water and butter to a boil. Mix last 5 ingredients into a paste and stir into the boiling part. Stir constantly until thick. Cool; add 1 cup sour cream.

Tasty Tomatoes

¼ c. chopped celery
2 Tbsp. chopped onion
½ c. salad dressing

½ c. sour cream
1 tsp. Ranch dressing mix
shredded cheddar cheese

Mix first 5 ingredients. Slice tomatoes and drop 1 Tbsp. topping on each slice. Sprinkle with cheese.

Lime Cottage Cheese Salad

1 small pkg. lime Jell-O
½ c. boiling water
2 c. mini marshmallows

1 c. drained pineapples
2 c. whipped topping
1 c. small curd cottage cheese

Dissolve Jell-O in boiling water; add marshmallows to melt. Stir in pineapples. Chill until slightly thickened. Fold in cottage cheese and whipped topping.

Quick and Delicious Jell-O Dessert

7 oz. cherry Jell-O
7 oz. orange Jell-O
7 oz. lemon Jell-O

4 oz. cream cheese
½ c. sugar

4 c. water
4 c. water
2 c. water

1 c. whipped topping

Fix three kinds Jell-O in separate bowls at one time, using only 2 c. water for lemon Jell-O. Cool cherry Jell-O and pour in Tupperware Cold Cut Keeper. Cream cream cheese and sugar. Add whipped topping and lemon Jell-O. Pour on top of set cherry Jell-O. After lemon layer sets, pour orange Jell-O on top.

Lime Crust Salad

2 c. flour
½ c. brown sugar
1 c. butter
1 c. pineapple

1 small pkg. lime Jell-O
8 oz. cream cheese
½ c. sugar
2 c. Rich's topping

Mix flour, brown sugar and butter. Press into oblong pan. Bake for 12-15 minutes. Drain pineapple in saucepan. Bring to boil. Dissolve lime Jell-O in pineapple juice and cool. Mix cream cheese with sugar. Blend in Jell-O and stir in pineapple. Whip topping and mix all together. Put on top of crust and serve.

Sparkling Summer Salad

2 (3 oz.) boxes pineapple Jell-O
2 large bananas
1 can crushed pineapples, drained
3 c. mini marshmallows

1 c. pineapple juice
¼ c. sugar
2 Tbsp. flour
1 c. Rich's topping

Make boxes of Jell-O as directed and let cool until syrupy. Add pineapple, marshmallows and sliced bananas. Pour in a 9" x 13" pan and let gel. Take the juice and add sugar and flour and cook to thicken. Add the beaten topping to this mixture after it is cool. Spread on top.

Lizbet and Daughters—Country Cooking

Creamy Grape Salad

First Layer–
3 oz. grape Jell-O   1¾ c. boiling water

Second Layer–
8 oz. cream cheese   3 oz. grape Jell-O
1 c. sugar   1 c. boiling water
1 tsp. vanilla

Third Layer–
3 oz. grape Jell-O   1¾ c. boiling water

Mix together first layer and pour in pan. Mix together cream cheese and sugar. Add vanilla. Mix Jell-O and water and add to cream cheese mixture. Pour over first layer that has set. Mix together third layer and pour over top after second layer has set.

Cranberry Salad

½ lb. cranberries   ¼ c. chopped walnuts
3 apples   3 oz. cherry Jell-O
1 c. granulated sugar   1 c. boiling water
2 oranges   1 c. cold water
½ c. crushed pineapples

Wash and grind cranberries through food chopper. Pare and core apples and chop very fine. Mix cranberries and apples together. Add chopped oranges, pineapples, nuts and sugar. Dissolve Jell-O in boiling water and add cold water. When cool, add salad mixture. Serves 6 people.

Orange Ring Salad

1 pt. orange sherbet
1 lg. box orange Jell-O
2 c. hot water
1 can mandarin oranges, drained

1 can crushed pineapples, drained (reserve juice)
2 c. Cool Whip

Add water to Jell-O to dissolve, then add sherbet by spoonfuls to hot Jell-O. Add half of oranges and pineapples. Pour in a ring mold. Cook pineapple juice and a little water. Thicken with clear jel and let cool. Add Cool Whip and rest of oranges and pineapples. When ready to serve, put in center of mold.

Jell-O Pudding

First Layer–
8 oz. cream cheese
1 c. sugar
1 tsp. vanilla

⅓ c. Jell-O
1 c. hot water
8 oz. Cool Whip

Second Layer–
⅔ c. Jell-O
2 c. hot water

2 c. cold water

Cream together cream cheese, sugar and vanilla. Dissolve Jell-O in water and let set until partly set. Add cream cheese mixture to Jell-O and add Cool Whip. Put in pan until set. Mix together second layer. Let cool and put on top of first layer. Grape Jell-O is good.

Miracle drugs go a long way back:
Moses had two tablets that could cure the world's ills.

Lizbet and Daughters—Country Cooking

Rainbow Jell-O Salad

1 pt. sour cream

Bottom Layer–
3 oz. cherry Jell-O
1 c. boiling water
3 Tbsp. cold water
3 oz. lime Jell-O

3 oz. orange Jell-O
3 oz. lemon Jell-O
3 oz. lime Jell-O

Top Layer–
3 oz. strawberry Jell-O

Dissolve first pkg. Jell-O in boiling water. Place ⅓ cup sour cream in another bowl, gradually stirring in half of dissolved Jell-O mixture. Add cold water to remaining Jell-O. Pour sour cream mixture in an 11" x 7" glass pan. Let set in fridge for 20 minutes. Pour plain Jell-O on top. Let set 20 minutes more in fridge. Repeat steps with the rest of the Jell-O packages. Very colorful when finished.

Applesauce Salad

2 (3 oz.) boxes red Jell-O
3 c. water
3 c. applesauce

½ c. cinnamon candy
½ c. hot water

Dissolve Jell-O in water. In a separate bowl, dissolve candy with hot water. Mix together with applesauce. I like to add bananas before serving.

Strawberry Jell-O Salad

3 sm. boxes strawberry Jell-O
1 c. hot water
8 oz. cream cheese
8 oz. Cool Whip
1 c. crushed strawberries

Prepare 1 box Jell-O as directed on package. Pour into 9" x 13" pan. For second layer: Dissolve 1 box Jell-O with hot water. Add strawberries. Mix cream cheese and Cool Whip and fold into Jell-O and strawberries. Pour over first layer which has set. Prepare last box of Jell-O as directed. When cool, pour over second layer.

Grape Cottage Cheese Salad

4 small boxes grape Jell-O
1 box cottage cheese
2 c. whipped topping

Mix Jell-O as directed on box, but use grape juice instead of cold water. Pour half of Jell-O into 9" x 13" pan and let set. Put cottage cheese on top. Let rest of Jell-O thicken slightly, then beat whipped topping into thickened Jell-O and slowly pour on top of cottage cheese. Refrigerate until set.

Cool Whip – Cottage Cheese Salad

1 c. white sugar
1 can crushed pineapple
6 Tbsp. cold water
2 pkg. unflavored gelatin
2 lg. carrots, shredded
1 c. cottage cheese
1 c. nuts
1 lg. cont. Cool Whip
1½ c. Hellman's mayonnaise
1 c. chopped celery

In a large bowl, mix white sugar and pineapple. In saucepan, soak gelatin in cold water then bring to a boil. Pour over sugar and pineapple; stir. Set in refrigerator and let set slightly. Add all other ingredients and mix together.

Lizbet and Daughters—Country Cooking

Spring Salad

First Layer–
3 (3 oz.) boxes lime Jell-O
3 c. hot water
3 c. cold water
1 can crushed pineapples, drained

Second Layer–
2-3 c. whipped topping
8 oz. cream cheese

Third Layer–
reserved pineapple juice
water
3 egg yolks
2 Tbsp. flour
1 c. sugar
1 Tbsp. lemon juice

First layer: Combine Jell-O, water and pineapples. Pour in 9" x 13" pan. Second layer: Mix together and pour over cooled first layer. Third layer: Use pineapple juice and add enough water to make 1½ cups. Combine egg yolks, flour, sugar and lemon juice. Mix with a wire whisk. Cook over moderate heat until the consistency of mayonnaise. Cool and spread over second layer.

Pineapple Salad

First Layer–
3 (3 oz.) boxes pineapple Jell-O
1 can crushed pineapples, drained

Second Layer–
8 oz. cream cheese
1 c. sugar
2-3 c. whipped topping

Third Layer–
2 c. brown sugar
3 c. water
reserved pineapple juice
3 Tbsp. clear jel, heaping

First layer: Mix Jell-O according to directions on box (using only half the required amount of water). Add pineapple and put in 9" x 13" pan. Let set. Second layer: Cream together and spread on top of Jell-O. Third layer: Mix first 3 ingredients together. Bring to a boil and thicken with clear jel. Cool and spread on top of second layer. Delicious!

Coated Grapes

8 oz. cream cheese
1 c. powdered sugar
1 c. sour cream
1 tsp. vanilla
5-6 lb. grapes

Mix together first four ingredients and pour over grapes.

Lizbet and Daughters—Country Cooking

Meats & Main Dishes

If you are a typical housewife,
You've had this problem, no doubt.
You can't decide what next to make,
You say you're "all cooked out."
We had chicken just yesterday;
I made a casserole for lunch.
The children don't like liver so well.
Now what can I feed my bunch?
Sometimes it's hard to decide.
Do we want the potatoes mashed or fried?
Of course we need some dessert.
But what shall I bake?
Pies always take so much time,
And we're tired of plain old cake.
Oh, why do I have such a problem
Deciding what to cook?
The answer is very obvious,
If we care to take a look.
I think the greatest problem
In our society,
Very simply stated, is
Too much variety!

Basic White Sauce

2 Tbsp. butter
2 Tbsp. flour
2 c. milk
½ tsp. salt
⅛ tsp. pepper

Melt butter; add flour then milk, stirring constantly until thickened. Can also be used for cheese sauce by adding 1 c. Velveeta cheese and a little more milk.

Chicken Flour

4 c. flour
3 Tbsp. salt
1 Tbsp. paprika
5 tsp. garlic salt
2 Tbsp. Ac'cent
4 c. cracker meal
2 Tbsp. sugar
6 Tbsp. seasoned salt
1 Tbsp. black pepper

Roll any kind of meat in this mixture and fry. This is also good for fish.

Miracle drugs go back a long way.
Moses had two tablets that could cure the world's ills.

Lizbet and Daughters—Country Cooking

Chicken Breading

1 lb. white crackers
1 lb. Ritz crackers
2 pkg. original Shake 'n Bake
2 pkg. barbecue Shake 'n Bake

1 c. Bisquick
½ c. seasoned salt
paprika

Tomato Gravy

1 c. tomato juice
½ c. water
3 Tbsp. flour
½ tsp. salt

½ c. cream
2 c. milk
2 Tbsp. sugar, optional
pinch soda

Place juice and water in a saucepan and bring to a boil. Blend flour and salt with some of the milk; add cream and rest of milk. Stir into hot juice, stirring until thickened. May add 2 Tbsp. sugar and a little pepper. Serve over crackers, buttered bread or fried potatoes.

Dandelion Gravy

bacon
2 Tbsp. flour
1½ c. milk
1 Tbsp. sugar

salt to taste
vinegar to taste
2 hard-boiled eggs, diced
finely cut up dandelion greens

Cut up a few strips of bacon into a pan and fry. Use part of drippings to make pan gravy with flour. When brown, stir in milk. Let boil. Add sugar and salt and vinegar to taste. Add eggs. Just before serving add dandelion greens. Also good using lettuce or endive.

In real life, the greatest heroes are often found in ordinary people.

Batter for Deep Frying

1 c. flour
2 tsp. baking powder
2 eggs, separated
¼ tsp. salt
⅔ c. milk
1 Tbsp. butter, melted

Mix flour, baking powder and salt. Add beaten egg yolks and milk. Last add beaten egg whites and butter. This is good for fish or chicken.

Deep Fried Fish

1 tsp. salt
½ c. flour
2 eggs, beaten
¼ c. milk
Ritz crackers, crushed
Crisco oil

Roll fish in flour and salt mixture. Dip fish into mixture of eggs and milk. Roll in crackers. Deep fry in hot Crisco oil.

Barbecue Sauce

1 pt. warm water
½ c. salt
1 pt. vinegar
1 qt. salad oil
1 Tbsp. oregano
2 Tbsp. Worcestershire sauce
½ c. soy sauce
18 lb. chicken

Mix marinade well and soak chicken overnight in ice chest. Barbecue the next day. Strain the liquid and use to spray chicken while barbecuing.

Marinade for Chicken

1 c. barbecue sauce
1 c. sweet and sour dressing
1 c. Italian dressing

Mix all together and soak chicken tenders in this for several days. Grill. Delicious.

Lizbet and Daughters—Country Cooking

Grilled Thighs and Drumsticks

2½ c. packed brown sugar
2 c. water
2 c. cider vinegar
1 c. ketchup
1 c. vegetable oil
4 Tbsp. salt
3 Tbsp. prepared mustard

4½ tsp. Worcestershire sauce
1 Tbsp. soy sauce
1 tsp. pepper
1 tsp. liquid smoke
10 lb. chicken thighs and drumsticks
seasoned salt

In a large bowl combine the first 11 ingredients. Pour into 2 large resealable plastic bags. Add chicken. Seal bags. Turn to coat. Prepare grill for indirect heat. Drain and discard marinade. Sprinkle chicken with seasoned salt. Grill chicken, skin side down, covered, over indirect medium heat for 15 minutes. Turn; grill until juices run clear.

Crunchy Baked Chicken

chicken
salt
butter, melted

crushed soda crackers
seasoned salt

Sprinkle salt over chicken pieces. Let set overnight in refrigerator. Next day, dip chicken pieces in melted butter then in finely crushed soda cracker crumbs. Layer on cookie sheet. Sprinkle seasoned salt over all. Bake at 400° for 30 minutes. Finish baking at 350°.

Habit starts out as a thread.

As new threads are added,

it becomes a rope we cannot break.

Chicken Gumbo

9 slices bread, lightly toasted and cut up
4 c. cooked, cut up chicken
¼ c. butter
½ c. salad dressing
4 eggs, beaten
2 cans celery soup
1 c. milk
1 c. chicken broth
1 tsp. salt
9 slices Velveeta cheese

Grease casserole or roaster. Layer bread crumbs in roaster and put chicken on top of bread. Mix together butter, salad dressing, eggs, celery soup, milk, chicken broth and salt. Pour over bread crumbs. Layer cheese on top. Bake at 350° for 1¼ hours.

Southern Chicken Pie

chicken
3 tsp. butter, melted
3 tsp. flour

Crust–
2 c. flour
1 tsp. salt
2 tsp. baking powder

potatoes, optional
carrots, optional

salt and pepper to taste
3 c. warm chicken broth
1 c. milk

2 tsp. butter, melted
1 egg, lightly beaten
1 c. milk

peas, optional

Stew chicken until meat will drop off bones. Cut meat in bite-sized pieces. Put in baking dish. Mix butter, flour, salt and pepper and chicken broth. Cook until smooth and add milk. Pour over chicken and keep warm until crust is made. Pour crust batter over chicken and bake at 350° until nice and brown. Potatoes, carrots and peas can be cooked and added to meat for a tasty one dish meal.

Lizbet and Daughters—Country Cooking

Easy Chicken Potpie

1⅔ c. frozen mixed vegetables
1 c. cut up, cooked chicken
1 can cream of chicken soup

1 c. Bisquick baking mix
½ c. milk
1 egg

Heat oven to 400°. Mix vegetables, chicken and soup and put in an ungreased 9" pie pan or a small casserole. Stir remaining ingredients until blended. Pour over vegetables. Bake for 30 minutes or until golden brown. A quick and easy supper.

Chicken and Dumplings

1 qt. chicken

Dumplings–
1 egg
2 Tbsp. milk
½ tsp. salt

3 tsp. baking powder
flour to make stiff dough

Using a large kettle with a tight-fitting cover; remove a quart of chicken meat from the bones. Add broth and make gravy as usual. Beat dumpling ingredients together to make a good stiff dough. Drop by spoonsful into the boiling gravy. Place lid on and let covered for 5-8 minutes. It is important that the lid not be removed once. Remove lid and serve immediately.

Country Chicken and Biscuits

2½ c. diced chicken
1½ c. Velveeta cheese
1-2 cans cream of chicken soup
1 pkg. frozen mixed vegetables

2 c. cubed potatoes, cooked
salt
seasoned salt
oven ready biscuits

Mix all ingredients except biscuits and bake at 350° for 20 minutes. Arrange biscuits on top. Leave uncovered and return to oven and bake 20 minutes longer or until biscuits are done.

Chicken Casserole

2 lb. chicken breasts
16 oz. sour cream
1 can cream of chicken soup
1 (1 lb.) pkg. California Blend
1 (2 lb.) pkg. Tater Tots
Velveeta cheese

Cut chicken breasts in small pieces and fry. Put in bottom of roaster. Mix sour cream and soup together and spread over chicken. Cook the vegetables until soft. Drain and layer over chicken layer. Put Velveeta cheese over vegetables. Add Tater Tots on top. Bake at 350° for 1 hour.

Cheesy Chicken and Rice Casserole

1 can cream of chicken soup
1⅓ c. water
¾ c. uncooked white rice
2 c. fresh or frozen mixed vegetables
½ tsp. onion powder
4 boneless, skinless chicken breasts
½ c. shredded cheddar cheese

Stir soup, water, rice, vegetables and onion powder in a baking dish. Top with chicken. Season chicken as desired. Bake covered at 375° for 45 minutes or until done. Top with cheese.

Chicken and Rice Casserole

1 can cream of chicken soup
1 can cream of mushroom soup
1½ c. milk
1 c. rice
1 pkg. onion soup mix
¼ c. butter
2 lb. boneless chicken

Put rice, soup and milk into a greased casserole. Dip chicken in melted butter and place on top of rice mixture. Sprinkle soup mix over top. Bake for 2 hours. If you use cooked chicken, bake for only 1 hour.

Lizbet and Daughters—Country Cooking

Vegetable and Rice Dish

1 pt. canned chicken with broth
12 oz. mixed vegetables
1 c. rice

Bring 2 c. water, chicken and broth to a boil. Add 2 Tbsp. chicken base. Add rice and mixed vegetables. Simmer until vegetables are tender.

Chicken Rice Casserole

2 c. rice
2½ c. chicken broth
2 c. celery
1 c. mushroom soup
1½ c. Real mayonnaise
2 Tbsp. chopped onion
2 c. cooked chicken

Cook rice in chicken broth until tender. Sauté celery in butter. Put all ingredients together and mix gently. Put in greased casserole. Put on crushed cornflakes mixed with melted butter. Bake at 350° for 1 hour.

Mexican Chicken Roll-Ups

2½ c. cooked chicken
1½ tsp. taco seasoning
1 c. cheddar cheese
½ c. salsa
½ c. sour cream
½ can cream of mushroom soup
1 sm. onion
10 flour tortillas

Topping-
1 c. sour cream
1½ tsp. taco seasoning
½ can cream of mushroom soup

Combine and place ⅓ c. filling on each tortilla. Roll up and place seam side down in 9" x 13" pan. Pour topping ingredients over tortillas. Bake at 350° for 30 minutes. Sprinkle with ½ c. cheddar cheese. Serve with lettuce and chopped tomatoes.

Chicken Enchiladas

2 Tbsp. butter
3 oz. cream cheese, softened
1 Tbsp. milk
½ tsp. salt
¼ tsp. ground cumin
2 c. cubed, cooked chicken

6 flour tortillas
1 can cream of chicken soup
8 oz. sour cream
1 c. milk
½ c. jalapeño peppers, optional
1 c. cheddar cheese

Combine softened cream cheese, milk, salt, cumin and chicken. Stir well. Spoon ⅓ c. chicken mixture onto each tortilla. Roll up. Place filled tortillas seam side down in a baking dish. In a bowl combine cream of chicken soup, sour cream, milk and peppers. Pour the soup mixture evenly over the tortillas. Cover. Bake at 350° for 35 minutes or until heated through. Remove; sprinkle with cheese. Return to oven until cheese is melted.

Turkey or Chicken Supreme

2 c. cooked chicken
1 c. uncooked macaroni
2 cans cream of chicken soup
2 c. milk
½ c. chopped onion

½ tsp. salt
¼ tsp. pepper
3 Tbsp. butter
1 c. grated cheese

Combine all ingredients. Put in greased casserole. Bake at 350° for 1½ hours.

Chicken or Ham Roll

biscuit dough

cooked, cut up chicken or ham

Use your favorite biscuit recipe. Roll out, then spread with cut up, cooked chicken or ham. Roll up as you do to make rolls, then cut in slices. Put in a greased pan and bake at 350°. Make gravy with chicken broth if using chicken. If using ham, make a white sauce with Velveeta cheese for gravy. Top hot rolls with gravy.

Lizbet and Daughters—Country Cooking

Chicken Nuggets

3 boneless, skinless chicken breasts
1¾ c. finely crushed round crackers
½ tsp. seasoned salt
dash of pepper
½ c. butter, melted

Cut chicken into 1" pieces. Combine crushed crackers, salt and pepper. Dip chicken pieces into butter then into crumb mixture. Place chicken pieces ½" apart on foil-lined sheets. Bake at 400° for 20-25 minutes or until golden brown. Serve hot or cold.

Underground Ham Casserole

5-6 c. cubed ham
4 Tbsp. butter
½ c. diced onion
1 Tbsp. Worcestershire sauce
2 cans cream of mushroom soup
1 c. milk
1 c. Velveeta cheese
1 lb. bacon, crumbled
1 c. Velveeta cheese, sliced
4 qt. mashed potatoes
1 pt. sour cream

Cook onions in butter until soft; add ham, mushroom soup, milk and Worcestershire sauce. Add 1 c. Velveeta cheese and heat until cheese is melted. Pour all in a large roaster. Mash potatoes, using no salt or milk, just mix with sour cream. Spread on top of ham mixture. Top with bacon and cheese slices. Bake at 350° until heated through.

Mashed Potato Casserole

3 lb. potatoes, peeled,
   cooked and mashed
½ c. butter
8 oz. cream cheese
2 eggs, beaten
½ c. milk
½ c. sour cream
salt to taste
2 lb. hamburger
salt and pepper to taste
1 can mushroom soup

Combine first 7 ingredients and spread in bottom of casserole. Brown hamburger and season with salt and pepper, adding 1 can mushroom soup to the gravy made from hamburger (pan gravy). Mix with hamburger and put on top of mashed potatoes. Bake until heated through. Can be made a day ahead.

Potluck Potatoes

2 lb. potatoes
1 can cream of mushroom soup
½ c. butter
1 tsp. onion salt
¼ tsp. pepper
1 pt. sour cream
2 c. Velveeta cheese
1 tsp. seasoned salt

Slice potatoes; cook until almost tender. Put the rest of ingredients together and heat until cheese is melted. Put in layers in casserole and cover with 2 c. crushed cornflake crumbs mixed with ½ c. melted butter. Bake at 350° for 45 minutes.

Lizbet and Daughters—Country Cooking

Potato Stack Casserole

6 lb. hash browns, thawed, or 8 lb. potatoes, cooked, cooled and shredded
2 c. sour cream

2 c. milk
2 pkg. Ranch dressing mix
4 lb. hamburger
2 pkg. taco seasoning

Cheese Sauce–
½ c. butter
4 Tbsp. flour
4 c. sour cream

2½ c. milk
6 c. Velveeta cheese

Spread potatoes in bottom of casserole. Mix sour cream, milk and Ranch dressing mix and pour on top of potatoes. Brown hamburger and taco seasoning and layer over top. For cheese sauce, melt ingredients together. Bake casserole at 350° for 2 hours or until hot. When ready to serve put cheese sauce over top, then layer with crushed Doritos.

Norwegian Parsley Potatoes

small red potatoes
butter

minced parsley
salt to taste

Boil potatoes until soft and peel strip around center of each potato. Put butter in skillet; stir potatoes until covered. Sprinkle with minced parsley and salt. A good way to use those small potatoes. Delicious.

Ranch Potato Casserole

6-8 med. potatoes
½ c. sour cream
½ c. prepared Ranch dressing

¼ c. bacon, crumbled
2 Tbsp. parsley
1 c. shredded cheddar cheese

Topping:
½ c. shredded cheese
¼ c. butter, melted

2 c. crushed cornflakes

Cook potatoes until tender; quarter and set aside. Combine sour cream, dressing, bacon, parsley and 1 c. cheese. Place potatoes in a greased 9" x 13" baking dish. Pour sour cream mixture over potatoes and toss gently. Top with cheese. Combine cornflakes and melted butter and sprinkle over casserole. Bake at 350° for 40-50 minutes.

Tasty Potato Casserole

2 lb. hash browns, cooked
½ c. butter, melted
1 tsp. salt
¼ tsp. pepper

½ c. chopped onions
1 can cream of chicken soup
2 c. milk
2 c. grated cheddar cheese

Topping–
2 c. cornflakes, crushed

¼ c. butter, melted

Combine all ingredients. Put in casserole and bake at 350° for 45 minutes. Combine topping ingredients and put on top of potatoes for last 15 minutes.

Lizbet and Daughters—Country Cooking

Quick Scalloped Potatoes

potatoes
butter
oil
salt
pepper

seasoned salt
flour
milk
Velveeta cheese

Peel potatoes. Slice thinly or put through Salad Master. Melt butter and a few drops oil in skillet. Add potatoes and fry until browned and soft. Add salt, pepper and seasoned salt. Sprinkle a little flour on top and stir. Add some milk and heat again. Top with Velveeta cheese if you like. Simple and quick if company stops in unexpectedly.

Make-Ahead Potatoes

12 lg. potatoes, boiled
8 oz. cream cheese
8 oz. sour cream

1 tsp. onion powder
¼ c. butter, melted
salt to taste

Combine potatoes, sour cream, cream cheese and onion powder and whip or mash until fluffy. Add a small amount of milk if necessary. Bake at 350° for 1 hour. To fill a Lifetime roaster, use 30 potatoes, 16 oz. cream cheese and 16 oz. sour cream.

*Always remember to forget the troubles that pass away,
But never forget to remember the blessings that come each day.*

Hearty Twice Baked Potatoes

8 lg. potatoes
½ lb. bulk pork sausage
¼ c. butter, softened
2 c. shredded cheddar cheese
1½ c. diced fully cooked ham

6 strips bacon, cooked and crumbled
1 c. sour cream
½ c. Italian salad dressing
salt and pepper to taste

Bake potatoes at 400° for 1 hour. Meanwhile, in a skillet, cook sausage until no longer pink; drain. When potatoes are cool enough to handle, cut in half lengthwise. Scoop out pulp, leaving ¼" in shell. In a large bowl, mash the pulp with butter. Stir in rest of ingredients. Spoon into potato shells. Bake at 400° for 30 minutes or until golden brown. Can be made the day before and refrigerated.

Parmesan Potatoes

¼ c. Parmesan cheese
1½ tsp. salt
1 tsp. garlic salt

1 tsp. paprika
½ tsp. pepper

Cut potatoes into bite-sized pieces. Mix ingredients. Put potatoes in bowl; sprinkle mixture over top; cover and shake. Pour ¼ c. oil in 9" x 13" pan. Add potatoes; do not stir. Bake at 350° uncovered for 50 minutes.

Cheddar Parmesan Potatoes

¼ c. flour
¼ c. Parmesan cheese
1 Tbsp. paprika
¾ tsp. salt

pinch garlic salt
6 Tbsp. butter, melted
potatoes, sliced in wedges
shredded cheddar cheese

Slice potatoes and put in bowl with dry ingredients; cover and shake. Put melted butter in bottom of 9" x 13" pan. Place potatoes in pan. Bake uncovered at 350° until potatoes are soft. Sprinkle cheddar cheese on top. Return to oven until cheese is melted.

Lizbet and Daughters—Country Cooking

Potato Stacks

baked potatoes
2 lb. hamburger, browned
½ c. chopped onion
seasonings to taste
1 pkg. taco seasoning

1 can chili hot beans
1 pkg. California Blend vegetables
2 cans cheese sauce
16 oz. sour cream

Mix hamburger, onion, seasonings, taco seasoning and chili hot beans. Prepare vegetables and make cheese sauce. Pass around in order given. Everyone makes their own.

Potato Roll Meatloaf

2 med. potatoes
2 lb. ground beef
1 c. oatmeal
1½ c. tomato sauce, divided
¾ tsp. pepper, divided

1 egg, slightly beaten
1½ c. shredded cheddar cheese
1½ tsp. salt, divided
2 tsp. Worcestershire sauce
1 sm. onion, finely chopped

Cook potatoes until just beginning to soften. Set aside to cool. Peel and shred. Should equal about 2 c. In a large bowl lightly mix ground beef, oatmeal, ¼ c. tomato sauce, ½ tsp. pepper, egg, 1 tsp. salt, Worcestershire sauce and onion. Roll meat mixture between 2 sheets of waxed paper into 9" x 12" rectangle. Remove top sheet. Set aside. In a medium bowl, lightly mix together potatoes, cheese, ½ tsp. salt, ¼ c. tomato sauce and ¼ tsp. pepper. Spread potato mixture evenly over meat mixture to within 1" of the edges. Beginning at the 9" side, roll up meatloaf, lifting away from the waxed paper as you go. Crimp and seal ends. In bottom of 9" x 13" baking dish, pour ½ c. tomato sauce. Place meatloaf in baking dish. Pour ½ c. tomato sauce over loaf. Bake uncovered at 350° for 1 hour.

Beef and Potato Loaf

4 c. shredded potatoes
1 Tbsp. chopped onion
1 tsp. salt
½ tsp. pepper
1 tsp. parsley
1 lb. hamburger
¾ c. milk
½ c. cracker crumbs or oatmeal
½ c. ketchup
¼ c. chopped onion
1 tsp. salt

Arrange potatoes, onion, salt, pepper and parsley in a 2 qt. baking dish. Mix remaining ingredients together. Spread hamburger mixture evenly over potatoes. Decorate with more ketchup if desired. Bake at 350° for 1-1½ hours or until potatoes are soft.

Potato Pancakes

2 c. leftover mashed potatoes
2 Tbsp. flour
2 eggs

Mix together. Drop by spoonful onto hot griddle and fry until golden brown on both sides. Delicious served with applesauce or butter and syrup.

Penny Saver Casserole

6 hot dogs, thinly sliced
4 med. potatoes, cooked and diced
1 c. peas
½ c. butter
2 Tbsp. minced onion
1 tsp. mustard
1 can cream of mushroom soup

Combine potatoes, onions and butter in casserole. Then add peas, mustard and soup to the first mixture. Dot with sliced hot dogs. Cover and bake at 350° for 25 minutes.

Lizbet and Daughters — Country Cooking

German Pizza

¼ c. butter
3 c. raw, shredded potatoes
ham or any meat
4 eggs
cheese
salt and pepper to taste
onions, optional
peppers, optional

Melt butter in a large Lifetime skillet. Add potatoes. Layer meat over potatoes. Beat eggs and pour over meat. Put lid on and heat over low heat, as you do not stir this. When potatoes are soft, add cheese on top. An easy supper and very good. If you use ham for your meat, try using mozzarella cheese.

Tasty California Blend Vegetables

30 Ritz crackers
5 Tbsp. butter
2 lb. California Blend vegetables
salt to taste
6 slices Velveeta cheese

Crush crackers. Melt butter and add to crackers. Reserve 2 heaping Tbsp. crumbs and put rest of crackers in a baking pan, pressing evenly over the bottom. Heat vegetables until soft. Drain and put on top of crackers. Salt to taste. Top with cheese and reserved crumbs. Bake at 350° for 45 minutes.

Green Beans

1 pkg. frozen green beans
1 med. onion, thinly sliced
½ c. fresh mushrooms
2 Tbsp. butter

Melt butter in saucepan. Add green beans, onion and mushrooms. Cook over low heat until beans are tender.

Green Bean Supreme

1 qt. canned beans
1 lb. hamburger
1 can cream of mushroom soup
salt and pepper

Fry hamburger and stir until crumbly. Add salt to hamburger to taste. Mix beans, hamburger and soup together and heat. A very easy and tasty dish.

Escalloped Cabbage

1 sm. head cabbage
1 tsp. salt
1¾ c. white sauce
⅓ c. bacon, crumbled

1½ c. chopped green peppers
1 c. shredded cheese
1 c. buttered bread crumbs

Basic White Sauce–
2 Tbsp. butter
2 Tbsp. flour

1¼ c. milk
salt and pepper to taste

Cut cabbage into eighths and cook in salt water for 8 minutes. Drain. Place a layer of cabbage in baking dish then white sauce, green pepper and cheese. Repeat. Sprinkle top with bread crumbs and bacon. Bake at 350° for 10-20 minutes or until top is browned. For white sauce, melt butter; stir in flour, stirring constantly until paste begins to bubble but not brown. Add milk and boil until thick.

String Bean Patties

1 qt. canned beans
2 eggs
1½ c. quick oatmeal

½ pkg. saltine crackers
½ tsp. seasoned salt

Use potato masher to mash the beans. Mix all together and form into patties. Roll in flour and fry in vegetable oil. If too thin, add more crackers or oatmeal. Patties can be eaten plain or with salad dressing. Very good.

Lizbet and Daughters—Country Cooking

Quick Baked Beans

1 can chili hot beans
1 can pork and beans
½ c. ketchup

1 tsp. mustard
3 Tbsp. brown sugar

Mix beans with ketchup, mustard and brown sugar. Heat on stove top or in oven.

Delicious Baked Beans

1 sm. can kidney beans
1 sm. can butter beans (lima)
1 med. can pork and beans
½ lb. bacon, cut in strips
2 sm. onions, chopped

1 c. brown sugar
1 c. ketchup
1 tsp. mustard
pineapple tidbits, undrained, optional

Mix beans together; don't drain off juice. In skillet start cooking bacon, but don't brown. Do not drain grease; add rest of ingredients. Heat through. Pour over beans and mix well. Bake uncovered at 350° for at least one hour or longer if desired.

Stuffed Green Peppers

6 green peppers
2 lb. hamburger, browned
1 c. rice

1 qt. tomato juice
salt and pepper to taste

Cut top off each pepper. Take out seeds and clean. Cook pepper upright in salt water for 5 minutes. Drain. Brown hamburger and onions; drain. Add remaining ingredients and cook for a few minutes. Stuff peppers with mixture. Set upright in baking pan. Pour rest of mixture over peppers. Bake at 350° for 45 minutes or until rice is soft. Good served with cut up tomatoes and sour cream.

Zucchini Casserole

1 box chicken flavored
    Stove Top stuffing
½ c. butter
1 c. sour cream

1 can cream of chicken soup
1 c. grated carrots
6 c. grated, unpeeled zucchini
3-4 c. chicken pieces

Melt butter and stir in Stove Top stuffing. Let set for several minutes. Combine chicken, sour cream and soup. Stir in zucchini and carrots. Add stuffing mixture and mix well. Pour into greased casserole and bake uncovered at 350° for 1 hour.

Zucchini Patties

⅔ c. Bisquick baking mix
¼ c. Parmesan cheese
2 eggs

2 c. grated zucchini
1 sm. onion, chopped
salt and pepper

Combine ingredients and drop by spoonful into heavy skillet containing a thin layer of hot oil or butter. Spread out and flatten as you turn them with spatula. Fry until golden brown on both sides.

Onion Patties

¾ c. flour
1 Tbsp. sugar
1 Tbsp. cornmeal
2½ c. finely chopped onions

2 tsp. baking powder
1 tsp. salt
¾ c. milk

Mix dry ingredients together, then add milk. Batter should be fairly thick. Add onions and mix thoroughly. Drop by spoonful into hot skillet with shortening. Flatten slightly when you turn them.

Lizbet and Daughters—Country Cooking

Squash Patties

3 c. shredded squash
1 c. flour
2 tsp. baking powder

1 egg
½ c. milk
salt and pepper to taste

Mix all together. Form into patties and fry in skillet until golden brown.

Shipwreck

1½ lb. hamburger, fried with onions and salt
1 qt. cubed potatoes
1 pt. carrots
1 pt. peas

celery, chopped
1 can cream of chicken soup
1 can cream of mushroom soup
milk
Velveeta cheese

Add salt to potatoes, carrots and peas separately. Cook each vegetable until soft. Put hamburger and vegetables in layers in a casserole dish. Add soups and milk. Bake at 350° until hot, then put Velveeta cheese on top.

El Paso Casserole

1¾ lb. Velveeta cheese
2 lb. chipped ham

1½ lb. noodles

White Sauce–
1 c. butter
1 c. flour

½ gal. milk
1 can cream of celery soup

Cook noodles in your favorite broth. Blend cheese and ham in white sauce. Pour over noodles in oiled pan. Sprinkle with toasted bread crumbs. Bake at 350° for 25 minutes.

Yummasetti

1 lb. wide noodles
2 lb. hamburger
2 cans mushroom soup
1 can tomato soup
Velveeta cheese
salt and pepper to taste

Cook noodles. Drain. Fry hamburger. Mix all together and bake at 350° for 1 hour. Put Velveeta cheese on top when almost done and put back in oven so cheese melts.

Wigglers

9 slices bacon
3 onions, chopped
1 c. chopped celery
3 c. peas
2 cans cream of mushroom soup
3 lb. hamburger
3 c. diced carrots
3 c. diced potatoes
2 lb. spaghetti, cooked
1½ qt. tomato juice

Fry bacon and crumble. Fry hamburger and onions in bacon grease. Put in casserole; add rest of ingredients except bacon and tomato juice. Arrange Velveeta cheese slices and bacon over top. Pour tomato juice over all. Bake at 370° for 1½-2 hours.

Ham and Noodles

½ c. chopped onions
2 Tbsp. butter
1 can cream of chicken soup
1 c. sour cream
8 oz. noodles
2 c. diced ham
½ lb. Swiss cheese, shredded

Sauté onions in butter. Add the soup and sour cream. Boil noodles and drain. Put half of noodles in greased casserole. Next put half of onion mixture on, then ham and cheese. Layer again, with onion mixture on top. Bake at 350° for 1½ hours.

Lizbet and Daughters—Country Cooking

Taco Skillet Meal

1 lb. hamburger
1 pt. tomato juice
1 c. uncooked rice
1 c. shredded cheddar cheese
lettuce
onions

1 pkg. taco seasoning
¾ c. water
2 Tbsp. brown sugar
sour cream
salsa

Brown hamburger in skillet with lid. Add tomato juice, water, seasonings and rice. Simmer for 20 minutes or until rice is tender, stirring several times. Top with cheese and let melt. Serve with lettuce, onions, sour cream and salsa.

Haystack

2 c. crushed Ritz crackers
chopped lettuce
chopped onions
chopped tomatoes
2 c. cooked rice

2 lb. ground beef, browned
1 pt. pizza sauce (add to beef)
2 cans cheddar cheese soup
shredded cheese
sour cream

Layer on plates in order given.

Taco Bake

Crust-
2 c. flour
3 tsp. baking powder
1 tsp. salt

2 lb. hamburger
1 sm. onion
1 pkg. taco seasoning
1 can kidney beans
⅓ c. brown sugar

4 Tbsp. shortening
¾ c. milk

1 tomato
1 green pepper
1 c. sour cream
⅔ c. salad dressing

Mix first 5 ingredients together for dough and spread in 9" x 13" pan. Fry together hamburger, onion and taco seasoning. Add beans and brown sugar. Spread on top of dough. Chop tomato and green pepper and spread on top of meat mixture. Mix sour cream and salad dressing together and spread over all. Top with Velveeta or mozzarella cheese. Bake at 350° for 35 minutes or until done.

Spanish Rice

1 lb. hamburger
1 sm. onion, chopped
½ c. diced green pepper
1 c. rice
shredded cheese of your choice

salt and pepper to taste
½ tsp. chili powder
dash of Italian seasoning
tomato juice
⅓ c. water

Brown hamburger and onion. Add green pepper, tomato juice and rice. Add the seasonings and simmer until rice is done. Add water if it gets too dry.

Lizbet and Daughters—Country Cooking

Mock Turkey

2 lb. hamburger
2 cans cream of chicken soup
1 can cream of mushroom soup
4 c. milk
1 loaf bread, toasted
salt and pepper to taste

Brown hamburger in butter. Mix all together and place in casserole dish. Bake at 350° for 45 minutes.

Enchiladas

2 lb. hamburger
green peppers
onions
2 Tbsp. taco seasoning
2 c. cheddar and mozzarella cheese
6 oz. cream cheese
18 soft taco shells

Brown hamburger; add peppers, onions, taco seasoning and salt to taste. Stir in cheeses and cream cheese until melted. Put ⅓ c. hamburger mixture on each shell and roll up. Place side by side in a greased pan. Top with more peppers and cheeses. Bake at 350° for 20 minutes. Serve with lettuce, taco sauce and sour cream.

Beef Stew

1 pt. canned beef chunks
2 c. chunked potatoes
2 c. sliced carrots
1 lg. onion
1 pt. water
1 tsp. beef seasoning
½ tsp. pepper

Cook all together until vegetables are soft. Thicken slightly with 1 heaping Tbsp. flour and enough water to make a paste.

Meatball Stew

1½ lb. hamburger
1 c. soft bread crumbs
¼ c. chopped onions
1 egg, beaten
1 tsp. salt

1 can tomato soup
1 can beef broth
4 med. potatoes, pared and quartered
4 carrots, sliced
2 Tbsp. chopped parsley

Combine the first 5 ingredients. Shape into 24 meatballs. Brown meatballs in butter in a 4 qt. pan. Add soup, broth and vegetables. Bring to boil; cover and simmer for 30 minutes or until vegetables are tender. Add parsley.

Tater Tot Casserole

1 lb. hamburger
½ pkg. onion soup mix
1 pkg. frozen mixed vegetables

1 can cream of mushroom soup
Velveeta cheese
1 pkg. frozen Tater Tots

Put raw hamburger in bottom of 9" x 9" baking dish. Sprinkle soup mix over hamburger. Layer mixed vegetables, mushroom soup and Velveeta cheese in order given. Bake for 1 hour at 350°, then top with Tater Tots. Return to oven and bake for 30 minutes longer.

Lizbet and Daughters—Country Cooking

Frankfurter Bake

8 oz. noodles
¼ c. butter
2 Tbsp. flour
1 c. milk
1 c. Velveeta cheese
½ tsp. salt

1 lb. hot dogs, sliced
¼ c. brown sugar
1 Tbsp. prepared mustard
¼ c. salad dressing
1 pkg. Tater Tots

In a large kettle cook noodles. Drain; return to kettle. In a saucepan melt butter and stir in flour. Add milk, cheese and salt. Heat until cheese is melted. Stir sauce and hot dogs into noodles. Combine brown sugar, mustard and salad dressing. Put noodles into casserole and pour sauce mixture evenly over noodles. Arrange Tater Tots on top. Bake at 350° for 25 minutes.

Ground Beef Grand Style

1 can biscuits or Tater Tots
1½ lb. ground beef
8 oz. cream cheese or Velveeta
1 can mushroom or chicken soup

¼ c. milk
¼ c. ketchup
½ c. chopped onions
1 tsp. salt

Brown ground beef with onions. Combine soup, milk, salt and ketchup; mix with ground beef and put in pan. Top with cheese and biscuits. Bake at 350°-400° for 45 minutes or until biscuits are brown.

Porcupine Meatballs

1 lb. ground beef
1 tsp. salt
½ tsp. pepper
1 onion, minced

½ c. rice
1 can tomato soup
½ c. water

Mix meat, rice, salt, pepper and onion. Shape into balls and put in a skillet with lid. Mix soup and water and pour over meatballs. Cover and cook over low heat until meatballs are done.

Bubble Up Pizza

2 lb. sausage or hamburger
1 qt. pizza sauce
4 tubes biscuit rolls
mozzarella cheese
onions
mushrooms
peppers
pepperoni
olives

Cut each biscuit in 6 pieces. Mix all together except cheese. Put in casserole. Bake at 350° for 1 hour or until biscuits are done. Add mozzarella cheese and bake until melted. Yummy.

Mushroom Pizza

1 tube crescent rolls
½ lb. fresh mushrooms
3 Tbsp. butter, melted
¼ c. Parmesan cheese
¼ tsp. Italian seasoning

Press crescent rolls in a 12" round pizza pan. Fry mushrooms and butter together and put on top of crescent rolls. Top with cheese and Italian seasoning. Bake at 375° for 15-20 minutes.

Pizza

1 c. warm water
1 tsp. white sugar
1 Tbsp. yeast
1½ tsp. salt
¼ c. vegetable oil
3 c. bread flour

Let rise 20-30 minutes rolled out on cookie sheet. Top with pizza sauce and *raw* hamburger, ham, peppers, onions or whatever you like. Wait to put cheese on until pizza is almost done. Do not prebake dough. Use only lean hamburger.

Pizza Cups

1 can pizza sauce
1 lb. hamburger or sausage
1 can biscuits
1 pkg. mozzarella cheese
mushrooms
pepperoni

Brown and drain meat. Stir in pizza sauce. Place biscuits in greased muffin tin, pressing to cover bottom and sides. Spoon about ¼ c. meat mixture into each cup. Add mushrooms, pepperoni and cheese. Bake at 350° for 10 minutes or until golden brown.

Stromboli

1 loaf frozen bread dough
¼ lb. ham
¼ lb. pepperoni
½ lb. mozzarella cheese
1 lb. hamburger, browned
mushrooms
peppers
onions

Thaw bread dough in refrigerator overnight. Press out on greased cookie sheet. Spread middle half of dough with toppings. Bring dough together at top and seal edges. Bake at 325° for 30 minutes or until golden. Brush with butter when done.

Taco Shells

1½ c. cold water
1 c. all-purpose flour
½ c. cornmeal
¼ tsp. salt
1 egg

Mix all together with hand beater and fry like pancakes. Pour scant ¼ c. dough in pan and rotate pan to make a nice round ring. We love it with tomatoes, hamburger (browned), cheddar cheese, lettuce and onions. Pour taco sauce over all. Wrap up taco shell and eat.

Lasagna

9-10 noodles
1 lb. hamburger
mushrooms
2 Tbsp. cottage cheese
1 c. mozzarella cheese

1 lg. + 1 sm. jar spaghetti sauce
¾ c. peppers
2 eggs
Velveeta cheese
1 c. sharp cheddar cheese

Brown hamburger; add large jar spaghetti sauce, peppers and mushrooms and simmer for 10 minutes. Cook noodles until tender; add a few drops of cooking oil. Cool. Beat eggs. Add cottage cheese. Put in layers: hamburger sauce, cheddar cheese, mozzarella cheese, noodles, cottage cheese mixture and Velveeta cheese. Repeat until ingredients are all used up. Pour small jar spaghetti sauce on top.

Mexican Lasagna

1 lb. hamburger, browned
16 oz. refried beans
12 uncooked lasagna noodles
2½ c. water

2½ c. pizza sauce
2 c. sour cream
1 c. shredded mozzarella cheese

Combine hamburger and beans. Place 4 or 5 of the uncooked noodles in bottom of a 9" x 13" baking pan. Spread half of the beef mixture over noodles. Cover with remaining noodles. Spread remaining beef mixture on top. Combine water and pizza sauce. Pour over all. Cover tightly with foil. Bake at 350° for 1½ hours or until noodles are tender. Spoon sour cream over casserole; top with cheese. Bake uncovered for 5 minutes or until cheese is melted.

The person who never makes a mistake must get tired of doing nothing.

Lizbet and Daughters—Country Cooking

No-Fuss Lasagna

1½ lb. hamburger, fried
    and seasoned with salt
2 tsp. oregano
¾ tsp. garlic powder, optional
3 c. pizza sauce, divided
2½ c. water

12 uncooked lasagna noodles
4 oz. cream cheese
¼ c. milk
½ c. finely chopped onion
1 c. mozzarella cheese

Add 2½ c. pizza sauce to hamburger mixture. Layer noodles and meat alternately in cake pan, beginning and ending with 4 noodles. Put water over all, then spread with ½ c. pizza sauce. Cover thickly with foil and bake at 350° for 1½ hours or until noodles are tender. Mix cream cheese, milk and onion and spread over top. Sprinkle cheese on top and return to oven until cheese is melted. 1 can refried beans or mild chili beans may be added to hamburger mixture and 1 c. sour cream may be substituted for cream cheese and milk.

Meatballs

4 lb. hamburger
2¾ c. quick oatmeal
3 eggs
¾ c. evaporated milk
⅔ c. milk

¼ c. chopped onion
2¾ tsp. salt
¾ tsp. garlic salt
¾ tsp. black pepper

Barbecue Sauce-
¾ Tbsp. lemon juice
¾ Tbsp. vinegar
1⅓ c. ketchup
1 c. brown sugar

¾ tsp. garlic salt
2 Tbsp. Worcestershire sauce
⅓ tsp. liquid smoke
¼ c. barbecue sauce

Shape into balls and fit tightly in baking pan. Cover with sauce. Bake, uncovered, at 350° for 1 hour.

Saucy Meatballs

1 lb. hamburger
½ c. dry bread crumbs
¼ c. milk
1 egg

¼ tsp. salt
½ tsp. Worcestershire sauce
2 Tbsp. chopped onion

Sauce-
1 can mushroom soup
⅓ c. milk

½ c. sour cream

Mix ingredients for meatballs. Shape into 20 1½" balls. Bake in ungreased 9" x 13" pan at 400° for 20 minutes. For sauce, mix soup and milk in casserole. Add meatballs to soup mixture. Bake at 350° for 30 minutes. Remove and top with sour cream. Serve. We like this with mashed potatoes. Use sauce for gravy.

Meatloaf

2 lb. hamburger
¼ c. minced onion
1 c. oatmeal or crackers
1 egg, beaten

2½ tsp. salt
¼ tsp. pepper
1 tsp. mustard
¼ c. ketchup

Glaze-
½ c. brown sugar
1½ tsp. prepared mustard

1 Tbsp. Worcestershire sauce
¼ c. ketchup

Mix and form into loaf. Bake at 350° for 1 hour. After baking for 30 minutes, spread glaze on top and bake until done.

Lizbet and Daughters—Country Cooking

Poor Man's Steak

3 lb. hamburger
1 c. cracker crumbs
1 c. cold water or milk

1 Tbsp. salt and 1½ tsp. pepper
1 can mushroom soup
1 Tbsp. Worcestershire sauce

Mix well, all except soup. Press into cookie sheet. Chill and cut in squares. Roll in flour and fry in a small amount of grease until golden brown. Place in a baking dish. Dilute soup with ¾ can water and Worcestershire sauce and spread over meat. Bake at 350° for 1 hour.

Salisbury Steak

3 lb. hamburger
1 c. crushed soda crackers
1 c. milk

1 scant Tbsp. salt
pepper

Sauce-
⅔ qt. water
3 Tbsp. dry onion soup mix

5 Tbsp. soy sauce
1 sm. can mushrooms

Mix and press on tray and refrigerate overnight. Cut in squares and roll in flour and brown in skillet. Place in roaster and bake in sauce at 350° for 1½ hours. For delicious gravy, thicken sauce with cornstarch and water mixture at serving time.

Yummy Summer Sausage

2 lb. ground beef
1 c. cold water
2 Tbsp. Tenderquick
1 tsp. garlic salt

1 tsp. pepper
1 tsp. onion salt
2 tsp. liquid smoke
1 tsp. mustard seed

Let this mixture set in a covered bowl for 24 hours in refrigerator. Roll into three equal rolls. Wrap each roll in foil and poke holes with a fork along the bottom of the rolls for the grease to drip out. Place the rolls on a broiler pan rack and bake for 325° for 1½ hours. Let cool. Unwrap and store in plastic bags in refrigerator.

Venison Roast

5 lb. deer meat
salt and pepper to taste
½ c. butter
2 Tbsp. flour
slices of onions and apples

Put meat in casserole. Add salt and pepper. Brown butter in saucepan; add flour. Stir and pour over meat. Add slices of onions and apples. Bake at 350° for 2 hours or until done.

Barbecue on a Budget

3 or 4 lb. boneless chuck roast
2 env. onion soup mix
1 c. salad oil
½ c. cider vinegar
2 Tbsp. brown sugar
2 tsp. Worcestershire sauce
1 c. ketchup

Combine soup mix, oil, vinegar, sugar and Worcestershire sauce. Pour over chuck roast in glass dish. Cover and refrigerate overnight. To cook, place meat and marinade in roaster; add ketchup. Bake at 300° for 4 hours. Serve with sauce.

Barbecue Chuck Roast

3 lb. chuck roast
¼ c. ketchup
1 tsp. prepared mustard
1 tsp. salt
½ tsp. pepper
½ tsp. garlic powder
⅓ c. red wine vinegar
2 Tbsp. cooking oil
2 Tbsp. soy sauce
1 Tbsp. Worcestershire sauce

Marinate for 12 hours. Pierce meat. Bake at 350° for 3 hours.

Lizbet and Daughters—Country Cooking

Juicy Roast

frozen roast
1 c. water

1 env. dry onion soup mix

Put roast in roaster and sprinkle dry onion soup over it. Put in water. Bake at 200° for 7-8 hours. Flavorful and juicy.

Pork Chop Supreme

6-8 pork chops
½ c. water

1 can cream of chicken soup

Dressing:
4 c. bread crumbs
⅓ c. chopped celery
¼ c. butter, melted
2 eggs, beaten

1 sm. onion, chopped
2 Tbsp. parsley flakes
salt and pepper to taste

Brown pork chops and put in roaster. Make dressing by putting all ingredients together. Spoon dressing over pork chops. Dilute soup with ½ c. water and pour over pork chops and dressing. Cover and bake at 350° for 1 hour.

Smoky Ribs

4-6 lb. pork ribs
2 Tbsp. butter
3 cloves garlic, chopped, or garlic powder
¼ c. water
1 tsp. Worcestershire sauce

1 Tbsp. hickory liquid smoke
2 Tbsp. brown sugar
1 c. ketchup
1 tsp. salt
1 tsp. pepper

Place ribs in a large saucepan and cover with water. Bring to a boil; reduce heat and simmer for 20 minutes or until almost tender. Meanwhile, prepare sauce in saucepan. Bring to a boil; reduce heat. Cover and simmer for 10 minutes, stirring occasionally. Place ribs on grill and cook for 20 minutes, turning and brushing with sauce. Delicious.

Ham Loaf

2½ lb. ham loaf mix
2 eggs
salt and pepper to taste

2 c. cracker crumbs
1 tsp. seasoned salt
¼ c. milk

Pineapple Glaze–
1⅓ c. brown sugar
2 tsp. dry mustard

1 c. pineapple juice

Mix ham loaf ingredients well. Put in well greased pan. Combine glaze ingredients and pour over meat. Bake at 350° for 1½-2 hours.

Beef or Deer Jerky

1½ lb. meat (no fat),
    sliced into thin strips
¼ c. soy sauce
1 Tbsp. steak sauce
1 Tbsp. Worcestershire sauce

1 Tbsp. liquid smoke
½ tsp. black pepper
½ tsp. onion salt
½ tsp. garlic salt

Combine above ingredients and marinate meat for 1 day in refrigerator. When marinated, put on oven racks with toothpicks and dry in a 250° oven for 1½-2½ hours. Put foil in oven to catch drips.

Steak Marinade

1 c. soy sauce
½ c. vegetable oil
1 tsp. garlic powder
1 tsp. dry mustard

1 tsp. Ac'cent
½ tsp. cloves
½ tsp. ginger

Sprinkle meat tenderizer on meat if desired. This is also good for pork chops. Can marinate for up to 4 days.

Pineapple Sauce for Ham

1 c. pineapple juice
¾ c. water
⅓ c. brown sugar
2-3 Tbsp. clear jel

1 tsp. dry mustard
1 Tbsp. vinegar
pinch of salt

Bring to boil. Put ham in a casserole and cover with sauce. Bake at 325° for 1 hour or until done. I like to have the ham sliced thick since it's juicier this way. Enough for 20 ham slices.

Chicken Barbecue Sauce

¼ c. butter
1 c. vinegar
1 c. water

2¼ Tbsp. salt
1 Tbsp. Worcestershire sauce

Bring to a boil. Spray on meat often while barbecuing.

Barbecue Sauce

1 pt. ketchup
2 Tbsp. mustard
1¾ c. brown sugar
5 Tbsp. liquid smoke
3 Tbsp. Worcestershire sauce

1 tsp. garlic salt
3 Tbsp. vinegar
1 c. barbecue sauce
fresh or minced onion

Stir all together and pour over hamburgers. Bake at 350° for ½-1 hour. Also good to use on hamburgers when grilling.

Big Mac Sauce

1 c. Miracle Whip
¼ c. creamy French dressing
⅓ c. sweet pickle relish
1 tsp. minced onion
1 Tbsp. sugar
¼ tsp. pepper

Use only the orange colored Kraft Creamy French Dressing. Never use the red colored type. Make sauce in advance and chill. Must be served cold. Tastes better the second day. Good on sandwiches.

Pickled Tongue and Heart

2 c. vinegar
2 c. water
¾ c. sugar

Scald tongue in boiling water to remove skin. Pressure cook each at 10 lb. pressure for 1 hour. Cool and cut into bite-sized chunks. Put in brine. This is enough for 1 heart and 1 tongue.

Corny Dogs

⅔ c. self-rising cornmeal
1 c. flour
1⅓ tsp. baking powder
1 tsp. sugar
¾ c. milk
1 egg
16 hot dogs

Mix first 6 ingredients together. Roll hot dogs in batter. Drop in hot oil and fry until golden brown.

Lizbet and Daughters—Country Cooking

Favorite Barbecued Burgers

Sauce-
- 1 c. ketchup
- ½ c. packed brown sugar
- ⅓ c. sugar
- ¼ c. honey
- ¼ c. molasses
- 2 tsp. mustard
- 1½ tsp. Worcestershire sauce
- ¼ tsp. salt
- ¼ tsp. liquid smoke
- ⅛ tsp. pepper

Burgers-
- 1 egg, beaten
- ⅛ tsp. salt
- ⅓ c. quick oatmeal
- ¼ tsp. onion salt
- ¼ tsp. garlic salt
- ¼ tsp. pepper
- 1½ lb. ground beef

In a saucepan combine sauce ingredients. Bring to a boil. Remove from heat. Set aside 1 c. barbecue sauce to serve with burgers. In a bowl combine the egg, oats, ¼ c. of sauce, salts and pepper. Mix in ground beef. This sauce is also good on barbecued ribs.

Baked Ham and Swiss Sandwiches

- ½ c. butter, softened
- ¼ c. chopped onion
- ¼ c. prepared mustard
- 1 Tbsp. poppy seeds
- ½ tsp. Worcestershire sauce
- ham
- Swiss cheese
- 8 sandwich buns

Combine butter, onion, Worcestershire sauce, mustard and poppy seeds. Spread on sandwich buns. Add ham and cheese. Wrap in foil and bake at 350° for 15-20 minutes.

Chicken Salad Sandwiches

1 qt. cold boiled chicken
2 c. celery
salt and pepper to taste

4 or 5 hard-boiled eggs
mayonnaise

Cut up chicken, celery and eggs. Mix together, then add mayonnaise until desired consistency.

Pizza Burgers

1 lb. hamburger
½ c. chopped onion
½ tsp. garlic powder
1½ tsp. oregano
1 can tomato soup

1 sm. can mushroom pieces
shredded mozzarella cheese
pepperoni
hamburger buns

Brown hamburger and onions. Add next 4 ingredients. Put on hamburger buns. Top with pepperoni and cheese. Bake at 350° for 10 minutes or until cheese melts.

Barbecued Beef Sandwiches

½ c. ketchup
2 Tbsp. brown sugar
2 Tbsp. vinegar

2 tsp. mustard
chopped onion or onion salt

In skillet heat 1 qt. canned beef. Pour off broth. Add rest of ingredients. Simmer for about 15 minutes for variety. Put filling and a thin slice of Velveeta cheese between hamburger buns. Wrap in foil. Bake at 400° for 10-15 minutes. If sandwich filling is dry add more ketchup.

Lizbet and Daughters—Country Cooking

Sloppy Joes

2½ lb. hamburger
1 med. onion, chopped
2½ Tbsp. Worcestershire sauce
⅓ c. brown sugar

½ c. ketchup
1 Tbsp. mustard
1 can cream of mushroom soup

Brown hamburger and onion. Add rest of ingredients. Simmer for 30 minutes.

Spam Burgers

1 (1 lb.) can Spam
½ lb. Muenster cheese
1 sm. onion
¼ c. pickle relish

6 Tbsp. mayonnaise
4 Tbsp. ketchup
3 Tbsp. milk

Grate Spam. Cut up cheese and onion. Mix all together and spread on half of bun. Bake at 350° for 10-15 minutes. Makes 24 open faced sandwiches.

Cornmeal Mush

3 c. water
1 tsp. salt

1 c. cornmeal
1 c. milk

Heat water to boiling in saucepan. Mix cornmeal and salt with milk and add to boiling water, stirring constantly. Cook over low heat for 5 minutes. Pour into pan and let cool. Slice and fry.

Waste not, want not, use it up wear it out, make it do.

Cornmeal Mush

4 c. water
1 tsp. salt
1 c. cornmeal
½ c. flour

Put water on to boil, saving 1 c. to mix with cornmeal and flour. Pour mixture into boiling water, stirring constantly until it boils thoroughly. Turn burner to low heat; cover kettle, stirring occasionally. Cook for 1 hour. Eat hot with butter and syrup or milk, or pour in dish to cool. Slice and fry.

Quiche

½ lb. bacon
1 Tbsp. butter
1 c. chopped onions
3 eggs
1 tsp. salt
2 c. half and half
½ lb. Swiss cheese
salt and pepper to taste
1 (9") pie crust

Cook bacon until crisp. Crumble and put aside. Sauté onions in butter until soft. Mix eggs, salt and half and half. Shred cheese and add to mixture. Add onions and pour into unbaked crust. Bake for 10 minutes at 450°. Reduce heat to 325° and bake for 25 minutes or until firm. Serve warm.

Kabobs

4 boneless chicken breasts
8 oz. pineapple chunks
½ c. Heinz 57 sauce
¼ c. honey
butter
green pepper chunks
ham chunks

In a small saucepan blanch green peppers in boiling water for 1 minute; drain. Cut each chicken breast in 4 pieces. Thread chicken chunks, ham chunks, pineapple and pepper pieces alternately onto skewers. Combine 57 sauce and honey. Brush kabobs with melted butter. Grill; baste with mixture. Also good to marinate chicken and ham in Italian dressing, then threading on skewers.

Lizbet and Daughters—Country Cooking

Creamed Eggs and Toast

6 hard-boiled eggs
butter
½ c. flour
3 c. milk

½ tsp. salt
salt and pepper
Velveeta cheese
ham or bacon

Combine flour, butter, milk, salt, pepper and cheese and make as a gravy. Stir well and let come to a boil. Add chopped eggs and meat. Serve over toast.

Egg Dutch

5 eggs
1 tsp. salt
1 heaping Tbsp. flour

1 c. milk
½ tsp. pepper

Put in bowl in order given; beat with beater. Pour into heated greased pan. Cover with lid. Place over medium heat. Cut and turn when about half done.

Cookies & Bars

Grandmother's Cookies and Mine

Her cookies were molasses or the ginger kind,
Maybe some buttermilk or sugar cookies too,
Stored in crocks or tins so carefully for you.
Mine—chocolate chip, Debbies are some you'll find,
Some made with Eagle Brand are a delightful kind.
The list goes on, there are so many more,
To decide which to bake is actually a chore.
Baked on nonstick or air filled cookie sheet,
Stored in Tupperware to keep soft, can't be beat.
They served the same purpose of being a treat
When children came searching for something to eat.

Triple Treat Cookies

1 c. brown sugar
1 c. sugar
1 c. butter
1 c. peanut butter
2 eggs

2 tsp. soda
1 tsp. salt
3 c. flour
1 c. chocolate chips

Filling–
½ c. peanut butter
1 tsp. vanilla
⅓ c. milk

2-3 c. powdered sugar
2 Tbsp. butter, softened

Mix all together and shape into balls. Bake at 350°. Do not overbake. For filling: Mix and spread between 2 cookies to make sandwiches.

Peanut Butter Cookies

2 c. butter
2 c. brown sugar
2 c. peanut butter
2 c. white sugar

5 eggs
2 tsp. soda
6 c. flour
2 tsp. salt

Cream together first four ingredients, then add eggs. Stir in dry ingredients. Make into rolls and let stand overnight. Slice and bake. Makes a large amount. You can also roll into balls and press down with fork.

Peanut Butter Temptations

½ c. peanut butter
½ c. butter
½ c. sugar
½ c. brown sugar
1 egg

½ tsp. vanilla
1¼ c. flour
¾ tsp. soda
½ tsp. salt

Mix in order given and put in small muffin cups. Fill about ¾ full. Bake at 350° for 10-12 minutes. Take from oven and let cool a little, then press peanut butter cups in center of each one. Remove from muffin pan.

Lizbet and Daughters—Country Cooking

Peanut Butter Honey Cookies

½ c. butter flavored shortening
1 c. peanut butter
2 eggs
1 tsp. baking powder
½ tsp. salt

¾ c. honey
1 c. sugar
1½ tsp. baking soda
2½ c. flour
1½ c. chocolate chips

Mix all together and drop on cookie sheet. Bake at 350°.

Peanut Blossom Cookies

1¾ c. bread flour
1 tsp. soda
½ tsp. salt
½ c. peanut butter
2 T. milk

½ c. sugar
½ c. brown sugar
½ c. shortening
1 egg
1 tsp. vanilla

Combine all ingredients in large bowl. Mix well. Shape into balls, using a rounded teaspoon for each. Roll balls in sugar. Place on ungreased cookie sheet. Bake at 375° for 10-12 minutes. After baked, top immediately with a Hershey kiss. Takes about 48 kisses. Press firmly so cookie cracks around edges.

Double Treat Cookies

1 c. sugar
1 c. brown sugar
1 c. shortening
1 c. peanut butter
3 eggs
1 tsp. vanilla
2 c. flour

dash of salt
2 tsp. soda
2½ c. oatmeal
1 c. mini chocolate chips
1 c. mini M&M's
1 c. nuts, optional

Cream together sugars and shortening. Add rest of ingredients. Bake at 350° until slightly brown.

Monster Cookies

½ c. butter
1 c. brown sugar
1 c. granulated sugar
3 eggs
1½ c. peanut butter
1 tsp. light Karo

2 tsp. soda
3 c. oatmeal
1¾ c. bread flour
chocolate chips
M&M's

Mix together and let set for 1 hour before baking. Bake at 350°. Do not overbake.

Monster Cookies

¾ c. butter
1 c. white sugar
1 c. brown sugar
4 eggs
1 lb. chunky peanut butter

1 c. flour, optional
2½ tsp. soda
4 c. oatmeal
½ lb. M&M's
12 oz. chocolate chips

Mix all ingredients together. Add more oatmeal if necessary to make a stiff dough. Form teaspoon size balls and roll in powdered sugar. Bake at 350° for 10 minutes. Do not overbake.

Dad's Chocolate Chip Cookies

⅔ c. butter
⅔ c. butter-flavored Crisco
1 c. white sugar
1 c. brown sugar
2 eggs
2 tsp. vanilla

1 tsp. salt
1 sm. box instant vanilla pudding
1 tsp. baking soda
3½ c. all-purpose flour
2 c. chocolate chips

Cream butter, shortening and sugars. Add eggs one at time, beating well. Add vanilla and instant pudding. Add flour, salt, baking soda and chocolate. Shape into balls, but do not flatten. Bake at 350°.

Lizbet and Daughters—Country Cooking

Chocolate Chip Pudding Cookies

10 c. flour
4 tsp. baking soda
4 c. butter
1 c. sugar
3 c. brown sugar
8 eggs
12 oz. instant vanilla pudding
3 c. chocolate chips

Cream sugars and butter together. Add pudding mix and eggs. Stir in flour and baking soda. Add chocolate chips. Drop by teaspoon on cookie sheet. Bake at 350°.

Chocolate Chip Oatmeal Cookies

2 c. brown sugar
1 c. shortening
2 eggs
1 tsp. soda
5 Tbsp. sweet milk
1 tsp. salt
1 tsp. baking powder
1 tsp. vanilla
2 c. flour
3 c. oatmeal
1 c. chocolate chips

Mix in order given. Bake at 350°. Do not overbake!

Soft Chocolate Chip Cookies

4 c. brown sugar
4 eggs
1½ c. vegetable oil
1½ tsp. vanilla
6 c. flour
3 tsp. soda
1½ tsp. salt
2 c. chocolate chips

Mix vegetable oil with brown sugar. Add eggs and beat well. Add vanilla, soda and salt. Mix in flour and chocolate chips. Dough will be very stiff. Form balls and press down just a little. Bake at 350°.

Just Right Chocolate Chip Cookies

⅔ c. butter
⅔ c. butter flavored Crisco
¾ c. sugar
¾ c. brown sugar
2 eggs
2 tsp. vanilla

3 c. flour
1 tsp. soda
½ tsp. salt
1 pkg. instant vanilla pudding
12 oz. chocolate chips

Beat shortenings together until fluffy. Add sugars, eggs and vanilla. Add pudding mix. Gradually add the rest of dry ingredients. Stir in chocolate chips. Drop by heaping tablespoon onto ungreased cookie sheet. Bake at 350° for 14-18 minutes. Do not overbake.

Soft Batch Sandwich Cookies

2 c. butter Crisco
½ c. sugar
1½ c. brown sugar
2 tsp. vanilla
4 eggs

2 tsp. soda
2 boxes instant French vanilla pudding
1 c. oatmeal
4½ c. flour
12 oz. chocolate chips

Filling–
¾ c. Crisco
1 c. marshmallow créme
dash of salt

1 tsp. vanilla
3 c. powdered sugar

Cream Crisco, sugars, pudding and vanilla. Beat until smooth, then add eggs. Add dry ingredients gradually. Add chocolate chips. Shape into balls and press flat. Bake at 350° for 8-10 minutes. For filling: Mix and put between two cookies.

Lizbet and Daughters—Country Cooking

The Best Cookies Ever

2 c. brown sugar
2 eggs
1 tsp. soda
2 c. flour
1 c. coconut
1 tsp. vanilla

1 c. butter
1 Tbsp. hot water
2 tsp. baking powder
2 c. oatmeal
1 c. chocolate chips
½ tsp. salt

Cream together brown sugar, butter and eggs. Add hot water. Sift soda, baking powder and flour together and add to mixture. Add remaining ingredients. Refrigerate 1 hour. Roll in 1-2" balls, then roll in powdered sugar. Bake at 375° for 8-9 minutes. Hint: Do not overbake. Always leave baked cookies on cookie sheet for about 2 minutes.

Double Chocolate Jumbo Crisps

1¼ c. butter
1½ c. sugar
1 egg
1 tsp. vanilla
6 Tbsp. cocoa
½ tsp. soda

½ tsp. salt
1 c. flour
¼ c. water
3 c. quick oats
1 c. mini chocolate chips

Mix in order given and bake at 350°. Make whoopie filling and put between 2 cookies.

Chocolate Crinkles

1 c. cocoa
½ c. cooking oil
2 c. granulated sugar
4 eggs

2 c. flour
½ tsp. salt
2 tsp. baking powder
2 tsp. vanilla

Mix oil, cocoa and granulated sugar. Blend in eggs one at a time. Add vanilla. Stir in flour, baking powder and salt. Chill several hours or overnight. Drop by teaspoon in powdered sugar and then in granulated sugar and roll in balls and place on cookie sheet. Bake at 350°.

Cocoa Sandwich Cookies

2¼ c. butter
2¼ c. sugar
3 eggs
6 c. flour

1½ tsp. salt
1 c. cocoa
3 tsp. soda

Filling–
1 egg
4 Tbsp. milk
4 Tbsp. flour

4 c. powdered sugar
Crisco
marshmallow topping

Roll in balls and press down with a sugared glass. Bake at 350°. For filling: Beat egg and milk thoroughly. Add rest of ingredients.

Oreo Cookies

1 white or yellow cake mix
3 Tbsp. water
½ c. cocoa

2 eggs
2 Tbsp. cooking oil
Nestle Quik

Filling–
2 egg whites, beaten
3 c. powdered sugar

1 tsp. vanilla
1 c. Crisco

Mix in following order: Cake mix, eggs plus water, cooking oil and cocoa. Let stand for 20 minutes. Shape into balls. Flatten with glass dipped into Nestle Quik. Bake about 8 minutes at 300°. For filling: Combine all ingredients and frost between 2 cookies.

When working for the Lord, the pay may not be so good, but the retirement plan is out of this world.

Lizbet and Daughters—Country Cooking

Whoopie Pies

1 c. brown sugar
1 c. sugar
1 c. shortening
2 tsp. vanilla
2 tsp. soda
½ tsp. salt

2 eggs
1 c. cocoa
4 c. flour
1 c. thick sour milk
1 c. cold water

Filling–
1 egg white, beaten
1 Tbsp. vanilla
2 Tbsp. flour
2 Tbsp. milk

2 c. powdered sugar
¾ c. Crisco
marshmallow créme

Cream together sugars, salt, shortening, vanilla and eggs. Sift together flour, soda and cocoa. Add this to the first mixture alternately with water and sour milk. Add slightly more flour if milk is not thick. Drop by teaspoons. Bake at 350°. For filling: Beat egg white, sugar and vanilla. Add remaining ingredients. Beat well.

Molasses Cookies

2½ c. brown sugar
1 c. butter
¼ c. lard
1 c. Brer Rabbit molasses
2 tsp. cinnamon

1 Tbsp. soda
3 eggs
4 c. Calla Lily flour
2 c. bread flour

Mix together sugar, butter and lard. Add eggs and mix well, then add molasses, cinnamon and soda. Add flour last. Roll into balls and roll in sugar to bake. They're better if dough is chilled overnight.

Disappearing Molasses Cookies

3 c. shortening
1 c. Brer Rabbit molasses
8 tsp. soda
1 tsp. cinnamon
4 c. sugar
5 eggs
8½ c. flour
2 tsp. salt

Melt shortening and add sugar, molasses, eggs, cinnamon and salt. Mix. Add flour and soda. Make in balls. Roll in white sugar. Place on cookie sheet. Do not press down. Bake at 350°.

Delicious Molasses Cookies

2 c. sugar
2 c. butter
2 c. Brer Rabbit molasses
2 eggs
2 tsp. soda
2 tsp. cinnamon
1 tsp. ginger
1 tsp. cloves
1 tsp. nutmeg
8 c. flour

Shape into balls and roll in sugar. Bake at 350° for about 10 minutes. Do not overbake.

Sandwich Molasses Cookies

1 c. butter Crisco
2 c. brown sugar
2 eggs
½ c. sour cream
½ c. Grandma's molasses
½ tsp. salt
3 tsp. soda
1 tsp. baking powder
2 tsp. cinnamon
¼ tsp. ginger
5 c. flour

Filling–
¾ c. Crisco
1 c. marshmallow créme
dash of salt
1 tsp. vanilla
3 c. powdered sugar

Cream Crisco and sugar. Add eggs, sour cream and molasses. Add dry ingredients. For filling: Mix and put between two cookies.

Lizbet and Daughters—Country Cooking

Butterscotch Crunch Sandwich Cookies

2 c. shortening
2 c. brown sugar
2 c. sugar
2 tsp. vanilla
4 eggs, beaten

3 c. flour
2 tsp. salt
2 tsp. soda
6 c. oatmeal

Filling–
½ c. butter, softened
4 oz. cream cheese

1 tsp. maple flavoring
2½ c. powdered sugar

Mix well. Drop by tablespoon on ungreased cookie sheet. Bake at 400° for 10 minutes. Do not overbake.

Butterscotch Cookies

4 c. brown sugar
4 eggs
1 tsp. salt
2 tsp. soda

1 c. butter
7-8 c. all-purpose flour
2 tsp. vanilla
1½ tsp. baking powder

Cream together butter and sugar. Add eggs and vanilla; beat until fluffy. Add dry ingredients and mix to a smooth dough. Shape in long rolls 2½-3" in diameter. Chill overnight. Slice and bake at 350°. These are also good to make into balls and roll in powdered sugar. Press down lightly.

Butterscotch Cookies

2 c. brown sugar
1 c. melted butter
2 eggs
1 tsp. vanilla

4 c. flour
1 tsp. soda
1 tsp. cream of tartar

Cream sugar and butter, add eggs and vanilla. Mix flour, soda and cream of tartar. Add to creamed mixture. Makes a stiff dough. Shape in rolls and wrap in waxed paper. Chill overnight in refrigerator. Slice and bake at 350°. Do not overbake. These cookies are good iced with caramel frosting, or use the marshmallow frosting recipe and spread between 2 cookies for a sandwich cookie. They are also good without any frosting.

Butterscotch Delights

2½ c. sugar
2½ c. brown sugar
2 c. butter
2½ tsp. soda
2½ tsp. baking powder
5 eggs

1 Tbsp. vanilla
¼ c. milk
5 c. bread flour
2 tsp. salt
5 c. quick oats

Frosting–
8 Tbsp. butter
4 c. powdered sugar

4 Tbsp. hot water

Mix sugars and butter. Add eggs and vanilla, then dry ingredients and milk. Bake at 375°. For frosting: Melt butter and add powdered sugar and hot water.

Lizbet and Daughters—Country Cooking

Hot Water Cookies

2 c. brown sugar	2 tsp. baking powder
1 c. granulated sugar	½ tsp. salt
1½ c. shortening	1 tsp. vanilla
1 c. boiling water	1 tsp. maple flavoring
3 eggs, well beaten	6½-7 c. flour
2 tsp. soda	

Penuche Frosting-

½ c. butter	1 c. brown sugar
2½ Tbsp. flour	2 c. powdered sugar
¼ tsp. salt	1 tsp. vanilla
½ c. milk	

Mix all cookie ingredients together and bake at 350° for 10-15 minutes. Frost with penuche frosting. For frosting: Mix together butter, flour and salt. Cook for 1 minute. Add milk and cook until thick. Remove from heat and add brown sugar then powdered sugar. Stir until thick and creamy and add vanilla.

Butter Sugar Cookies

3 eggs	1 Tbsp. vanilla
2 c. sugar	6 c. flour
2 c. butter	2 tsp. baking powder

In a bowl cream eggs, sugar, butter and vanilla. Add flour and baking powder. Roll out dough and use cookie cutter. Frost with favorite frosting. Note: Do not put dough in fridge or it will get too stiff.

When working for the Lord, the pay may not be so good, but the retirement plan is out of this world.

Dutch Sugar Cookies

1 c. lard
2½ c. brown sugar
3 eggs
1 c. sour milk

6 c. flour
1 tsp. soda
1 tsp. salt
2 tsp. baking powder

Mix in order given, blending well. Chill dough, then roll out. Bake at 350°.

Buttermilk Cookies

1 c. shortening
2 c. brown sugar
2 eggs
1 Tbsp. vanilla

4 c. flour
2 tsp. baking powder
2 tsp. baking soda
1 c. buttermilk

Brown Sugar Frosting–
1 c. brown sugar
1 c. granulated sugar

1 c. light cream

Mix shortening and sugar. Add vanilla and eggs. Dissolve soda in buttermilk. Add baking powder to flour. Add liquid and flour alternately. Bake at 375°. These are good with brown sugar frosting. For frosting: Combine all ingredients and boil to soft ball stage (235°). Cool, then stir until thick.

Snickerdoodles

1 c. butter, softened
2 c. sugar
2 eggs
¼ c. milk

1 tsp. vanilla
3¾ c. flour
½ tsp. soda
½ tsp. salt

Cinnamon Sugar Mixture–
½ c. sugar

3 tsp. cinnamon

Cream butter and sugar until fluffy. Add eggs. Blend in milk and vanilla. Add dry ingredients. Cool dough. Form into 1" balls and roll in cinnamon sugar mixture. Bake at 350°. Do not overbake.

Lizbet and Daughters—Country Cooking

Spellbinders

3 c. bread flour
3 tsp. baking powder
2 tsp. baking soda
2 c. brown sugar
2 c. butter

2 eggs
2 c. rolled oats
2 c. coconut
2 c. nuts
1 c. crushed cornflakes

Icing-
4 Tbsp. butter
2 c. powdered sugar

2 Tbsp. hot water
½ tsp. vanilla

Mix together all ingredients except cornflakes. Roll into balls and roll in cornflake crumbs. Do not flatten. Bake at 350°. For icing: Melt butter; add powdered sugar, water and vanilla.

Maple Leaf Cookies

1 lb. butter
4 c. brown sugar
8 eggs
6 tsp. soda

1 tsp. salt
12 Tbsp. cream
10½ c. flour
4 Tbsp. maple flavoring

Frosting-
2 egg whites, beaten
1 Tbsp. vanilla
1 tsp. cream of tartar
2 Tbsp. flour

2 c. powdered sugar
½ c. Crisco
¾ c. marshmallow topping

Combine ingredients in order given. Do not overbake. Use a maple leaf design cookie cutter or they can be put through a press. For frosting: Beat egg whites, vanilla, cream of tartar, flour and powdered sugar. Add Crisco and marshmallow topping. Cream until smooth.

To find out what a poor loser you are, try dieting.

Pumpkin Cookies

1 c. shortening
2 c. cooked pumpkin
2 c. brown sugar
4 c. flour

2 tsp. baking powder
1½ tsp. soda
2 tsp. cinnamon

Mix together first three ingredients, then add sifted dry ingredients. Add nuts and dates if desired. Frost with caramel frosting. Bake at 350°.

Vanilla Cream Wafers

½ c. butter
1 c. brown sugar
2 eggs, beaten
2 sq. chocolate, optional
1 tsp. vanilla

2 Tbsp. sour cream
1¼ tsp. soda
½ tsp. salt
2¾ c. flour

Mix together, then roll out as thin as possible and bake at 350°. When cool put 2 cookies together with powdered sugar frosting. These are very good when put through a cookie press, and spread with frosting below.

Cream Wafer Cookies

5 c. white sugar
2½ c. butter
10 eggs, beaten
10 Tbsp. milk

5 tsp. vanilla
7 tsp. soda
2 tsp. salt
13¾ c. flour

Frosting–
2 lb. powdered sugar + 2 c.
2 c. Crisco
2 eggs, beaten

milk
2 c. marshmallow créme

Cream together sugar and butter. Add rest of ingredients. Either use cookie press or roll out as a cutout. Put two together with frosting.

Lizbet and Daughters—Country Cooking

Pecan Tarts

2 c. flour
1 c. butter

6 oz. cream cheese

Filling–
3 c. brown sugar
dash of salt
4 Tbsp. butter, melted

4 eggs
1 tsp. vanilla

For dough: Mix and form balls the size of walnuts. Chill. Shape in cupcake tins. For filling: Beat eggs in melted butter. Add sugar, vanilla and salt. Put 1 tsp. nuts in bottom of prepared dough in pans and fill up with syrup. Bake until filling appears set.

Date Pinwheel Cookies

1 c. butter
1 c. sugar
1 c. brown sugar
3 eggs
1 tsp. vanilla

4 c. flour
1 tsp. soda
1 tsp. baking powder
½ tsp. salt

Filling–
1½ c. dates
⅔ c. water

½ c. sugar
1 c. chopped nuts

Cream butter and sugars. Blend in eggs and vanilla. Beat until light, then add flour and rest of ingredients. Roll out into two rolls. Spread with filling and roll up. Chill overnight. Slice and bake at 400° for 8-10 minutes. For filling: Cook dates, water and sugar together for 10 minutes. Let cool, then add nuts.

Date or Raisin Filled Cookies

1 c. shortening
1½ c. brown sugar
2 eggs
4 c. flour
1 c. rolled oats

2 tsp. baking powder
½ tsp. soda
¼ c. milk
2 tsp. vanilla

Filling–
2 c. chopped dates or raisins
1 c. sugar

¼ c. flour
1 c. water

Cream shortening and sugar together. Add vanilla and eggs. Beat until fluffy. Add dry ingredients and milk. Chill dough a few hours or overnight. Roll out ¼" thick on lightly floured board. Cut with round cookie cutter and fill with cooled filling. Top each cookie with another cookie with a hole the size of a thimble in the middle. Press edges securely. Bake at 375° until a golden brown. Can frost with a brown sugar frosting if desired. Yield: 2½ to 3 dozen cookies. For filling: Combine all ingredients and cook until thickened, stirring constantly. Put 1 teaspoon on each cookie.

Easy Filled Drop Cookies

1 c. butter
2 c. brown sugar
¼ c. water
¼ c. maple syrup

1 tsp. soda
2 eggs
3½ c. flour
¾ tsp. salt

Filling–
2 c. chopped dates
¾ c. water

¾ c. granulated sugar

Mix together dough ingredients. For filling: Cook on low heat and cool. On cookie sheet put 1 teaspoon batter, then a little date mixture. Put another teaspoon batter on top and bake at 350°.

Lizbet and Daughters—Country Cooking

Trilbies

2 c. shortening
3 c. brown sugar
6 c. flour
4 c. rolled oats

1 tsp. salt
2 tsp. soda
1 c. buttermilk
1 tsp. vanilla

Date Filling–
2 c. chopped dates
1 c. sugar

1 c. water
2 Tbsp. flour

Cream shortening and sugar together and add vanilla. Add dry ingredients alternately with buttermilk. Mix thoroughly. Chill for a few hours or overnight. Roll out ⅛" thick on lightly floured board. Cut with round cookie cutter and place 1" apart on cookie sheet. Bake at 375° until a golden brown. When cookies are cool, spread with date filling. For filling: Combine and cook until thick. Cool before spreading on cookies. Top with another cookie. Yield: 8 dozen.

Thumbprint Cookies

1 c. butter
½ c. brown sugar
2 egg yolks
1 tsp. vanilla

2 c. flour
½ tsp. salt
2 egg whites
1 c. nuts, chopped fine

Mix butter, sugar, egg yolks and vanilla thoroughly. Blend in flour and salt. Roll into 1" thick balls and dip into slightly beaten egg whites and roll in chopped nuts. Place 1½" apart on cookie sheet. Press thumb gently into center of ball. Makes a little pocket to fill with frosting. Bake 10-12 minutes or until set at 350°. Cool and fill holes with frosting.

Honey Cookies

2 c. honey
4 tsp. soda
½ tsp. ginger
½ tsp. allspice
6½ c. flour

1 c. butter
2 eggs, beaten
2 tsp. vanilla
½ tsp. cinnamon

Frosting–
1⅓ c. granulated sugar
4 Tbsp. water

2 egg whites, beaten
red food coloring

Cook honey and butter for 1 minute. Remove from heat and add soda. (Put in a large bowl as it will rise.) Let set to cool, then add remaining ingredients. Roll out, cut with cutter and bake at 350°. Frost with your favorite frosting or with this frosting. For frosting: Boil sugar and water together till it threads, then pour over egg whites. Beat till smooth and thick. Add food coloring for a pink tint.

Orange Cookies

2 c. sugar
1 c. butter
2 eggs
2 tsp. baking powder

5 c. flour
1 orange, juice and rind
1 tsp. soda
1 c. buttermilk or sour cream

Grate peel of orange and juice the orange. Dissolve soda in buttermilk or sour cream. Mix in order given and bake at 350°. Ice with icing made with powdered sugar and orange juice.

*If a rooster sits on a barnyard fence and crows,
it is a sign that company is coming.*

Lizbet and Daughters—Country Cooking

Peanut Butter Dream Bars

Crust–
3 c. quick oats
2¼ c. flour
1½ c. butter, melted

1½ tsp. soda
1½ c. brown sugar
¾ tsp. salt

Additional Ingredients–
⅓ c. peanut butter
1 c. M&M's

1 can sweetened condensed milk

Combine crust ingredients to make crumbs. Measure out 1½ cups. Set aside. Press remaining crumbs in a jelly roll pan. Bake at 350° for 12 minutes. Mix peanut butter and milk. Spread over baked crust. Mix 1½ c. reserved crumbs with M&M's and sprinkle over peanut butter layer. Bake 20 minutes longer. Note: Also good to add 1 cup chocolate chips and 2 Tbsp. butter to the evaporated milk, then omit the peanut butter and M&M's.

Monster Cookie Bars

½ c. butter, melted
1½ c. peanut butter
1 c. sugar
1¼ c. brown sugar
3 eggs

1 tsp. Karo
4 c. oatmeal
2 tsp. baking soda
1 c. M&M's
¾ c. chocolate chips

Mix in order given and put in jelly roll pan. Bake for 15-20 minutes.

Granola Bars

½ c. mini M&M's
½ c. mini chocolate chips
5 c. quick oatmeal
4½ c. Rice Krispies
1 c. coconut
1 c. chopped nuts, optional

1 pkg. crushed graham crackers
¾ c. butter
½ c. peanut butter
½ c. honey
2 bags mini marshmallows

Chill M&M's and chocolate chips. Toss oatmeal, Rice Krispies, coconut, nuts and graham crackers together. Melt butter, peanut butter, honey and marshmallows. Mix all together, adding chips and M&M's last. Press into greased jelly roll pan. Cut into squares. Note: To keep M&M's and chocolate chips from melting, store them in freezer.

Fruit Bars

1 c. butter
1¾ c. sugar
4 eggs
1 tsp. vanilla
½ tsp. almond extract

3 c. flour
1½ tsp. salt
1½ tsp. baking powder
1 can cherry pie filling

Cream together butter and sugar. Add eggs, one at a time, beating well after each one. Add remaining ingredients, except pie filling. Remove 1 c. batter. Put rest of batter onto cookie sheet; spread pie filling over dough. Drop remaining batter by spoonfuls on top. Bake at 350°. Make a glaze using 1½ c. powdered sugar and drizzle over cooled cake. This is good with any pie filling.

Lizbet and Daughters—Country Cooking

Sour Cream Raisin Bars

1 c. butter, softened
1 c. packed brown sugar
1¾-2 c. flour
1¾-2 c. quick oats

1 tsp. baking powder
1 tsp. soda
⅛ tsp. salt

Filling–
4 egg yolks
1½ c. raisins
1 c. white sugar

1-2 Tbsp. clear jel or cornstarch
2 c. sour cream

In a large mixing bowl, cream butter and brown sugar. Beat in flour, oats, baking powder, soda and salt. Mixture will be crumbly. Set aside 2 c. of the crumbs. Pat remaining crumbs in 9" x 13" baking pan. Bake at 350° for 15 minutes. Cool. Combine filling ingredients in a saucepan. Bring to a boil and cook, stirring constantly, for 5-8 minutes. Pour over crust. Sprinkle with reserved crumbs. Return to oven for 15 minutes. You can substitute ½ c. brown sugar and ½ c. white sugar for 1 c. brown sugar.

Toffee Topped Bars

½ tsp. soda
2 c. brown sugar, packed
2 c. flour
½ c. butter, softened
1 tsp. baking powder
½ tsp. salt

1 tsp. vanilla
1 c. milk
1 egg
1 c. chocolate chips
½ c. nuts
¼ c. coconut

Mix sugar and flour. Add butter and make crumbs like pie dough. Set aside 1 c. crumbs. To rest of mixture add soda, baking powder, salt, vanilla, milk and egg. Stir lightly with a fork. Put in 9" x 13" pan. Sprinkle chocolate chips, nuts and coconut on top. Then sprinkle 1 c. crumbs on top of that. Bake at 350° for 35 minutes.

Triple Layer Cookie Bars

½ c. butter
1½ c. graham cracker crumbs
2⅔ c. flaked coconut

1 can sweetened condensed milk
12 oz. chocolate chips
½ c. creamy peanut butter

Preheat oven to 350° or 325° for glass dish. In 9" x 13" pan melt butter in oven. Sprinkle graham cracker crumbs evenly over butter. Top with coconut, then condensed milk. Bake for 25 minutes or until lightly browned. Melt chocolate chips and peanut butter over low heat in medium saucepan. Spread evenly over hot coconut layer. Cool 30 minutes. Cut into bars.

Zucchini Brownies

4 eggs
2 c. sugar
2 tsp. soda
1 tsp. salt
1 tsp. vanilla
1 c. nuts

1½ c. oil
2 c. flour
2 tsp. cinnamon
4 Tbsp. cocoa
3 c. shredded zucchini

Frosting–
½ c. butter
2 Tbsp. cocoa
2-3 c. powdered sugar

6 Tbsp. milk
1 tsp. vanilla

Beat oil, eggs and sugar together. Stir in dry ingredients. Add vanilla, nuts and zucchini. Mix together and spread in 10" x 15" jelly roll pan. Bake at 350° for 30 minutes. For frosting: Heat butter, milk and cocoa. Bring to a boil. Remove from heat. Add powdered sugar and vanilla. Beat until smooth.

Lizbet and Daughters—Country Cooking

Pumpkin Bars

4 eggs, beaten
1 c. pumpkin
1 tsp. baking powder
1 tsp. salt
1 tsp. soda

2 tsp. cinnamon
1 c. salad oil
2 c. sugar
2 c. flour

Frosting-
3 oz. cream cheese
1 tsp. vanilla
½ c. butter

2 c. powdered sugar
chopped nuts, optional

Combine all ingredients and bake at 350° until done.

Brownie Cheesecake Bars

1½ c. flour
1½ c. sugar
⅔ c. butter, melted
⅔ c. Hershey's cocoa
3 eggs, divided
½ c. milk
3 tsp. vanilla, divided

½ tsp. baking powder
1 c. chopped nuts
8 oz. cream cheese
2 Tbsp. butter
1 Tbsp. cornstarch
1 can sweetened condensed milk

Heat oven to 350°. In mixing bowl beat flour, sugar, butter, cocoa, 2 eggs, milk, 2 tsp. vanilla and baking powder until well blended. Stir in nuts and spread in pan. In small bowl blend cream cheese, 2 Tbsp. butter and cornstarch until fluffy. Gradually add condensed milk, remaining egg and 1 tsp. vanilla, beating until smooth. Pour over brownie batter. Bake 35-40 minutes or until top is lightly browned. Cool and refrigerate. Cut into bars.

Cream Cheese Brownies

1 cake mix
8 oz. cream cheese
1 egg
½ c. sugar
1½ c. chocolate chips

Mix cake mix as directed on box. Pour into 9" x 13" pan. Beat together cream cheese, egg and sugar. Drop on cake batter with a spoon, then swirl with a knife. Sprinkle with chocolate chips. Bake at 350° until done.

1-2-3- Coffee Bars

2 eggs
2⅔ c. brown sugar
1 tsp. salt
1 tsp. baking soda
1 c. vegetable oil
1 c. warm coffee
3 c. flour
1 tsp. vanilla

Mix in order given and put into greased jelly roll pan. Sprinkle with nuts and miniature chocolate chips. Bake at 350°. Cut into bars.

Lemon Bars

1 c. butter
½ c. powdered sugar
2 c. flour
4 eggs, beaten
2 c. sugar
⅓ c. lemon juice
¼ c. flour
½ tsp. baking powder

Melt butter. Add flour and powdered sugar. Mix well. Pat into 9" x 13" cake pan. Bake till light brown, approximately 10 minutes, at 350°. Mix eggs, sugar, lemon juice, flour and baking powder. Put this on baked crust and bake 20-25 minutes. Sprinkle with powdered sugar. Cool.

Lizbet and Daughters—Country Cooking

Tri-Level Brownies

1½ c. flour
1¼ c. brown sugar
1¼ c. butter, melted

2½ c. oatmeal
¾ tsp. baking powder

Filling–
¼ c. cocoa
1¾ c. sugar
¾ c. butter, melted
3 eggs

1⅔ c. flour
½ tsp. salt
½ c. milk

Icing–
⅜ c. cocoa
3½ c. powdered sugar
½ c. butter, melted

2½ tsp. vanilla
⅜ c. hot water

Mix crust and press lightly in large cookie sheet. Mix filling and pour over crust. Bake at 350° for 25 minutes. Frost.

Whole Wheat Chip and Coffee Bars

2 eggs
2 c. brown sugar
1 c. cooking oil
2 tsp. vanilla
2 tsp. instant coffee
1 c. cold water

1 tsp. salt
1 tsp. baking soda
1 c. whole wheat flour
2 c. all-purpose flour
1 c. chocolate chips

Coffee Glaze–
½ tsp. instant coffee
4 tsp. water

1 c. powdered sugar
1 Tbsp. butter, softened

In large bowl beat eggs until light and fluffy. Gradually add brown sugar, oil and vanilla. Beat well. Dissolve coffee in cold water and gradually stir into egg mixture. Add dry ingredients. Beat until well combined. Pour batter into a greased cookie sheet. Sprinkle chocolate chips evenly on top. Bake at 350° for 20 minutes. For coffee glaze: Dissolve coffee in water. Combine powdered sugar and butter and add to coffee mixture, beating until smooth. Cool bars slightly, then drizzle with coffee glaze.

Coffee Bars

2 c. brown sugar
2 eggs
½ c. butter
1 c. strong hot coffee

3 c. flour
1 tsp. soda
1 tsp. baking powder
1 c. raisins

Frosting–
½ c. butter
2 c. powdered sugar

strong hot coffee

Mix together and pour into greased jelly roll pan. Bake at 350°. Frost and cut in squares when cool.

Chocolate Marshmallow Bars

½ c. butter
1 c. brown sugar
1 egg
1 tsp. vanilla
¼ c. cocoa

2 c. flour
½ tsp. soda
½ tsp. salt
½ c. milk
3 c. miniature marshmallows

Icing–
½ c. brown sugar
½ c. butter

2 tsp. cocoa
¼ c. milk

Combine sugar, butter, milk, egg and vanilla. Add dry ingredients. Spread on cookie sheet and bake at 350°. When baked, top with miniature marshmallows and return to oven for 1-2 minutes. For icing: Boil until it forms large bubbles. Cool and add powdered sugar to thicken. Frosting should be quite thin.

Lizbet and Daughters—Country Cooking

Fruit Swirl Bars

1½ c. sugar
1 c. butter
4 eggs
1 tsp. almond flavoring

1 tsp. vanilla
3 c. flour
1 tsp. baking powder

Glaze–
1 c. powdered sugar

2 Tbsp. milk

Spread ⅔ of batter in cookie sheet, then spread 3-4 c. of your favorite pie filling over this. Drop remaining batter by tablespoon on pie filling. Bake at 350° for 30 minutes or until light brown. Drizzle with glaze while warm.

Double Chocolate Bars

1 c. butter
1½ c. sugar
4 eggs
2 tsp. vanilla
½ tsp. baking powder
1½ c. flour

4 Tbsp. cocoa
½ tsp. salt
4 c. marshmallows
12 oz. chocolate or butterscotch chips
1 c. peanut butter
3 c. Rice Krispies

Cream butter and sugar. Beat in eggs and vanilla. Add flour, cocoa, baking powder and salt. Spread into cookie sheet. Bake at 350° for 15-20 minutes. Sprinkle marshmallows evenly on top and bake 2 minutes. Cool. In saucepan combine chips and peanut butter. Heat until chips are melted. Add Rice Krispies. Spread mixture on top of chilled bars.

Betty Crocker Bars

1 yellow cake mix
2 eggs
⅓ c. water

¼ c. butter, melted
1 c. peanut butter
12 oz. chocolate chips

Bake at 350° for 40 minutes. Do not overbake or they will be dry.

Sunny Graham Chewies

1⅔ c. graham cracker crumbs
2 Tbsp. flour
½ c. butter
1½ c. brown sugar, packed
½ c. nuts

dash of salt
¼ tsp. baking powder
2 eggs
1 tsp. vanilla

Combine 1⅓ c. crumbs, flour and butter in bowl. Blend till particles form like rice. Pack into 9" square pan. Bake 20 minutes at 350°. Combine sugar, remaining crumbs, nuts, salt and baking powder. Blend. Add beaten eggs and vanilla with brown sugar mixture. Blend well. When crust has been baked, pour brown sugar mixture over crust. Return to oven and bake 20 minutes or more. Cool and cut into bars.

Reese's Pieces Bars

1 c. butter
1 c. sugar
1 c. brown sugar
2 eggs
⅔ c. peanut butter
1 tsp. vanilla

2 c. flour
½ tsp. soda
½ tsp. salt
2 c. quick rolled oats
2 c. chocolate chips

Peanut Butter Mixture-
¾ c. powdered sugar
¾ c. peanut butter

4-6 Tbsp. milk

Cream butter and sugars well. Add eggs, peanut butter and vanilla. Stir in flour, soda, salt and rolled oats. Bake in an 11" x 17" cookie sheet at 350° for 25 minutes. After removing from oven sprinkle immediately with chocolate chips. Mix peanut butter mixture until runny. When chocolate chips are melted, spread them, then drizzle peanut butter mixture on top and swirl.

Lizbet and Daughters—Country Cooking

Raisin Bars

11 c. bread flour
5 c. white sugar
1 lb. butter
1 tsp. salt
2 lb. raisins

3 c. water
5 eggs, beaten
1 pt. Grandma's molasses
3 Tbsp. soda
½ c. boiling water

In a large bowl, mix together flour, sugar, butter and salt like pie crumbs. Cook raisins in water until soft. Add to crumbs when cool. Add eggs and molasses. Pour water over soda and add to mixture. Let set overnight or longer. Make in ½" thick rolls the length of your cookie sheet. Garnish top with beaten egg; add a little water to egg. Bake at 350°. Once baked, let set a little, then cut into squares. Note: ½ lb. dough for small cookie sheet. ¾ lb. dough for large cookie sheet.

Fudge Brownies

1¼ c. butter
4 c. sugar
8 eggs
2 c. flour

1¼ c. baking cocoa
1 tsp. salt
2 tsp. vanilla
2 c. chopped walnuts

Icing–
½ c. butter
3 Tbsp. cocoa
3 c. powdered sugar

5 Tbsp. milk
1 tsp. vanilla

In a mixing bowl, cream butter and sugar. Add eggs. Combine flour, cocoa and salt. Add to creamed mixture and mix well. Stir in vanilla and walnuts. Spread in a greased 10" x 15" baking pan. Bake at 325° for 40-45 minutes or until done. For icing: Cream cocoa and butter. Add powdered sugar, milk and vanilla. Beat until smooth. Spread over warm brownies. Sprinkle with nuts if desired.

Double Deck Brownies

Bottom–
2 c. flour
1 tsp. soda
1 tsp. salt

4 c. rolled oats
2 c. brown sugar
2 c. butter, melted

Top–
3 c. sugar
4 eggs
1 c. butter, melted
¾ c. cocoa
1 tsp. baking powder

1 tsp. salt
2 tsp. vanilla
2¾ c. flour
1 c. milk

24 oz. chocolate chips

1½ c. peanut butter

Mix bottom layer ingredients and press into two jelly roll pans. Variation: Substitute ½ c. peanut butter for ½ c. butter. Bake at 350° for 5-10 minutes. Mix top layer ingredients; pour on bottom layer. Bake at 350° until done. Do not overbake. Melt chocolate chips, add peanut butter and spread on top.

One Bowl Brownies

2 c. sugar
1⅓ c. all-purpose flour
¾ c. cocoa
1 tsp. baking powder
½ tsp. salt

½ c. chopped nuts
⅔ c. vegetable oil
4 eggs, beaten
2 tsp. vanilla

In a large bowl combine sugar, flour, cocoa, baking powder, salt and nuts. Add oil, eggs and vanilla. Stir just until moistened. Do not overmix. Spread in a greased 9" x 13" baking pan. Bake at 350° for 20-25 minutes or until a toothpick inserted near the center comes out clean.

Lizbet and Daughters—Country Cooking

Sinfully Delicious Brownies

2 pkg. chocolate cake mix
½ c. chopped nuts
⅓ c. butter, melted
1 can evaporated milk
2 (14 oz.) pkg. vanilla caramels

12 oz. chocolate chips
½ c. chopped nuts
⅓ c. butter, melted
½ c. flaked coconut
2 eggs

Mix one cake mix, nuts, butter, ½ c. milk and 1 egg. Spread in a greased and floured pan. Bake at 350° for 12-15 minutes. Heat caramels and remaining milk, stirring constantly, until caramels are melted. Pour half of caramels over baked layer. Sprinkle chocolate chips over caramel mixture. Mix remaining cake mix, nuts, butter, caramel mixture and egg. Drop by spoonful on chocolate chips. Sprinkle with coconut. Bake for 25-30 minutes.

Pecan Pie Bars

Crust–
3 c. flour
1 c. butter

½ c. sugar
½ tsp. salt

Filling–
4 eggs
1½ c. brown sugar
1½ tsp. vanilla
2 Tbsp. flour

1½ c. light Karo
3 T. melted butter
2 c. chopped pecans

Prepare crust in large bowl. Mix crust mixture until it resembles coarse crumbs. Press evenly into 10" x 15" x 1" cookie sheet and bake at 350° for 20 minutes. For filling: Mix flour and sugar. Add slightly beaten eggs, Karo, vanilla, nuts and butter. Spread evenly over crust and bake 25-30 minutes longer. Cool and cut into bars.

Can't Leave Alone Bars

1 yellow cake mix
3 eggs
⅓ c. oil
½ c. butter

1 can sweetened condensed milk
1 c. butterscotch chips
1 c. chocolate chips

Mix first three ingredients. Press half in 9" x 13" pan. Melt butter, milk and chips. Put on top of cake batter. Put rest of cake batter on top of chocolate mixture and bake at 350°.

Seven Layer Bars

1 c. graham cracker crumbs
6 oz. chocolate chips
6 oz. butterscotch chips
1 c. coconut

1 c. chopped nuts
1 can sweetened condensed milk
½ c. butter

Melt butter in 9" x 13" pan, then add each layer listed in order given. Do not stir. Bake at 325° for 25-30 minutes.

Rhubarb Dream Bars

2 c. flour
1 c. butter
¾ c. powdered sugar
4 eggs

2 c. sugar
½ c. flour
½ tsp. salt
4 c. diced rhubarb

Mix first three ingredients and press into 10" x 15" pan. Bake at 350° for 15 minutes. Beat together eggs, sugar, flour, salt and rhubarb. Spread on hot crust. Bake at 350° for 40-45 minutes.

Lizbet and Daughters—Country Cooking

Mud Hen Bars

Crust-
½ c. butter
1 c. sugar
1 egg
2 egg yolks

1½ c. flour
1 tsp. baking powder
¼ tsp. salt

Topping-
1 c. nuts
½ c. chocolate chips
1 c. brown sugar

1 c. mini marshmallows
2 egg whites

Mix crust ingredients and press in a 9" x 13" pan. Bake at 350° for 10-15 minutes. Then cover with nuts, chocolate chips and marshmallows. Beat egg whites until stiff. Add brown sugar and mix. Spread on top and bake at 350° till done, approximately 30 minutes.

Toll House Marble Squares

1½ c. butter
1 c. brown sugar
1 c. sugar
3 eggs

3 c. flour
1½ tsp. soda
½ tsp. salt
chocolate chips

Preheat oven to 350°. Cream butter and sugars. Add eggs and dry ingredients. Put in a 10" x 16" pan and sprinkle chocolate chips on top. Put in oven for a few minutes to melt chocolate chips. Swirl chips over batter with a fork. Return to oven and finish baking.

*A boatman had his one oar marked "faith"
and the other one "works".
It took both to reach the other shore.*

Rhubarb Custard Bars

2 c. all-purpose flour
¼ c. sugar

1 c. cold butter

Filling-
2 c. sugar
7 Tbsp. flour
5 c. diced rhubarb

1 c. whipping cream
3 eggs, beaten

Topping-
6 oz. cream cheese
½ c. sugar

½ tsp. vanilla
1 c. whipping cream, whipped

In a bowl combine flour and sugar. Cut in butter until mixture is in coarse crumbs. Press in 9" x 13" greased pan. Mix filling ingredients and pour into crust. Bake at 350° for 40-45 minutes or until custard is set. Cool. For topping: Beat cream cheese, sugar and vanilla until smooth. Fold in whipped topping and spread on top.

Fudge Nut Bars

2 c. butter
4 c. brown sugar
4 eggs
4 tsp. vanilla

4 c. flour
2 tsp. soda
2 tsp. salt
6 c. oatmeal

Fudge Nut Filling-
1 can sweetened condensed milk
1 large pkg. chocolate chips
1 c. nuts

2 Tbsp. butter
2 tsp. vanilla
½ tsp. salt

Cream together butter and sugar. Add eggs and vanilla. Stir in dry ingredients. Spread a thin layer of dough in two large cookie sheets. For filling: In saucepan melt chocolate chips, milk, butter and salt over low heat. Stir in vanilla and nuts. Spread over bottom layer. Dot with remaining dough. Bake at 350° for 25-30 minutes. Do not overbake.

Lizbet and Daughters—Country Cooking

Candy Bar Cookies

Crust-
1 pkg. chocolate chip cookie mix
¼ c. cocoa
1 egg

Caramel Layer-
14 oz. caramels
⅓ c. evaporated milk
⅓ c. butter
1⅔ c. powdered sugar
1 c. chopped nuts

Chocolate Drizzle-
½ c. chocolate chips
2 tsp. Crisco

Mix ingredients for crust and press in a 9" x 13" pan. Bake at 350° for 14-16 minutes. For caramel layer, melt first three ingredients, then add powdered sugar and nuts. Pour over cookie crust. For chocolate drizzle, melt chocolate chips and Crisco over hot water and drizzle over top.

Chocolate Twinkies

4 c. flour
4 tsp. soda
4 Tbsp. cocoa
2 c. cold water
2 c. white sugar
1 tsp. salt
1½ c. Miracle Whip
2 tsp. vanilla

Cream Filling-
2 c. powdered sugar, heaping
1 c. Crisco
2 tsp. vanilla
4 Tbsp. flour
2 egg whites

Sift flour, sugar, soda and cocoa together. Add remaining ingredients. Mix well and spread in two sheet pans lined with wax paper. Bake at 350°. Cool. For filling: Mix powdered sugar, flour and Crisco thoroughly. Beat egg whites until stiff and add. Add vanilla. Mix until creamy. Spread on cake. Put other cake on top and cut into squares.

Twinkies

1 yellow cake mix
1 sm. pkg. instant pudding
4 eggs

¾ c. oil
¾ c. water

Filling–
2 egg whites
2 c. powdered sugar

1 c. Crisco
1 tsp. vanilla

Mix first five ingredients and bake in 9" x 13" pan at 350°. Cool and slice through middle and fill with filling. For filling: Mix together until creamy. Marshmallow créme can be added if desired.

Trail Mix Bars

6 c. Crispix cereal
1½ c. raisins
½ c. sunflower seeds
1 c. honey

¾ c. white sugar
1 (16 oz.) can chunky peanut butter
1 tsp. vanilla

Combine cereal, raisins and sunflower seeds in a large bowl. Combine honey and sugar in a medium saucepan. Heat over medium heat for 3-5 minutes. Add peanut butter and vanilla. Stir until peanut butter is melted. Pour over cereal mixture and mix well. Press mixture into greased 10" x 15" pan. When cool, cut into squares.

Lizbet and Daughters—Country Cooking

No Bake Cookies

½ c. milk
2 c. granulated sugar
¼ c. butter
1 bag mini marshmallows
½ c. peanut butter

1 tsp. vanilla
½ c. coconut
3 Tbsp. cocoa
3 c. quick oats

Combine milk, cocoa, sugar and butter. Bring to a boil, and boil for 1 minute. Remove from heat. Add marshmallows and stir until melted. Add remaining ingredients. Drop by teaspoon and shape on cookie sheet. Let cool.

Russian Tea Balls

1 c. butter, softened
½ c. powdered sugar
1 tsp. vanilla

2¼ c. flour
¾ c. chopped nuts
¼ tsp. salt

Mix together butter, powdered sugar and vanilla. Stir in flour, nuts and salt. Chill the dough. Roll into 1" balls and bake on ungreased cookie sheet. Do not brown. While still warm, roll in powdered sugar. Cool. Roll in powdered sugar again.

Father is the head of the home,
Mother is the heart of the house.

Cakes & Frostings

A Love Cake for Mother

1 can obedience

1 can of running errands (willing brand)

1 can thoughtfulness

several pounds of affection

1 pt. neatness

1 bottle "keep sunny all day long"

some holiday, birthday and everyday surprises

Mix well; bake in hearty, warm oven and serve to Mother every day.

Bunny Cake

Figure 1   Figure 2

Bake your favorite cake in 2 round layer pans. Line pans with waxed paper. When cool cut one layer as shown in Figure 1. Use outside pieces for ears and inside piece for bow. Frost with fluffy frosting or 1 tub frosting and 2 c. Cool Whip whipped together. Decorate with licorice, dollar candy for eyes or whatever you wish. This was a favorite for a children's birthday. It makes big smiles.

Flowerpot Cupcakes

1 Funfetti cake mix
36 ice cream cones, with flat bottoms
1 can pink vanilla Funfetti frosting
assorted candies

Preheat oven to 350°. Prepare cake mix according to package directions. Place ice cream cones in muffin cups. Fill cones with batter to 1" from top. Bake 20-25 minutes. Frost and sprinkle with candy bits.

Magic Cupcakes

1 chocolate cake mix
8 oz. cream cheese
½ tsp. salt
¾ c. sugar
1 beaten egg
6 oz. chocolate chips

Prepare cake mix according to directions. Fill cupcake tins ⅔ full. Combine cream cheese, salt, sugar and egg until fluffy. Stir in chocolate chips. Drop 1 Tbsp. of mixture in each cupcake. Bake at 350° for 12-15 minutes.

Lizbet and Daughters—Country Cooking

Diabetic Cake

1 cake mix

1 can diet pop

Topping-
1 box sugarfree instant pudding
1½ c. 2% milk

2 c. lite Cool Whip

For white or yellow cakes use Diet Sprite or Sierra Mist. For dark it is best with Coke or Dr. Pepper, must be diet. Mix cake mix and pop together with wire whisk. Bake at 350°. For topping: Mix pudding with milk. Add Cool Whip. Keep refrigerated.

Cream Filled Coffee Cake

1 c. scalded milk
1½ c. water
½ c. butter
1 tsp. salt
3½ c. bread flour

2 eggs
½ c. sugar
2½ Tbsp. yeast
3 c. doughnut mix

Topping-
1 c. brown sugar
⅓ c. flour

1 tsp. cinnamon
1 Tbsp. melted butter

Frosting-
8 oz. cream cheese
2 c. powdered sugar

12 oz. Cool Whip

Dissolve yeast in water. Scald milk. Add butter, sugar and salt. Stir till butter is melted. Add eggs. Cool to lukewarm then add yeast and doughnut mix. Let rise once. Put in 4-5 foil pie pans. Put topping on and let set for 30 minutes. Bake at 350°. Cool and split cakes and fill with frosting.

Walnut Wonder Coffee Cake

2 c. flour
1 tsp. soda
1 tsp. baking powder
½ tsp. salt
1 c. butter, softened

1 c. sugar
2 eggs
1 tsp. vanilla
1 c. sour cream

Topping-
⅓ c. brown sugar
¼ c. sugar
1 tsp. cinnamon

⅓ c. chocolate chips
½ c. chopped nuts

Cream Filling-
1 box instant vanilla pudding
1 c. milk

4 oz. cream cheese
3 c. whipped topping

Combine flour, salt, baking powder and soda. Cream butter and sugar. Add eggs and vanilla. Alternate sour cream with dry ingredients. Pour batter into two round 8" pans. Mix topping ingredients and sprinkle over batter. Bake at 350° for 35 minutes. Cut through middle and put cream filling in center. For filling: Mix pudding with milk; add to softened cream cheese. Add whipped topping.

Coffee Cake

½ c. sugar
½ c. butter
2 Tbsp. yeast
1 Tbsp. salt

2 eggs
2 c. hot water
6½ c. bread flour

Crumbs-
1½ c. flour
½ c. butter

¾ c. brown sugar

Dissolve butter, salt and sugar in hot water. Add yeast when lukewarm, then beaten eggs and flour. Let stand for 2 hours. Put dough in pans. Top with crumbs. Bake at 350°. Makes five small or four large coffee cakes. When cold, slice in half and fill with your favorite filling.

Finnish Coffee Cake

1¼ c. white sugar
2 eggs
1 c. buttermilk or sour milk
½ tsp. salt
1 tsp. baking powder

1 c. vegetable oil
1 tsp. vanilla
2 c. flour
½ tsp. baking soda

Cinnamon Mixture–
2 tsp. cinnamon

4 Tbsp. sugar

Glaze–
1 c. powdered sugar
hot water

½ tsp. vanilla

Beat eggs, oil, sugar, vanilla and buttermilk. Add dry ingredients. Pour half of batter into greased 9" x 13" pan. Top with half of cinnamon mixture. Pour remaining batter into pan and top with remaining cinnamon mixture. Bake at 350° for 20-25 minutes. Poke holes with fork into hot cake and drizzle with glaze.

Raspberry Cream Coffee Cake

2¼ c. flour
¾ c. sugar
¾ c. butter
¼ c. flour
½ tsp. baking powder

½ tsp. soda
½ tsp. salt
1 c. sour cream
1 egg, beaten
1½ tsp. almond flavoring

Filling–
8 oz. cream cheese
½ c. sugar

1 egg

Combine 2¼ c. flour, sugar and butter. Reserve 1 c. crumbs for topping. Add remaining ingredients to remaining crumb mixture. Mix well and spread in a 9" x 9" baking pan. Use one and one half recipe for 9" x 13" pan. For filling: Beat well and pour over batter. Spoon ½ to 1 cup raspberry pie filling on top of filling. Sprinkle ½ c. slivered almonds on top, along with the remaining crumbs. Bake at 350° for 55-60 minutes. I like to use the red raspberry filling in a tube.

Maple Nut Twist Coffee Cake

¾ c. milk
¼ c. butter
1 Tbsp. yeast
1 egg, beaten

½ tsp. salt
1 tsp. maple flavoring
3 Tbsp. sugar
3 c. flour

Filling–
¼ c. butter, creamy
½ c. brown sugar
1 tsp. cinnamon

1 tsp. maple flavoring
⅓ c. nuts

Glaze–
1 c. powdered sugar
1-2 tsp. milk

1 Tbsp. butter
½ tsp. maple flavoring

Heat milk and butter until very warm. Mix yeast with enough warm water to dissolve. Mix together milk and butter, yeast mixture, egg, salt, maple flavoring and sugar. Add flour. Divide dough in three parts. Pat one part on round pizza size pan; Spread filling. Put on another layer of dough, filling and dough. Cut into it with scissors, then twist each piece a few times. Let rise, then bake and top with glaze.

Blueberry Coffee Cake

1 rounded Tbsp. yeast
1 tsp. sugar
¼ c. warm water
1 egg, beaten
½ c. melted butter

⅓ c. milk
¼ c. sugar
½ tsp. salt
2½-3 c. bread flour
2 c. blueberries

Filling–
16 oz. cream cheese
⅔ c. sugar

2 egg yolks
1 tsp. vanilla

Mix together yeast, sugar and water. Let dissolve. Add egg, butter, milk, sugar, salt and bread flour. Keep dough soft. Set aside. Mix cream cheese, sugar, egg yolks and vanilla. Roll ⅔ of dough to fit into 9" x 13" pan. Keep enough dough to cut in strips to put on top of filling. Put on filling, then add the blueberries last. Arrange strips as you wish on top.

Lizbet and Daughters—Country Cooking

Gingerbread

½ c. butter
½ c. sugar
1 egg, beaten
2½ c. flour
1½ tsp. soda
1 tsp. cinnamon

1 tsp. ginger
½ tsp. cloves
½ tsp. salt
1 c. Brer Rabbit molasses
1 c. hot water

Sauce–
5 c. water

2 c. brown sugar

Cream butter and sugar. Add egg. Mix in dry ingredients. Add molasses and water. Bake at 350° for about 45 minutes. For sauce: Bring to a boil and thicken with clear jel. Add vanilla and lemon juice to make it glossy. Serve over warm cake with whipped topping.

Strawberry Shortcake

2 c. flour
4 tsp. baking powder
¾ tsp. salt
1 Tbsp. sugar

⅓ c. butter
⅔ c. milk
1 egg, beaten

Topping–
½ c. sugar
½ c. flour

3 Tbsp. butter

Make crumbs with first five ingredients. Add milk and egg. Pour into small cake pan. Make topping and spread on top of batter and bake at 350°. Serve with fresh fruit and milk.

Cherry Crumb Cake

2 c. flour
1 c. sugar
2 tsp. baking powder
½ tsp. salt
2 egg whites, beaten

½ c. butter
2 egg yolks
⅓ c. milk
1 can cherry pie filling

Mix flour, sugar, baking powder, salt and butter until crumbs form. Reserve ½ c. of this for topping. Combine egg yolks and milk with remaining crumb mixture. Beat smooth and fold in beaten egg whites. Spread in greased baking pan. Spread cherry pie filling over this and top with remaining crumbs. Bake at 350° for 40-45 minutes.

Lazy Cake

1½ c. flour
¼ tsp. salt
2 tsp. soda
1 tsp. vanilla
3 Tbsp. cocoa

1 c. sugar
7 Tbsp. cooking oil
1 Tbsp. vinegar
1 c. cold water

Sift dry ingredients into a 9" x 9" ungreased cake pan. Mix with fork. Make three holes in the dry ingredients. Into one pour vanilla, the next oil and into the third the vinegar. Pour over this 1 c. cold water and mix with fork. Do not beat. Bake at 350° for 25-30 minutes or until done.

Lizbet and Daughters—Country Cooking

Carrot Cake

2 c. sugar
1½ c. Wesson oil
2 c. flour
3 c. shredded carrots

4 eggs
1 tsp. salt
2 tsp. cinnamon
2 tsp. soda

Icing–
¼ c. butter
4 oz. cream cheese

1 Tbsp. milk
3 c. powdered sugar

Beat together eggs, sugar and oil till smooth. Mix flour, salt, cinnamon and soda together. Add to egg mixture. Beat about five minutes. Fold in carrots last. Pour in greased and floured pan. Bake at 350° for 40-50 minutes. For icing: Beat until smooth and spread on cake.

Cocoa Crumb Cake

2 c. flour
1½ c. brown sugar
½ c. butter
1 egg, beaten

1 c. buttermilk
1 large Tbsp. cocoa
1 tsp. soda
1 tsp. vanilla

Mix together first three ingredients like pie crust. Reserve ¾ c. for topping. Add rest of ingredients to the remaining crumbs. Put into large cake pan or pie pans. Top with crumbs. Bake at 350° for 30-40 minutes.

When Mom ain't happy, nobody's happy.

Granny Cake

1½ c. sugar
2 c. flour
1 tsp. baking soda
1 tsp. baking powder

½ tsp. salt
1 can crushed pineapples, undrained
2 eggs

Topping-
½ c. brown sugar

½ c. chopped nuts

Frosting-
½ c. sugar
6 Tbsp. butter

¾ c. evaporated milk
1 tsp. vanilla

Mix together and spread in cookie sheet. Sprinkle topping over batter and bake at 350° for 15 minutes. Shortly before cake is done, remove from oven; poke holes in cake with a fork, and pour frosting mixture over cake. Return to oven for about 5 minutes.

Heath Bar Cake

2 c. flour
2 c. brown sugar
½ c. butter
1 egg
¾ c. milk

1 tsp. soda
1 tsp. vanilla
½ c. chopped nuts
6 Heath bars, chopped

Cut butter into flour and sugar. Reserve 1 cup of this mixture to use for topping of cake. Combine egg, milk, soda and vanilla. Add this to the crumb mixture and mix well. Place in greased 9" x 13" pan. Sprinkle the rest of the crumbs, nuts and Heath bars on top. Bake at 350° until done. You can cut cake in half and fill with whoopie pie filling. For a different flavor, add ¼ c. strawberry jam to filling.

Lizbet and Daughters—Country Cooking

Honey Chocolate Cake

1 c. honey	2 tsp. soda
1 c. hot water	¼ tsp. salt
½ c. vegetable oil	¾ c. cocoa
2 eggs	2½ c. flour

Mix eggs, honey and oil together. Add water and the dry ingredients which have been sifted. Blend real well. Bake at 350° until done.

Amish Cake

½ c. butter	2 c. buttermilk
2 c. brown sugar	2 tsp. soda
3 c. flour	2 tsp. vanilla

Topping-

6 Tbsp. butter	½ c. coconut
1 c. brown sugar	½ c. nuts
4 Tbsp. milk	

Mix butter and sugar together. Add buttermilk, soda, vanilla and flour alternately. (Milk with 2 tsp. vinegar can be used instead of buttermilk.) Bake at 375°. For topping: Mix together and spread on hot cake. Put back in oven till bubbly.

Lemon Streusel Cake

1 lemon cake mix
1 c. water

Streusel Mix-
½ c. flour
½ c. powdered sugar
2 Tbsp. melted butter

Drizzle-
⅔ c. cream cheese
1 tsp. lemon juice

3 eggs
½ c. vegetable oil

1 tsp. lemon extract
3 drops yellow food coloring

3 drops yellow food coloring

Spoon ⅓ of cake batter in a greased, floured 9" x 13" pan. Sprinkle with ⅓ of streusel mix. Repeat layers two more times, ending with streusel. Bake at 375° for 42-48 minutes. Combine cream cheese, lemon juice and food coloring in small saucepan. Cook over low heat, stirring constantly, until thin. Drizzle over cake.

Butterscotch Cake

1 yellow cake mix
1 sm. box instant butterscotch pudding

1 c. nuts
1 c. butterscotch chips
½ c. granulated sugar

Mix cake according to directions. Add pudding mix. Put in greased loaf pan. Put topping mixture of nuts, chips and sugar on top of batter and bake at 350° until cake is done.

One of the healthiest ways to gamble is with a spade and a package of garden seeds.

Lizbet and Daughters—Country Cooking

Oatmeal Cake Supreme

1½ c. quick oatmeal	3 eggs
1½ c. flour	1½ tsp. soda
1¾ c. boiling water	½ tsp. cinnamon
¾ c. butter	1½ tsp. vanilla
1½ c. sugar	¼ tsp. salt
1½ c. brown sugar	

Topping-
1 c. coconut	1 tsp. vanilla
½ c. melted butter	1 c. nuts
1 c. brown sugar	¼ c. cream

Soak oatmeal in boiling water while you cream butter and sugars. Add eggs and vanilla and beat well. Sift flour, soda, cinnamon and salt together. Add to oatmeal mixture. Bake at 350° in greased 9" x 13" pan for about 30 minutes. Mix topping while cake is baking. Spread topping on hot cake. Return to oven for another 5 minutes or until lightly brown.

Dutch Apple Cake

3 eggs	1 tsp. soda
1 tsp. vanilla	1-2 tsp. cinnamon
1 c. salad oil	3 c. chopped apples
2 c. sugar	½ c. chopped nuts, optional
2 c. flour	

Topping-
½ c. brown sugar	
½ c. sugar	1 c. hot water
2 Tbsp. flour	¼ c. butter
	1 tsp. vanilla

Beat together eggs, vanilla, oil and sugar. Add flour, soda and cinnamon and blend well. Fold in apples and nuts. Bake in a greased 9" x 13" pan at 350° for 40-50 minutes. Blend topping ingredients except vanilla and cook until sauce thickens and becomes clear. Add vanilla. Prick cake with a fork as soon as it comes out of the oven. Pour warm sauce over cake and serve warm.

Spice Cake

¾ c. shortening
1¼ c. brown sugar
1 c. white sugar
3 eggs
3 c. cake flour
1½ tsp. soda
¾ tsp. nutmeg
¾ tsp. salt
¾ tsp. cloves
1½ c. buttermilk

Cream shortening and sugars until fluffy. Beat in eggs thoroughly. Sift together dry ingredients. Stir in alternately with buttermilk. Pour into greased 9" x 13" pan. Bake at 350° for 35-40 minutes. This cake is delicious frosted with brown sugar frosting.

Pumpkin Pudding Cake

1 yellow cake mix
1 pkg. instant butterscotch pudding
4 eggs
¼ c. water
¼ c. oil
1 c. canned pumpkin
1 tsp. cinnamon
¼ tsp. ginger

Combine all ingredients in large bowl. Blend well, then beat at medium speed for 4 minutes. Pour into greased and floured tube pan. Bake at 350° for 40-45 minutes. Cool in pan for 15 minutes. Top with Smooth and Creamy Frosting.

Pumpkin Pecan Cake

1 spice cake mix
1 c. canned pumpkin
½ c. salad oil
1 pkg. instant vanilla pudding mix
3 eggs
½ c. water
1 c. pecans, chopped

Mix and beat at medium speed for 5 minutes. Pour into greased and floured Bundt pan and bake at 350° for 40-45 minutes. Let cool in pan for 10-15 minutes. Loosen center and sides with spatula, invert and tip onto wire rack to cool. Top with Smooth and Creamy Frosting.

Lizbet and Daughters—Country Cooking

Alaska Sheet Cake

1 c. butter
1 c. water
2 c. sugar
2 c. plus 2 Tbsp. flour
1 tsp. salt

½ c. buttermilk
1½ tsp. soda
1 tsp. vanilla
3 eggs

Frosting-
6 Tbsp. butter
5 Tbsp. milk
3 c. powdered sugar

1 tsp. vanilla
1 c. nuts, optional

Put the butter and water in a saucepan and bring to a boil. Pour into bowl containing the rest of ingredients. Blend and put in a greased, floured cookie sheet. Put frosting on cake while still warm. For frosting: Bring butter and milk to a boil. Add powdered sugar and vanilla.

Mayonnaise Cake

2 c. flour
2 tsp. soda
5 Tbsp. cocoa
1 c. sugar

1 c. mayonnaise or salad dressing
1 c. cold water
1 tsp. vanilla

Measure and mix flour, soda and cocoa together and sift. Add sugar, salad dressing, water and vanilla. Beat well. Bake at 350°.

Yellow Sponge Cake

1½ c. sifted flour
1 c. sugar
½ tsp. baking powder
¼ tsp. salt

Icing–
¾ c. milk
⅓ c. flour
½ c. butter

6 egg yolks, beaten
½ c. water
6 egg whites, beaten
1 tsp. vanilla

¾ c. sugar
1 tsp. vanilla

Sift together flour, sugar and baking powder. Set aside. Beat the egg yolks until fluffy, then add the flour and cold water; first the flour, then water until the flour is gone. Fold in the beaten egg whites. Pour into angel food pan and bake at 350° for 1 hour or until done. For icing: Cook milk and flour until thick. Cool, then beat in the butter and sugar. Add vanilla. Beat until fluffy.

Chocolate Cake

⅔ c. sugar
½ c. water
½ c. cocoa
1 c. sugar
¾ c. sour milk

½ c. Crisco
2 eggs
2 c. flour
1 tsp. soda

Boil together first three ingredients. Dissolve soda in sour milk. When first mixture is cool, add remaining ingredients. Mix well and pour into greased pan. Bake at 350° for 30 minutes.

Lizbet and Daughters—Country Cooking

Graham Streusel Cake

2 c. graham cracker crumbs
¾ c. chopped nuts
¾ c. brown sugar, packed
1¼ tsp. cinnamon
¾ c. butter, melted

1 cake mix—any kind
1 c. water
¼ c. vegetable oil
3 eggs

Vanilla Glaze–
1 c. powdered sugar

1-2 Tbsp. water

Mix crumbs, nuts, brown sugar, cinnamon and butter. Reserve. Blend cake mix, water, oil and eggs until moistened. Pour half of the batter into greased 13" x 9" pan. Sprinkle with half of the reserved crumb mixture. Spread remaining batter evenly over crumb mixture. Sprinkle with remaining crumbs. Bake at 350°. Mix glaze and pour over cake.

Angel Food Cake

1 c. sifted flour
1½ c. sifted powdered sugar
2 c. egg whites
1½ tsp. cream of tartar

1 c. sugar
½ tsp. vanilla
½ tsp. almond flavoring

Sift flour and powdered sugar together three times. Set aside. Place egg whites, cream of tartar and salt in a large mixing bowl and beat until foamy. Gradually add sugar, two tablespoons at a time. Continue beating until meringue holds stiff peaks; fold in flavoring. Gradually sift flour and sugar mixture over egg whites. Mix gently by hand. Bake in 10" tube pan at 350° for 35-40 minutes or until top springs back when lightly touched. Invert on a funnel and let cool.

Texas Sheet Cake

2 c. granulated sugar
2 c. flour
½ tsp. salt
1 c. butter
1 c. water

2½ Tbsp. cocoa
2 eggs
1 Tbsp. vinegar
1 tsp. vanilla
1 tsp. soda

Icing-
½ c. butter
4 Tbsp. cocoa
6 Tbsp. milk

1 lb. powdered sugar
1 tsp. vanilla

Sift together sugar, flour and salt in a large bowl. Bring butter, water and cocoa to a boil. Beat eggs, vinegar, vanilla and soda. Add both mixtures to flour mixture, beating well while adding. Put in greased cookie sheet and bake at 350°. For icing: Bring butter, cocoa and milk to a boil, then add rest of ingredients and spread on cake while warm.

Banana Cake

1 c. sugar
½ c. butter
4 Tbsp. sour milk
2 eggs, well beaten
2 c. flour
1 c. mashed bananas

1 tsp. soda
2 tsp. baking powder
1 tsp. cream of tartar
dash of salt
1 tsp. vanilla
½ c. chopped nuts

Cream sugar and butter. Add eggs, milk and vanilla. Add sifted dry ingredients. Add bananas and nuts. Bake at 350° for 40 minutes or until done.

Lizbet and Daughters—Country Cooking

Quick Banana Cake

1 yellow cake mix
1 pkg. instant vanilla pudding
4 eggs
½ c. oil
1 c. water
2 bananas, mashed

Mix in order given and bake at 350° for 30-40 minutes.

Zucchini Cake

¼ c. butter
½ c. vegetable oil
1¾ c. sugar
2 eggs
1 tsp. vanilla
½ c. sour milk
2½ c. unsifted flour
4 Tbsp. cocoa
½ tsp. baking powder
1 tsp. soda
½ tsp. cinnamon
2 c. finely chopped zucchini
¼ c. chocolate chips
¼ c. chopped nuts

Cream butter, oil and sugar. Add eggs, vanilla and milk. Stir in dry ingredients. Last stir in zucchini. Pour in a greased cake pan. Sprinkle chocolate chips and nuts over top. Bake at 350° for 40-50 minutes.

Jell-O Cake

1 white cake mix
1 (3 oz.) box Jell-O
¾ c. hot water
½ c. cold water
1 box instant vanilla pudding
1½ c. milk
8 oz. Cool Whip

Mix cake and bake according to directions. After cake is baked use a fork to prick holes in cake 1" apart. Dissolve Jell-O in hot water, then add cold water. Pour over baked cake. Mix together last three ingredients and put on top. You may use a lemon cake mix with lime Jell-O.

Ho-Ho Cake

1 chocolate cake mix

Filling-
5 Tbsp. flour
1 c. sugar
½ c. shortening

1¼ c. milk
½ c. butter

Topping-
½ c. melted butter
6 Tbsp. cocoa
2 Tbsp. hot water

3 c. powdered sugar
1 tsp. vanilla
1 egg, beaten

Mix and bake cake as directed. Bake in 10" x 15" jelly roll pan. Cool. Cook flour and milk until thick. Cool. Combine sugar, butter and shortening. Beat until fluffy (about 4 minutes). Beat another 4 minutes after adding cooled flour and milk mixture. Spread over cake. Mix topping ingredients together and beat until fluffy. Spread over second layer.

Pineapple Sheet Cake

2½ c. all-purpose flour
2 c. sugar
2 eggs
1 c. chopped nuts

2 tsp. baking powder
½ tsp. salt
1 tsp. vanilla
20 oz. crushed pineapple, undrained

Cream Cheese Icing-
8 oz. cream cheese, softened
3½ c. powdered sugar
½ c. butter, softened

1 tsp. vanilla
½ c. nuts

In large mixing bowl, combine all ingredients. Mix until smooth. Pour into a greased 10" x 15" baking pan. Bake at 350° for 35 minutes. Cool. For icing: Combine cream cheese, sugar, butter and vanilla in a small mixing bowl. Beat until smooth. Spread over cake and sprinkle with nuts.

Lizbet and Daughters—Country Cooking

Earthquake Cake

1½ c. coconut
1 c. chopped nuts
½ c. butter, softened

2 c. powdered sugar
1 German chocolate cake mix
8 oz. cream cheese, softened

Grease a 9" x 13" x 3" pan. (If you use a 9" x 13" x 2" pan, cake will run over.) Cover bottom of pan with coconut. Sprinkle chopped nuts over coconut. Prepare cake mix as directed on box. Pour over coconut and nut mixture. Combine butter, powdered sugar and cream cheese. Stir until smooth. Spoon over cake mix. Bake at 350° for 1 hour.

Chocolate Mocha Torte

½ c. cocoa
½ c. boiling water
2½ c. all-purpose flour
1½ tsp. baking soda
½ tsp. salt

1¾ c. sugar
⅔ c. butter
2 eggs
1 tsp. vanilla
1 c. buttermilk

Filling–
5 Tbsp. flour
1 c. milk
1 c. sugar
1 c. butter

½ tsp. instant coffee granules
2 tsp. water
1 tsp. vanilla
2 tsp. cocoa

Make a paste of cocoa and water. Cool and set aside. Sift together flour, soda and salt. Cream the sugar and butter. Add eggs and vanilla. Blend in cocoa mixture. Add flour mixture alternately with the buttermilk. Blend until smooth. Pour into two greased and floured 9" cake pans. Bake at 350° for 35 minutes or until cake is done. For filling: Cook flour and milk over low heat, stirring constantly, until thick. Cool. Cream sugar and butter until light. Dissolve coffee in water; add with vanilla, cocoa and milk mixture to creamed mixture. Beat until fluffy. Split each cake layer in half. Divide filling into thirds and spread between layers. Frost with your favorite frosting.

Christmas Fruitcake

1 lb. butter
6 egg yolks
1 tsp. soda
2 oz. lemon extract
1 Tbsp. warm water
2 c. sugar
2 c. nuts
1 c. coconut
1 lb. mixed candied fruit
1 c. white raisins
3 c. all-purpose flour
6 egg whites

Mix together first six ingredients. In another bowl mix nuts, coconut, fruit and raisins. Add this mixture to first mixture with flour. Beat egg whites until stiff and fold in. Bake in greased bread pans lined with brown paper. Bake 1 hour at 250°. This makes 4 loaves. When cool, wrap in plastic wrap and store in cool place.

Turtle Cake

1 German chocolate cake mix
1 pkg. Kraft caramels
½ c. butter
1 can sweetened condensed milk
¾ c. chocolate chips

Prepare cake mix according to directions and pour half of mixture in cake pan. Bake at 350° for 20 minutes. Melt caramels with butter and milk. Pour over baked cake. Dot remaining batter over milk mixture. Sprinkle with chocolate chips. Bake at 250° for 20 minutes, then at 350° for 10 minutes.

Fluffy Lemon Cake

1 pkg. lemon cake mix
1 can sweetened condensed milk
1 (6 oz.) can frozen lemonade, thawed and undiluted
8 oz. Cool Whip
1 Tbsp. lemon juice
3 drops yellow food coloring

Make cake according to package directions. Bake in 9" x 13" pan at 350° for 30-35 minutes. Cool in pan 10 minutes, then remove from pan and let cool completely. Split cake in half; set aside. Combine remaining ingredients and blend well. Spread between layers and on top and sides of cake. Keep refrigerated.

Butter Pecan Dessert Cake

1 butter pecan cake mix

Filling–
8 oz. cream cheese
½ c. powdered sugar
1 c. Rich's topping, measured before whipping

Sour Cream Topping–
6 Tbsp. butter
¾ c. brown sugar
½ c. sour cream

Bake cake according to directions. Mix filling ingredients and put on top of cooled cake. For sour cream topping: Lightly brown butter. Add brown sugar and sour cream. Bring to a boil. Remove from heat and let cool. Spread on top of filling.

Pistachio Cake

1 white cake mix
2 boxes instant pistachio pudding
5 eggs
½ c. water
½ c. oil
½ c. milk
¾ c. chopped nuts, optional

Icing–
1 box instant pistachio pudding
1 c. milk
8 oz. Cool Whip

Mix all ingredients. Add nuts last. Bake at 350° in a well greased 9" x 13" pan for 50 minutes. Let cool. For icing: Mix pudding and milk. Add Cool Whip. Spread over cake. Keep refrigerated.

Cookies and Cream Cake

1 white cake mix

16 Oreos, crushed

Topping–
1 sm. pkg. vanilla instant pudding
¾ c. cold milk

8 oz. Cool Whip
6-8 crushed Oreos

Mix cake mix as directed on box. Add Oreos and bake at 350°. For topping: Mix together milk and pudding. Add Cool Whip and crushed Oreos. Put on top of cake.

Pumpkin Roll

3 eggs
⅔ c. cooked pumpkin
1 c. sugar
1 tsp. baking soda

¾ c. flour
1 tsp. salt
½ tsp. cinnamon

Filling–
8 oz. cream cheese
2 tsp. vanilla

1 c. powdered sugar
2 Tbsp. butter

Combine all ingredients. Pour in cookie sheet lined with waxed paper. Bake at 375° for 15 minutes. Turn out on towel sprinkled with powdered sugar. Refrigerate for 10 minutes. Unroll and spread with filling. For filling: Combine ingredients. Roll up same as a jelly roll.

Today I will act toward people as though this might be my last day on earth. I will not wait for tomorrow—tomorrow never comes.

Jelly Roll

1 c. bread flour
1 c. sugar
1 tsp. baking powder

½ tsp. salt
3 tsp. vanilla
6 eggs

Filling-
¾ c. bread flour
1¼ c. brown sugar
1½ c. warm water

5 Tbsp. butter
1 tsp. vanilla
1 tsp. maple flavoring

Separate eggs. Beat yolks well, then add ¾ c. sugar (reserve ¼ c. to beat with egg whites) and vanilla. Beat until creamy. Add flour, baking powder and salt. Beat egg whites until foamy, then gradually add remaining sugar until stiff. Mix together with other ingredients. Line a 16" x 11" pan with wax paper. Pour batter into pan and bake at 375° for 13 minutes or until light brown. When done invert onto a dish towel. Remove wax paper. Let cool for a minute, then put filling on top and roll up. For filling: Put first three ingredients into a saucepan. Heat until thick. Remove from heat and add butter and flavorings.

Chocolate Jelly Roll

¾ c. bread flour
¼ c. cocoa
1 tsp. baking powder
¼ tsp. salt

1 c. white sugar
5 Tbsp. water
1 tsp. vanilla
4 eggs

Filling-
4 oz. cream cheese
¼ c. powdered sugar

8 oz. Cool Whip

Separate eggs. Beat yolks well, then add ¾ c. sugar (reserve ¼ c. to beat with egg whites), vanilla and water. Beat again, then add baking powder, salt and sifted flour and cocoa. Beat egg whites until foamy, then gradually add remaining sugar until stiff. Mix together with other ingredients. Pour into a 16" x 11" pan lined with wax paper. Bake at 375° for 13 minutes. When done invert on a dish towel, then roll up. When cool fill with filling. For filling: Cream first two ingredients until smooth, then add Cool Whip.

Jelly Roll

5 eggs, separated
1 c. sugar
1¼ c. sifted cake flour
2½ tsp. baking powder

½ tsp. salt
1 tsp. vanilla
1 tsp. lemon flavoring

Filling–
1 (3 oz.) box Jell-O
2 c. water

½ c. sugar
clear jel

Beat egg whites, then add the yolks and beat some more. Beat in sugar, 1 Tbsp. at a time. Fold in sifted flour and baking powder. Add flavoring and bake on wax paper lined cookie sheet at 350° until done. Flop cake upside down on another sheet wax paper as soon as it can be handled. Peel off paper from cake and roll up cake. When cold, unroll and fill. Mother made these jelly rolls for all her daughters' weddings, and I also used this recipe for all our daughters' weddings.

Marshmallow Frosting

¾ c. Crisco
2 c. marshmallow créme
3-4 Tbsp. milk

1 tsp. vanilla
4 c. powdered sugar

Beat together until creamy.

Quick Chocolate Frosting

1 c. Nestle Quik
¼ c. butter, softened
1 tsp. vanilla

⅓ c. boiling water
2¾ c. powdered sugar

Combine Nestle Quik, butter, vanilla and boiling water. Stir well. Beat in powdered sugar.

Brown Sugar Frosting

1½ c. brown sugar
½ c. sugar
1 c. cream

Boil together until soft ball, tested in cold water. Let set until cool, then stir until gloss is gone and frosting is right consistency to spread. Grandmother Miller's frosting for her rolls and chocolate and spice cakes. Delicious!

Caramel Frosting

½ c. butter
1 c. brown sugar
¼ c. milk
1¾-2 c. powdered sugar

Melt butter and add brown sugar. Cook over low heat, stirring constantly, for about 3-4 minutes. Add milk. Stir until mixture comes to a boil. Remove from heat. Slowly add powdered sugar, beating after each addition, until thick enough to spread. Enough for a large cake.

Our Favorite Frosting

16 oz. chocolate or vanilla frosting, ready made
8 oz. Cool Whip

Mix together frosting and Cool Whip. Enough for a large cake. You can pile this on and it's not so rich. Refrigerate.

Butter Cream Frosting

1 Tbsp. coffee
2 Tbsp. hot water
½ c. butter, softened
8 oz. cream cheese
3 c. powdered sugar

1 tsp. vanilla
1 c. whipped topping
1 Tbsp. corn syrup
6 oz. chocolate chips
1 Tbsp. peanut butter

Blend coffee and in 2 Tbsp. water. Mix butter and cream cheese together and add to coffee. Add powdered sugar, vanilla and whipped topping. Spread on cake. Melt syrup, chocolate chips and peanut butter over low heat. Add water until right consistency to drizzle over frosting.

Fluffy Frosting

1 c. sugar
¼ tsp. cream of tartar
⅛ tsp. salt

⅓ c. hot water
3 egg whites

Combine first four ingredients in saucepan. Cook without stirring until a little of the mixture dropped in very cold water forms a soft ball (240° on candy thermometer). Meanwhile, beat egg whites until stiff, but not dry. Add syrup slowly to egg whites, beating constantly, until it holds its shape.

Smooth and Creamy Frosting

3 oz. instant vanilla pudding
¼ c. powdered sugar
1 c. cold milk

8 oz. Cool Whip
4 oz. cream cheese

Mix instant pudding and milk. Let stand until thickened. Mix powdered sugar and cream cheese. Add to thickened pudding. Add Cool Whip.

Coconut Pecan Frosting

1 c. evaporated milk
1 c. sugar
3 egg yolks
½ c. butter
1 tsp. vanilla
1⅓ c. coconut
1 c. chopped pecans or walnuts

Combine milk, sugar, egg yolks, butter and vanilla. Cook and stir over medium heat until thickened (about 12 minutes). Add coconut and nuts. Spread over cooled cake. Makes about 2½ cups. Delicious on German chocolate cake mix.

Frosting for Coffee Cakes

8 oz. cream cheese
2 c. powdered sugar
16 oz. Cool Whip

Cream together cream cheese and powdered sugar. Add Cool Whip. This is enough frosting for 4-5 coffee cakes, all depending on how much frosting you want in each cake.

Whoopie Pie Filling

2 eggs, beaten
2 c. powdered sugar
1 Tbsp. vanilla
1½ c. Crisco

Beat eggs, powdered sugar and vanilla well. Add Crisco and continue beating until smooth. Add marshmallow créme.

Cream Cheese Frosting

8 oz. cream cheese
¼ c. butter
1 tsp. vanilla
1 lb. powdered sugar

Beat ingredients until smooth and fluffy.

Sour Cream Caramel Frosting

¼ c. butter
½ c. sour cream

¾ c. brown sugar

Cook together for three minutes.

Chocolate Frosting

1¾ c. sugar
½ c. butter
1 Tbsp. light Karo

3 heaping Tbsp. cocoa
½ c. milk

Boil until soft ball stage. Cool, then stir until thick.

Starter "Herman"

2 c. flour
2 c. warm water

¼ c. sugar
1 pkg. yeast

Mix all ingredients and place in plastic or glass container. Let stand overnight in a warm place. Cover with lid, but not tightly. Refrigerate covered, but stir every day. The fifth day you have to feed "Herman" with 1 c. flour, 1 c. milk and ½ c. sugar. On the tenth day you can bake "Herman" with one of the following recipes. Before baking reserve 1 c. of "Herman" to start again, by feeding it like on the fifth day. You can also give 1 c. to someone else.

Lizbet and Daughters—Country Cooking

"Herman" Cake

1 c. sugar
2 eggs
2 c. "Herman"
2 c. flour
¾ c. milk
½ tsp. soda
½ tsp. baking powder
2 tsp. salt

⅔ c. oil
1½ tsp. cinnamon
1 c. nuts
1 c. raisins
1 Tbsp. flour
1 c. brown sugar
1 Tbsp. cinnamon
¼ c. butter, softened

Mix all ingredients together except last four, adding nuts and raisins last. Put in greased and floured 9" x 13" pan. Mix together last four ingredients. Sprinkle on cake. Bake at 350° for 30-40 minutes.

"Herman" Cinnamon Rolls

2 c. "Herman"
2 c. flour
½ tsp. salt
½ tsp. soda
4 tsp. baking powder
½ c. cooking oil

butter
cinnamon
sugar
½ c. melted butter
1 c. brown sugar
½ c. nuts

Combine "Herman", flour, soda, salt, baking powder and oil and knead lightly on floured board until dough is no longer sticky. Roll to ¼" thickness and spread with soft butter. Sprinkle with cinnamon and sugar and roll up jelly roll fashion. Cut into ½" slices. Combine melted butter, brown sugar and nuts. Spread in bottom of 9" x 13" pan. Place dough on top of mixture and bake at 350° for 30 minutes or until golden brown. Invert pan immediately and remove rolls.

"Herman" Cookies

½ c. shortening
1½ c. brown sugar
1½ c. sour milk
2 eggs
½ c. "Herman"
2 c. flour
1 tsp. soda
1 tsp. baking powder
1 tsp. salt
1 tsp. cinnamon
3 c. quick oats
1 c. raisins
½ c. milk

Cream together shortening and sugar. Add remaining ingredients and mix well. Drop batter by spoonfuls on greased cookie sheets and bake at 375° for 10 minutes.

Lizbet and Daughters—Country Cooking

Desserts

Seese wie zucker,
Glatt wie butter,
Gmixed mit rom
Und aw some nuts,
Macht an pudding shrecklich gut!

Sweet as sugar,
Smooth as butter,
Mixed with cream
and some nuts,
Makes a pudding scrumptiously good!

. . . . .

If there's not enough to save
And a little too much to dump,
Then there's nothing left to do but eat it;
That's what makes the housewife plump!

Notes

Triple Orange Dessert

1 box orange Jell-O
1 box instant vanilla pudding
1 box tapioca pudding
2½ c. water
1 can mandarin oranges
2 c. Cool Whip

Bring Jell-O, vanilla pudding, tapioca and water to a boil, then take from heat; cool. Add Cool Whip and mandarin oranges.

Lemon Fluff

1 can sweetened condensed milk
1 can lemon pudding or
   1 box cook-type lemon pudding
1 can crushed pineapple
1 c. miniature marshmallows
1 lg. Cool Whip

Mix well and chill. Makes a big bowl full.

try

Oreo Pudding

Crumbs–
1 lg. pkg. Oreo cookies, crushed
½ c. butter, melted

Pudding–
8 oz. cream cheese
3 c. milk
2 pkg. instant vanilla pudding
12 oz. Cool Whip
1 c. powdered sugar

Line bottom of 9" x 13" pan with crumbs. Reserve some for top. Mix cream cheese and powdered sugar. Mix instant pudding and milk. Add to cream cheese. Add Cool Whip and put on top of crumbs. Top with reserved crumbs.

Lizbet and Daughters—Country Cooking

Eclair Pudding

1 box graham crackers
9 oz. Cool Whip

2 boxes instant vanilla pudding
3½ c. milk

Topping-
1 c. chocolate chips
3 Tbsp. butter
3 Tbsp. milk

2 Tbsp. light Karo
1 tsp. vanilla
1½ c. powdered sugar

Prepare pudding; add Cool Whip. Line bottom of 9" x 13" pan with graham crackers. Put half of pudding mixture over crackers. Cover with another layer crackers. Add remaining pudding. Cover with another layer crackers. For topping, melt chocolate chips and butter. Add remaining ingredients, ending with powdered sugar. Stir well. Spread over crackers. Refrigerate at least 1 day before serving.

Pine Scotch Pudding

¾ c. sifted flour
½ tsp. salt
1 c. sugar
1 c. crushed pineapple, drained

1 tsp. baking powder
2 eggs, beaten
1 tsp. vanilla
1 c. chopped nuts

Sauce-
¼ c. butter, melted
1 c. firmly packed brown sugar
¼ c. pineapple juice
1 egg, beaten

¼ c. water
1 Tbsp. flour
1 tsp. vanilla

Combine dry ingredients. Combine eggs and sugar, beating until thick and ivory colored. (Beat egg whites first, then add yolks.) Add vanilla. Fold in pineapple and nuts. Gently fold in dry ingredients. Pour into well greased 8" x 13" pan. Bake at 325° for 30-35 minutes. Cool. To make sauce, mix first 6 ingredients well and bring to a boil, stirring constantly. Add vanilla. Chill until served. Pour over squares. Top with Cool Whip.

Maple Sponge Pudding

1 pkg. (1 Tbsp.) gelatin
1½ c. cold water
2 c. brown sugar
½ c. hot water
2 egg whites
1 c. chopped nuts
½ c. sugar
3 c. milk
1 Tbsp. flour
2 egg yolks
pinch salt

Put sugar and hot water in saucepan. Bring to a boil and boil for 10 minutes. Soak gelatin in cold water for 5 minutes. Pour syrup gradually on gelatin and mix. Cool and when starting to set, add beaten egg whites. Set aside to set. Cook remaining ingredients. When ready to serve, mix both parts together and add whipped cream and nuts.

Pumpkin Festival Dessert

Layer One–
1 c. flour
½ c. butter, softened
1 c. nuts

Layer Two–
2 c. Cool Whip
8 oz. cream cheese
1 c. powdered sugar

Layer Three–
3 pkg. instant vanilla pudding
1 c. canned pumpkin
3 c. milk
8 oz. Cool Whip

Layer one: Combine and press into 9" x 13" pan. Bake at 350° for 20 minutes. Cool. Layer two: Mix cream cheese and powdered sugar until smooth. Add Cool Whip and pour over crust. Layer three: Mix milk and pudding together. Add pumpkin and Cool Whip. Spread over layer two.

Lizbet and Daughters—Country Cooking

Pumpkin Torte

Layer One–
24 graham crackers, crushed
½ c. butter
½ c. sugar

Layer Two–
2 eggs, beaten
¾ c. sugar
8 oz. cream cheese or sour cream

Layer Three–
2 c. pumpkin
3 eggs, separated
¾ c. sugar, divided
1 Tbsp. unflavored gelatin
½ c. milk
½ tsp. salt
1 Tbsp. cinnamon
8 oz. whipped topping

Press layer one into 9" x 13" pan. Mix layer two and pour over crust. Bake at 350° for 20 minutes. Cook pumpkin, egg yolks, ½ c. sugar, milk, salt and cinnamon until it thickens. Remove from heat and add gelatin dissolved in cold water; cool. Beat egg whites and ¼ c. sugar. Beat into pumpkin mixture. Add 1 c. whipped topping. Pour over cooled crust. Top with rest of whipped topping.

Apple Dumplings

Pastry–
2 c. flour
1 tsp. salt
⅔ c. Crisco
2 Tbsp. butter
1 egg, slightly beaten
2-3 Tbsp. water
apples

Sauce–
2 c. brown sugar
2 c. water
¼ c. butter
½ tsp. cinnamon
2 Tbsp. clear jel

Mix dough; roll out and wrap around apple halves. Bake at 375° until dough is brown and apples are soft. For sauce, bring sugar, water and butter to a boil. Thicken with clear jel mixed with a little water. Serve sauce over dumplings with ice cream, or milk can be used. Rich and good.

Apple Pudding

2 c. brown sugar
2 eggs
½ c. vegetable oil
1 tsp. vanilla
2 tsp. soda

2 c. flour
2 c. diced, cooked apples
1 tsp. cinnamon
½ c. nuts
½ tsp. salt

Sauce–
3 c. water
1½ c. brown sugar

⅛ tsp. salt
4 Tbsp. clear jel

Bake at 350° for 55 minutes or until done. When cold use with cake as date pudding, using whipped topping as desired. For sauce: Boil first three ingredients together, then add clear jel that has been mixed with a little water. Cook until thickened.

Homemade Applesauce

4 medium apples
¾ c. water

¼ c. brown sugar
dash of cinnamon

Peel, core and cut apples into quarters. Put apples, sugar, cinnamon and water into saucepan. Cover and cook at medium heat (simmering) for 15-20 minutes. Let apples cool, then mash with potato masher.

Apple Crisp

¾ c. sugar
dash of salt
4 c. peeled, sliced apples

1 Tbsp. flour
⅛ tsp. cinnamon

Topping–
½ c. butter
½ c. brown sugar
1 c. rolled oats

¾ c. pastry flour
¼ tsp. baking powder

Mix apple mixture and put in 9" x 13" pan. Crumble together topping and spread on top. Bake at 375°.

Lizbet and Daughters—Country Cooking

Caramel Apple Slices

⅓ c. brown sugar
2 Tbsp. butter

2 large apples

In a large skillet, cook and stir sugar and butter over medium heat until sugar is dissolved and butter melted. Pare and cut each apple into 16 slices; add to brown sugar mixture. Cook uncovered over medium heat for 5-7 minutes or until tender, stirring occasionally. Serve warm.

Quick Butterscotch Apples

6 apples, peeled and halved
¼ c. sugar
2 c. water
½ c. brown sugar

2 Tbsp. clear jel
2 tsp. maple flavoring
Cool Whip

Cook apples and sugar in water until apples are tender. Take apples out and thicken the water with brown sugar and clear jel. Cook until thickened then add maple flavoring. Stir and pour over apples. Top with Cool Whip and serve warm.

Delicious Pudding

1 angel food cake, cut in pieces
1 jar caramel topping

8 oz. Cool Whip
Skors candy bars, chopped in pieces

Mix caramel topping and Cool Whip together. Put angel food cake and topping in layers. Sprinkle candy bars on top.

Cherry Berry on a Cloud

3 egg whites
¼ tsp. cream of tartar
¾ c. white sugar
3 oz. cream cheese, softened
½ c. powdered sugar
½ tsp. vanilla
1 c. whipping cream
1 c. miniature marshmallows

Cover baking sheet with heavy brown paper. Beat egg whites and cream of tartar until foamy. Beat in sugar, 1 Tbsp. at time. Continue beating until stiff and glossy. Do not underbeat. Bake for 1½ hours at 270°, then turn off heat and leave meringue in oven with door closed for 1 hour. Remove from oven, away from draft. Blend cream cheese, sugar and vanilla. Beat cream until stiff. Gently fold whipped cream and marshmallows into cream cheese mixture. Pile into meringue shell. Top with any flavored pie filling.

Cornstarch Pudding

2 rounded Tbsp. cornstarch
½ c. sugar
2 egg yolks
2 c. boiling milk

Mix cornstarch, sugar and ¼ c. milk together well, then add egg yolks and mix well. Stir mixture into remaining milk, and stir until thick. Good with cinnamon sprinkled over top.

Just about the time a mother thinks that work is getting less, she becomes a grandmother.

Lizbet and Daughters—Country Cooking

Date Pudding

1 c. dates, cut fine
1 tsp. soda
1 Tbsp. butter
1 c. hot water

1 c. sugar
1 c. flour
1 c. nuts, optional

Caramel Topping–
1 can cooked sweetened condensed milk

2 c. whipped Rich's topping

Mix dates, soda and butter. Pour hot water over dates. Add sugar, flour and nuts. Bake in a 9" x 13" pan. Mix together condensed milk and whipped topping. Layer cake with condensed milk mixture. Top with whipped topping and sprinkle with chopped nuts.

Date Pudding

2 c. dates
2 tsp. soda
2 c. boiling water
2 Tbsp. butter

2 eggs
2 c. brown sugar
2 c. flour

Mash first four ingredients with potato masher. Cool, then add eggs, brown sugar and flour. Pour into large cookie sheet. Bake at 350°.

Date Pudding Sauce

3 tsp. butter
1 c. brown sugar
3 tsp. clear jel

1½ c. water
1 tsp. vanilla
½ tsp. maple flavoring

Brown butter. Add brown sugar and 1 c. water. Mix clear jel and rest of water and add to boiling mixture. Add flavorings.

Chocolate Angel Dessert

1 angel food cake, cubed
1 sm. pkg. instant chocolate pudding
2 c. milk
8 oz. cream cheese
2 Tbsp. milk
2 c. Cool Whip
¾ c. powdered sugar

Slowly beat milk and pudding for 2 minutes. Chill for 5 minutes. Beat cream cheese, powdered sugar and milk together. Add Cool Whip and pudding. Alternate pudding and cake in bowl.

Angel Delight

1 angel food cake
6 oz. chocolate chips
3 Tbsp. water
3 Tbsp. white sugar
¼ tsp. salt
2 eggs, separated
2 c. whipped topping
1 tsp. vanilla

Break cake in small pieces. Melt chocolate chips in double boiler; add water, sugar and salt. When melted, put in heavy saucepan and bring to a boil. Beat egg yolks and add to mixture. Cool. Add beaten egg whites, whipped topping and vanilla. Alternate layers of cake and chocolate mixture. Store in refrigerator overnight.

Cherry Delight

24 graham crackers, crushed
4 Tbsp. butter
1 Tbsp. sugar
8 oz. cream cheese
½ c. powdered sugar
2 c. whipped topping
1 tsp. vanilla

Mix cracker crumbs, butter and sugar and press in flat pan. Mix cream cheese with sugar and vanilla till smooth. Fold in whipped topping and spread on crust. Top with 1 can cherry pie filling or thickened fruit of your choice.

Lizbet and Daughters — Country Cooking

Cherry Chiffon Dessert

1 can cherry pie filling
1 can crushed pineapple, drained
1 can sweetened condensed milk
8 oz. Cool Whip, thawed
1 c. mini marshmallows

In a large bowl combine all ingredients and mix well. Pour into large serving bowl. Chill for 30 minutes. Blueberry pie filling can also be used.

Baked Chocolate Fudge Pudding

3 Tbsp. shortening
¾ c. sugar
1 c. flour
1½ tsp. baking powder
½ tsp. salt
½ c. milk
1 c. brown sugar
¼ c. cocoa
¼ tsp. salt
1¼ c. boiling water

Cream together shortening and sugar. Mix milk with flour, baking powder and ½ tsp. salt and add to shortening. Put into an ungreased 8" x 8" pan. Mix brown sugar, cocoa and ¼ tsp. salt. Sprinkle on top of batter. Do not stir. Pour water over top of batter. Bake at 350° for 40-45 minutes. Serve with vanilla ice cream.

Peaches -n- Cream Cheesecake

¾ c. flour
1 tsp. baking powder
½ tsp. salt
3¼ oz. pkg. vanilla pudding (cook type)

3 Tbsp. butter, softened
1 egg
½ c. milk

Filling–
1 can sliced peaches
8 oz. cream cheese

½ c. sugar

Grease sides and bottom of 9" or 10" pie pan. Combine cake ingredients and pudding mix in large bowl. Mix well. Pour into pan. Drain peaches, reserving 3 Tbsp. juice. Arrange peaches on batter. To make filling combine cream cheese, sugar and 3 Tbsp. juice. Mix well, then spoon on batter and peaches to within 1 inch from edge. Combine 1 Tbsp. sugar and ½ tsp. cinnamon and sprinkle over top. Bake at 350° for 30-35 minutes or until crust is golden brown. Filling will be soft.

Overnight Salad

2 beaten eggs
½ c. sugar
5 Tbsp. flour
1 c. orange juice
1 pkg. mini marshmallows

8 oz. cream cheese
1 can crushed pineapples
1 small can mandarin oranges, drained
1 c. whipped topping

Cook eggs, sugar, flour and orange juice until thick. While hot add marshmallows and cream cheese. Stir until smooth. Cool, then add whipped topping, pineapples and oranges. Let stand overnight.

Lizbet and Daughters—Country Cooking

Cake Dessert

1 yellow or white cake mix
8 oz. cream cheese
1 small box vanilla instant pudding

2 c. whipped topping
1 c. milk

Topping–
2 c. water
1 c. sugar

⅓ c. clear jel
3 oz. box Jell-O

Mix cake mix according to directions and bake in a jelly roll pan. Mix milk and pudding. In a separate bowl mix softened cream cheese and whipped topping and add to pudding. Spread over baked cake. For topping cook together first three ingredients until thick. Add Jell-O of your choice. Add fruit and put on top of cream cheese layer.

Red Hot Cinnamon Apples

8 to 10 medium apples
1½ c. cinnamon imperials
3 c. water

½ c. clear jel
¾ c. water

In a saucepan measure candy and add 3 c. water. Stir occasionally until melted, then bring to a boil. Mix clear jel and ¾ c. water. Add to boiling mixture and cook until clear. In another saucepan place peeled and quartered apples and a small amount of water and cover. Simmer until apples are soft. Cool sauce and apples. Pour sauce over apples.

Custard

6 eggs, separated
4 c. milk
1 Tbsp. unflavored gelatin

1 c. sugar, half white, half brown
vanilla
1 Tbsp. flour

Soak gelatin in water. Cream sugar with egg yolks, then add 1 c. milk and cream well. Scald rest of milk. Add milk, vanilla and gelatin to first mixture. Add vanilla. Beat egg whites and fold into custard. Sprinkle cinnamon on top. Set casserole in a pan of water. Bake for 1 hour at 350°. Cool before using so it does not become watery. Double for 9" x 13" pan. Set in cookie sheet filled with water. Use only 7 egg whites.

Raspberry Cream Torte

1 angel food cake
12 oz. Cool Whip
6 oz. raspberry yogurt
⅓ c. powdered sugar
1 pt. fresh raspberries

Bake cake. Combine Cool Whip, yogurt and sugar until blended. Run a knife around side of cake and remove from pan. Split cake into thirds horizontally. Place bottom layer on a serving plate. Spread with 1 c. topping mixture. Top with second cake layer; spread with 1 c. topping mixture. Top with remaining cake layer. Frost top and sides of cake with remaining topping mixture. Garnish with raspberries.

Pineapple Rings

Take the labels off 6 cans sweetened condensed milk. Put in a kettle. Keep cans covered with water at all times, at least 1" over top of cans. Bring to a rolling boil. Boil for 3 hours. If water level gets low, add boiling water only. Take cans out of water; set aside and cool. Store in refrigerator till ready to use. Drain 1 can pineapple slices for each can of milk. Arrange drained pineapple slices on a tray. Open each end of can of milk; remove one end. Leave other end on to help you push it through the can. Push through, cutting ¼" slices off. Put on top of pineapple slices. Add a dab of whipped topping and top with a maraschino cherry. Caution: Keep can covered with water at all times when cooking or they will explode!
Or, put cans in pressure cooker, cover with water, and bring to 10 lb. pressure for 20 min. No more busted cans!

Why do you think God gave us two ears and only one mouth?

Lizbet and Daughters—Country Cooking

Chocolate Eclairs

½ c. butter
1 c. water
1 c. flour
¼ tsp. salt
4 eggs

Filling-
1 pkg. instant vanilla pudding
2½ c. cold milk
1 c. whipped cream
¼ c. powdered sugar
1 tsp. vanilla

Chocolate Icing-
2 squares semisweet chocolate
   (1 oz. each)
2 tsp. butter
1 c. powdered sugar
2-3 tsp. hot water

In a saucepan, combine butter and water. Bring to a rapid boil, stirring until the butter melts. Reduce heat to low; add flour and salt. Stir until mixture leaves sides of the pan and forms a stiff ball. Remove from heat. Add eggs, one at a time, and beat well. With a teaspoon spoon dough in 4" long x 1½" wide strips on a greased cookie sheet. Bake at 450° for 15 minutes. Reduce heat to 325° and bake for 20 minutes longer. Mix pudding with directions on box. Add whipped cream, sugar and vanilla. Fill cooled shells. For icing: Melt chocolate and butter in a saucepan on low heat. Stir in sugar. Add hot water; cool slightly. Spread over eclairs.

Cinnamon Pudding

1 c. white sugar
2 Tbsp. butter
1 egg
4 tsp. baking powder
1 c. milk
2 c. flour
1 tsp. cinnamon

Syrup-
2½ c. water
2 c. brown sugar
2 Tbsp. butter
2 tsp. vanilla

Cream sugar and butter. Add egg. Add dry ingredients and milk alternately. Pour in baking pan. For syrup: Bring to a boil and pour over batter. Bake at 350°. Serve with whipped cream or ice cream.

Grandma's Graham Cracker Pudding

Crust-
24 graham crackers, crushed
½ c. butter
⅓ c. brown sugar

Pudding-
2 c. milk
½ c. sugar
2 egg yolks
2 Tbsp. flour, heaping
½ tsp. salt
1 tsp. vanilla

Melt butter, then add cracker and sugar. Set aside. Cook the pudding till thickened. When cool, add 1 c. whipped cream. In serving bowl, layer pudding, then crumbs, alternately till full, leaving some crumbs for top. When made real special, Mother would add banana slices over pudding layer.

Pumpkin Pecan Smash Dessert - diabetic

15 oz. can pumpkin
12 oz. can evaporated milk
3 eggs
1 c. sugar or ½ c. baking Splenda
4 tsp. pumpkin pie spice
1 yellow cake mix
1½ c. pecans or walnuts
¾ c. butter, melted

Beat pumpkin, milk, eggs, sugar and spice with wire whisk until smooth. Pour in 9" x 13" pan. Sprinkle dry cake mix over pumpkin mixture. Sprinkle nuts over top. Last pour melted butter evenly over top. Bake 50-60 minutes or until done.

It is easier to smile than to frown.

It takes 64 muscles to frown and only 13 to smile.

Lizbet and Daughters—Country Cooking

Mini Cheesecakes

1 c. vanilla wafer crumbs
3 Tbsp. butter, melted
8 oz. cream cheese, softened
1½ tsp. vanilla
2 tsp. lemon juice
⅓ c. sugar
1 egg

Combine crumbs and butter. Press gently into bottom of 12 paper lined muffin cups. Combine cream cheese, vanilla, lemon juice, sugar and egg. Beat until smooth. Spoon into crusts. Bake at 375° for 12-15 minutes or until set. Cool; top with pie filling.

Lowfat Cheesecake

⅓ c. Jell-O
¼ c. boiling water
16 oz. yogurt
8 oz. Cool Whip

Mix together Jell-O and water till mostly dissolved. Then add yogurt and Cool Whip. I use graham cracker crust. Use same kind of Jell-O and yogurt.

Peanut Delight Dessert

First Layer-
⅔ c. chopped pecans
1 c. flour
½ c. butter

Second Layer-
⅓ c. peanut butter
8 oz. cream cheese
1 c. powdered sugar
2 c. Cool Whip

Third Layer-
1 pkg. instant vanilla pudding
1 pkg. instant chocolate pudding
3 c. cold milk

Fourth Layer-
2 c. Cool Whip
Hershey's candy bar
chopped peanuts

First layer: Blend together. Press in a 9" x 13" pan. Bake at 350° for 20 minutes. Cool. Second layer: Cream together peanut butter and cream cheese. Add remaining ingredients and spread over first layer. Third layer: Mix and spread over second layer. Cool to set. Fourth layer: Top with Cool Whip. Shred candy bar over top. Sprinkle with chopped peanuts.

Fruit Pizza

¾ c. flour
½ c. butter
1 tsp. baking powder
⅓ c. sugar
1 egg
½ c. sugar
8 oz. cream cheese
8 oz. Cool Whip

Glaze-
2 c. pineapple juice
  (water may be added)
½ c. sugar
1 Tbsp. clear jel
1-2 Tbsp. pineapple Jell-O

Cream together first five ingredients. Press in 9" x 13" pan. Bake at 350° for 10 minutes. Mix together remaining ingredients and spread on cooled crust. Arrange any kind of fruit on top. Top with glaze.

Lizbet and Daughters—Country Cooking

Simple Fruit Pizza Crust

1 yellow cake mix
½ c. butter, softened

1 egg

Mix and pat in pizza pan. Bake at 350° for 10 minutes. Take out as soon as crust is a little brown at edges. Very good and quick.

Fruit Pizza Crust

1½ c. powdered sugar
1 c. butter
1 egg
1 tsp. almond flavoring

½ tsp. salt
2½ c. Gold Medal flour
1 tsp. cream of tartar

Bake at 350°. Do not overbake. Enough for a cookie sheet.

Fruit Pizza

¾ c. sugar
½ c. butter
1 egg

1½ c. flour
1 tsp. baking powder
½ tsp. salt

Filling–
8 oz. cream cheese
1 c. powdered sugar

1 c. whipped topping

Mix crust and bake 8-10 minutes at 350°. If you want a thicker crust make 2 batches for a cookie sheet. Mix together filling ingredients and spread on cooled crust. Top with your favorite fruit and glaze.

Tropical Fruit Dessert

1¼ c. sugar
½ c. clear jel
4 c. water
1 env. tropical punch drink mix
1 c. pineapple tidbits
6 bananas
1 c. red seedless grapes

Combine sugar, clear jel and drink mix. Stir in the water. Bring to a boil, stirring constantly until clear. Cool. Chill in refrigerator. Add pineapples, bananas and grapes.

Rhubarb Torte

Crust-
2 c. flour
4 Tbsp. sugar
1 c. butter

Filling-
5 c. rhubarb, diced
6 egg yolks, beaten
2 c. sugar
7 Tbsp. flour
¼ tsp. salt
1 c. sweet cream

Meringue-
6 egg whites, beaten
¾ c. sugar
¾ tsp. salt
¼ tsp. cream of tartar
1 tsp. vanilla

Mix together crust ingredients. Press into a 9" x 13" pan. Bake at 350° for 10 minutes. Remove from oven. Spread rhubarb on top of crust. Beat egg yolks, then add sugar, flour, salt and cream. Pour over rhubarb. Bake until set (about 45 minutes). To make meringue first reduce oven to 325°. Beat egg whites until stiff. Slowly add sugar, salt, cream of tartar and vanilla. Pour on top of baked rhubarb. Brown slightly (about 10 minutes).

Lizbet and Daughters—Country Cooking

Rhubarb Crunch

4 c. chopped rhubarb
1 Tbsp. flour

1 c. sugar

Topping-
2 c. oatmeal
1 c. flour

1 c. brown sugar
½ c. melted butter

Mix rhubarb, flour and sugar and put in 9" x 13" pan. Crumble together topping ingredients and spread on top. Bake at 350° for 35-45 minutes. Serve with vanilla ice cream.

Minute Tapioca Pudding

½ c. minute tapioca
1 qt. milk
¼ c. sugar
2 eggs, beaten

1 Tbsp. cornstarch
¼ tsp. salt
1 tsp. vanilla

In a saucepan, stir tapioca and milk until boiling. Boil over low heat until tapioca is clear, stirring constantly. Beat eggs, sugar, cornstarch and salt together. Add to first mixture; boil and stir until thickened. Add vanilla.

Fluff Pudding

2 egg yolks, beaten
1 c. sugar
⅓ c. cold water
1 c. Rich's topping, whipped
1½ c. milk
1 Tbsp. gelatin

2 egg whites, beaten
1 tsp. vanilla
16 graham crackers, crushed
½ c. melted butter
1 Tbsp. brown sugar

Boil egg yolks, milk and sugar for 1 minute, stirring all the time. Dissolve gelatin in water. Pour into hot liquid. Let stand until cool. Add egg whites, topping and vanilla. Combine cracker crumbs, sugar and butter. Press in bottom of pan, reserving 2 Tbsp. to sprinkle over top. Pour pudding on cracker crust. Sprinkle reserved crumbs over pudding.

Russian Creme

1 c. sugar
2¼ c. water
2 env. or 2 Tbsp. gelatin
1½ c. sour cream

½ tsp. vanilla
¾ tsp. salt
1½ c. heavy cream or Rich's topping, whipped

Topping–
10 oz. frozen raspberries

4.75 oz. raspberry flavored Danish Dessert

Dissolve sugar, salt and gelatin in water over low heat. Remove from stove and stir in sour cream and vanilla until smooth. Chill until slightly thickened. Fold in whipped cream until well blended. Pour into a greased 6 cup mold. Chill until set. To make topping, drain raspberries, reserving juice. Use juice and prepare dessert mix according to directions on box. Chill topping and fold in raspberries. Store-bought pie filling can also be used.

Butterscotch Tapioca

6 c. boiling water
1 Tbsp. salt
¾ c. brown sugar
1 c. pearl tapioca

¾ c. sugar
¼ c. orange Jell-O
1 can condensed milk
Milky Way candy bars

Bring water, brown sugar and salt to a boil. Slowly add tapioca. Cook until clear. Mix sugar and Jell-O. Stir into tapioca. Stir just until sugar is dissolved. Add condensed milk (cooked for 2½ hours). Heat to boiling. Cool. When ready to serve add whipped cream and Milky Way candy bars. Best if stainless steel pan is used.

Lizbet and Daughters—Country Cooking

Caramel Tapioca

7 c. water
1 tsp. salt
1 c. milk or cream
½ c. butter
¼ tsp. soda
1½ c. tapioca

4 egg yolks, beaten
3 c. brown sugar
⅓ c. water
candy bars, optional
whipped topping

Boil water; add tapioca and salt. Cook until only a small white dot remains in tapioca. Remove from heat. Beat egg yolks and add milk. Add to tapioca and bring to a boil, stirring constantly. Set aside. Boil sugar, butter, water and soda. Add to tapioca mixture. Cool. Before serving, add whipped topping and candy bars, cut into small pieces.

Creamy Tapioca

5 c. milk
10 Tbsp. tapioca
2 eggs, beaten
1 c. Rich's topping, whipped

1⅓ c. sugar
1 tsp. salt
1 tsp. vanilla
cream cheese, softened

Simmer milk and tapioca (do not boil), stirring constantly. Add eggs, sugar, salt and vanilla. Bring to a boil. Cool. When cool, add whipped topping and some cream cheese to make it fluffy and delicious!

Delicious Custard

½ gal. scalded milk
1 c. sugar
1 c. brown sugar

1 Tbsp. flour
12 eggs

Beat eggs until light colored, then add rest of ingredients and beat until smooth. Put in 10" x 15" pan. Sprinkle with cinnamon. Variation: 1 tsp. vanilla may be added to custard instead of sprinkling cinnamon on top. Bake at 475° for 3 minutes. Turn off oven, but do not remove custard until cooled. Best if stainless steel pan is used.

Yogurt

1 gal. 2% milk
1 c. sugar
¼ c. plain yogurt

2 Tbsp. gelatin
½ c. water

Soak gelatin in water. Heat milk to 190°; cool to 130°, then add sugar, yogurt and the soaked gelatin. Heat oven to 275°, then turn off heat. Set yogurt in oven for 8 hours. Add your favorite tube pie filling.

Tapioca

6 c. water
1 c. tapioca
½ tsp. salt

1¼ c. sugar
3 oz. box Jell-O
whipped topping

Bring water and salt to a boil. Add tapioca and bring to a boil, stirring often. Cover and simmer over low heat for 25 minutes. Remove from heat; add sugar and Jell-O. When cool add whipped topping and bananas or fruit of your choice.

Crepes

2 c. Bisquick mix
4 eggs

1⅓ c. milk

Filling–
16 oz. cream cheese, softened
2 boxes instant pudding

2¾ c. milk

Mix Bisquick, eggs and milk until smooth. Put ¼ c. mix on hot greased griddle. Quickly pick up pan and rotate around so pancake becomes thin. Fry until golden on both sides. Put cut up paper towels between pancakes. Can be made the day before. Fill with cream cheese filling, roll up and top with your favorite pie filling and a dab of whipped topping. You may want to add some whipped topping to cream cheese mixture.

Lizbet and Daughters—Country Cooking

Hot Fudge Brownie Sundae

1 box brownie mix
vanilla ice cream
hot fudge topping

Bake brownies as directed. When cool cut in squares and put on plates. Top with ice cream and your favorite hot fudge sauce.

Hot Fudge Cake

1 chocolate cake mix
½ gal. vanilla ice cream
hot fudge topping

Mix cake mix according to directions. Bake and cool. Cut in half and put ice cream between layers. Freeze for 4-5 hours. When ready to serve top with your favorite hot fudge sauce.

Cheesecake Dessert

24 graham crackers, crushed
4 Tbsp. melted butter
1 Tbsp. sugar
16 oz. cream cheese
1 c. powdered sugar
2 eggs, beaten
1 tsp. vanilla

Topping–
1 can cherry pie filling
whipped topping

Combine graham crackers, sugar and butter and press into baking pan. Combine cream cheese, eggs, powdered sugar and vanilla. Mix well and pour over crust. Bake for 15 minutes at 350°. Remove from oven and cool. Cover with pie filling. Add a layer of whipped topping when ready to serve. Note: Any fruit filling is good for this.

Strawberry Cheesecake Trifle

1 angel food cake, baked
8 oz. cream cheese

1 c. powdered sugar
1½ c. whipped topping

Glaze-
2 c. water
¾ c. sugar

2 Tbsp. clear jel
3 oz. pkg. strawberry Jell-O

Mix cream cheese and powdered sugar. Add whipped topping. Prepare strawberry glaze and let cool. Add desired amount of sliced strawberries. In a glass bowl layer bite-size pieces of cake, cream cheese mixture and strawberries. Continue layering until dish is full. This is also good with thickened grapes or raspberries.

Lemon Cheesecake

Crust-
1 c. flour
½ c. butter

¼ c. brown sugar
½ c. nuts

Filling-
8 oz. cream cheese, softened
¾ c. powdered sugar

12 oz. Cool Whip

Topping-
3 c. cold milk

2 pkgs. instant lemon pudding

Blend flour, sugar and butter well. Add nuts. Put in a 9" x 13" pan and bake for 15 minutes. Mix cream cheese and powdered sugar well. Add Cool Whip. Spread over cooled crust. Mix milk and pudding. Pour over top. This is also good with butterscotch or butter pecan pudding.

Lizbet and Daughters—Country Cooking

Angel Food Cake Dessert

1 angel food cake
8 oz. cream cheese
¾ c. powdered sugar

1½ c. Rich's topping, whipped, or 8 oz. Cool Whip

Caramel Topping–
1 c. packed brown sugar
½ c. evaporated milk
2 Tbsp. butter

2 Tbsp. corn syrup
1 tsp. vanilla

Use your favorite angel food cake recipe and bake in a large loaf pan. When cool take out of pan and slice in half. Put cream cheese mixture in between and the topping on top. For topping: Cook 3 minutes. If too stiff when cool, add more milk. Variation: Caramel topping can be substituted with 1 can cooked sweetened condensed milk and 12 oz. Cool Whip, mixed together.

Butterfinger Pudding

1 pkg. graham crackers, crushed
26 saltine crackers, crushed
5 Butterfinger candy bars, crushed
½ c. butter, melted

2 small pkg. French vanilla pudding
2 c. milk
1 qt. vanilla ice cream, softened
12 oz. Cool Whip

Mix butter with crackers and candy bars. Put half of crumbs in bottom of 9" x 13" pan. Save other half to put on top. Beat pudding with milk and add the ice cream and Cool Whip. Pour on crumbs. Put other half of crumbs on top. Note: It helps to have candy bars cold when you crush them.

Happiness was meant to be shared.

Ice Cream Sandwich Pudding

24 ice cream sandwiches
12 oz. Cool Whip

hot fudge syrup

Arrange ice cream sandwiches in 9" x 13" pan. Spread with half of Cool Whip. Spoon fudge topping over Cool Whip. Repeat layers with ice cream sandwiches, Cool Whip and fudge. Cover and freeze. Set out a few minutes before serving.

Ice Cream Pudding

2 c. flour
½ c. butter
1 c. nuts
½ gal. vanilla ice cream, softened

1 box instant vanilla pudding
2 boxes butter pecan instant pudding
1 c. milk
2 c. whipped topping

Mix first three ingredients until crumbly. Put in bottom of 9" x 13" pan. Bake at 350° until light brown. Cool. Mix milk and puddings. Add topping and ice cream. Break up the crumbs and take out ½ c. for over top. Pour ice cream mixture over rest of crumbs. Add reserved crumbs on top. Freeze. Take out of freezer 25-30 minutes before serving.

Frozen Cheesecake

3 c. graham cracker crumbs
¾ c. melted butter
6 Tbsp. brown sugar
16 oz. cream cheese

1 c. sugar
1 c. whipped topping
4 eggs, beaten
1 tsp. vanilla

Mix together first three ingredients and press in 9" x 13" pan. Mix cream cheese and sugar together until creamy. Add whipping topping and beaten eggs. Add vanilla. Pour over crust and freeze. Remove from freezer 15 minutes before serving. Serve with any fruit glaze topping.

Lizbet and Daughters—Country Cooking

Frozen Oreo Cookie Dessert

1 small pkg. Oreo cookies, crushed
½ gal. vanilla ice cream
1 c. fudge sauce

⅓ c. melted butter
9-12 oz. Cool Whip

Fudge Sauce-
1 c. sugar
⅓ c. cocoa
2 Tbsp. flour

¼ tsp. salt
1 c. water
1 tsp. vanilla

Combine Oreo cookies with butter. Spread in a 9" x 13" pan, reserving ⅔ c. for topping. Top with softened ice cream. Put in freezer until firm. Pour cooked sauce over ice cream and freeze again. Cover with Cool Whip. Top with remaining Oreo crumbs. Freeze. Fudge sauce: Mix sugar, salt, cocoa, water and flour. Cook until thick,stirring constantly. Remove from heat and add vanilla. Cool.

Frosty Strawberry Dessert

First Layer-
1½ c. flour
½ c. nuts

½ c. butter
¼ c. brown sugar

Second Layer-
2 egg whites, beaten
2 c. crushed strawberries, fresh or frozen

¾ c. sugar
2 Tbsp. lemon juice
1 c. whipped topping

Mix flour, nuts, butter and brown sugar. Spread in pan and bake at 350° for 20 minutes, stirring occasionally. Place ⅔ of crumbs into a 9" x 13" pan. In a large bowl beat egg whites and add strawberries, sugar and lemon juice. Beat for 10 minutes. Beat whipped topping and fold into mixture. Pour over crumbs in pan. Sprinkle remaining crumbs evenly over top. Freeze at least 6 hours before serving.

Chocolate Peanut Log

1 c. vanilla wafers (33)
½ c. chopped salted peanuts
2 Tbsp. powdered sugar
3 Tbsp. butter, melted

½ gal. vanilla ice cream
1 jar fudge sauce or your favorite hot fudge sauce

Filling–
3 oz. cream cheese, softened
¾ c. powdered sugar
⅓ c. peanut butter

⅓ c. milk
½ c. whipped cream

Mix vanilla wafers, peanuts, powdered sugar and melted butter together. Put in layers: Crust, 3 cups ice cream, peanut butter filling, fudge sauce and 3 more cups of ice cream. Sprinkle with some crust crumbs.

Ice Cream Dessert

3 c. milk
2 pkg. instant vanilla pudding
1 pkg. instant butterscotch pudding

8 oz. Cool Whip
½ gal. vanilla ice cream

Crumbs–
1 pkg. graham crackers, crushed
2 Tbsp. sugar

2 Tbsp. butter, melted

Mix milk and puddings together. Mix ice cream and Cool Whip together. Have ice cream mixture ready to put pudding in right away so it doesn't get lumpy. Put on top of graham cracker crumbs. Freeze.

Homemade Ice Cream

2 boxes instant pudding mix
1 c. brown sugar
1 pt. half and half
milk

1 c. sugar
1 can sweetened condensed milk
2 Tbsp. vanilla

Prepare pudding mix according to instructions on box. Mix all ingredients well. Add enough milk to fill can ¾ full. Freeze. Easy to make and very good.

Lizbet and Daughters—Country Cooking

Ice Cream

6 egg yolks
½ c. cornstarch
½ c. flour
½ tsp. salt
¾ c. sugar
1 can sweetened condensed milk

Mix these ingredients with cold sweet milk to make a thin paste. Bring ½ gal. milk to the boiling point. Pour the milk over the egg mixture, stirring while you pour. This should get thick and smooth. Add more sugar and flavor to taste. Add sweetened condensed milk. Beat whites of 6 eggs and add ¼ c. sugar. Add enough milk to make 1½ gallons. Freeze. You can also use 1 qt. half and half instead of sweetened condensed milk.

Soft Custard Ice Cream

3 Tbsp. gelatin
¾ c. water
6 c. milk
3 c. sugar
4½ c. cream
3 tsp. vanilla
½ tsp. salt

Soften gelatin in water while you heat milk to scalding. Add gelatin and sugar, stir to dissolve. Add vanilla and salt. Cool, then add cream and chill before freezing. Makes 1½ gallons. Freeze in ice cream freezer.

Ice Cream

2 sm. boxes instant vanilla pudding
1 Tbsp. vanilla
1⅓ c. sugar
2 qt. milk
12 oz. Cool Whip

Mix together, adding Cool Whip last. Freeze.

Ice Cream Topping

1 (12 oz.) pkg. chocolate chips
½ c. butter
⅓ c. creamy peanut butter

Melt ingredients together. Serve over ice cream. Hardens when you put it on ice cream.

Hot Chocolate Fudge

1 can sweetened condensed milk
2 Tbsp. butter
1 tsp. vanilla
1 c. chocolate chips
2 Tbsp. water

Combine ingredients and cook slowly for 5 minutes, stirring constantly. Use as an ice cream topping.

Hot Fudge Sauce

30 wrapped caramels
1 c. milk chocolate chips
1 (5 oz.) can evaporated milk
½ c. butter

Melt over low heat, stirring occasionally.

Hot Fudge Sauce

2 c. powdered sugar
⅔ c. semisweet chocolate chips
12 oz. evaporated milk
½ c. butter
1 tsp. vanilla

Combine first four ingredients in a saucepan. Bring to a boil. Boil for 8 minutes. Remove from heat and stir in vanilla.

Hot Chocolate Sauce

1 c. sugar
3 Tbsp. cocoa
½ tsp. salt

1 c. water
3½ Tbsp. flour
1 tsp. vanilla

Cook first 5 ingredients for 3 minutes. Add vanilla.

Butterscotch Topping

1 c. brown sugar
2 Tbsp. Karo syrup

¼ c. rich milk
3 Tbsp. butter

Combine all ingredients. Stir until boiling and simmer for 3 minutes.

Butterscotch Topping

¾ c. sugar
½ c. light corn syrup
⅛ tsp. salt

¼ c. butter
1 c. cream
½ tsp. vanilla

Reserve half of cream. Mix together the other ingredients except vanilla. Cook in saucepan over low heat, stirring constantly, until 228°. Then stir in the rest of cream and continue cooking until a thick consistency. Remove from heat. Stir in vanilla and cook again to soft ball stage.

Pies

After the meal, it's time to pass the pie,
All look so scrumptiously good, oh my!
Of all these kinds, which shall I choose?
Those cream pies look so delightfully smooth,
Two crust fruit pies, nicely browned, are hard to beat.
Some choose the gooey, rich kind, so deliciously sweet.
Make up your mind, take the choice of your kind,
It all goes to your waist, not mine.

Sunshine Pie

A pound of patience you must find
Mix well with loving words, so kind
Drop in two pounds of helping deeds
And thoughts of other people's needs
A pack of smiles to make the crust
Then stir and bake it well you must
And now, I ask that you may try
The recipe of the Sunshine Pie.

Pie Crust

8 c. flour
2 c. lard and butter Crisco
1 Tbsp. salt
2 Tbsp. sugar
1 tsp. baking powder
1 egg
1 Tbsp. vinegar
3 Tbsp. Wesson oil

Mix together first five ingredients until crumbly. Beat egg with fork in one cup measure. Add vinegar, oil and enough water to fill cup. Add to crumbs.

Pie Crust Mix

5 lb. Flaky Crust flour
1 can butter flavor Crisco
1 Tbsp. cream of tartar
2 Tbsp. salt
½ c. brown sugar

Mix and store in container until ready to use. For one pie crust, mix 1½ cups mix and 2 Tbsp. water.

Pie Crust Mix

5 lb. all-purpose flour
½ c. sugar
3 lb. butter flavor Crisco
2 Tbsp. salt

Blend ingredients together. Store in a plastic container in a cool place. Needs no refrigeration. For one crust use 1½ cups crumbs and 2 Tbsp. cold water. Crumb mixture will keep indefinitely.

Oatmeal Pie Crust

1 c. quick rolled oats
¼ c. brown sugar
¼ c. melted butter

Mix together and press in 8" pie plate. Bake at 350° for 10 minutes. Cool before filling up with your favorite pie filling.

Lizbet and Daughters—Country Cooking

Graham Cracker Pie Crust

12 graham crackers, crushed
¼ c. butter, melted

½ c. brown sugar

Mix all together and line pan. Bake, being careful not to burn. Makes 2 pie crusts.

Rice Krispie Pie

2 c. Rice Krispies
1 Tbsp. melted butter

½ c. marshmallow créme

Melt butter and blend with marshmallow créme. Add Rice Krispies and mix. Put in greased pie pan and shape into pie crust. Fill the crust with ice cream and freeze. When ready to serve, top with fresh fruit or your favorite ice cream topping.

Fudge Sundae Pie

¼ c. light Karo
2 Tbsp. brown sugar

3 Tbsp. butter
2½ c. Rice Krispies

Sauce-
1 c. sugar
3 Tbsp. cocoa
½ tsp. salt
1 c. water

3½ Tbsp. flour
1 tsp. vanilla
¼ c. peanut butter

Combine syrup, sugar and butter and cook over low heat until mixture begins to boil. Take from heat and add Rice Krispies. Press evenly in a pie pan. For sauce: Mix together first five ingredients and cook for three minutes. Add vanilla and peanut butter. Spread ¾ of mixture over crust. Use 1 quart softened ice cream over chocolate mixture. Freeze. Before serving, drizzle remaining sauce over top.

Basic Cream Pie

2 c. milk
¾ c. sugar
2 egg yolks, beaten
2 Tbsp. flour
2 Tbsp. cornstarch
1 Tbsp. butter
vanilla

Scald 1½ c. milk in a saucepan. Combine sugar, flour and cornstarch. Stir in remaining milk and egg yolks. Stir into hot milk and cook until thickened. Remove from heat. Add vanilla and butter.
Variations-
Coconut: Add ¾ c. coconut.
Banana: Layer bottom of pie crust with sliced bananas.
Peanut Butter: Mix ⅓ c. peanut butter and ¾ c. powdered sugar. Put a layer in bottom of crust, reserving some for on top of pie.

Chocolate Cream Cheese Pie

3 sm. boxes instant
   chocolate pudding
4½ c. milk
16 oz. cream cheese
2 c. powdered sugar
16 oz. Cool Whip

Mix instant pudding and milk. Mix cream cheese and powdered sugar. Add Cool Whip and instant pudding mix. Makes three pies.

Chocolate Fudge Pie

½ c. butter
3 Tbsp. cocoa
1½ c. sugar
4 eggs, beaten
3 Tbsp. Karo
1 tsp. vanilla

Melt butter and cocoa in pan. Mix all ingredients together and bake at 375° for 30 minutes. Makes 1 pie. Serve with ice cream.

Lizbet and Daughters—Country Cooking

Dutch Chocolate Pie

1.55 oz. milk chocolate candy bar
½ c. butter
2 c. sugar
2 Tbsp. cornstarch
4 c. evaporated milk
2 eggs, separated
1 tsp. vanilla
dash of salt
2 unbaked pie crusts

In a large saucepan melt chocolate bar and butter. Combine sugar, cornstarch, milk, egg yolks, vanilla and salt. Stir into chocolate mixture. Beat egg whites and fold in last. Pour into pie shells. Bake at 450° for 12 minutes. Reduce heat to 350° and bake until almost set. Cool and refrigerate.

Pumpkin Pie

1 c. pumpkin
2 Tbsp. flour
2 c. brown sugar
4 eggs, separated
½ tsp. salt
2 Tbsp. melted butter
1½ tsp. pumpkin pie spice
2 c. milk
1 can evaporated milk

Mix flour, sugar and salt together. Add pumpkin, egg yolks, butter, spice and milk. Last fold in the stiffly beaten egg whites. Pour into 2 unbaked pie shells. Bake at 375° for 15 minutes. Reduce heat to 350° and bake until done.

Pumpkin Pie

6 eggs, separated
1 c. sugar
1 c. brown sugar
2 Tbsp. flour
1 c. pumpkin
1¾ c. milk
1¾ c. evaporated milk
1½-2 tsp. pumpkin pie spice

Mix sugars, flour and spice. Add rest of ingredients, adding beaten egg whites last. Bake at 450° until lightly brown. Reduce heat to 350° and bake until done. Two batches make 3 large pies. You do not have to heat the milk.

Bob Andy Pie

1 c. brown sugar
2½ c. milk
2 egg yolks
3 Tbsp. flour
2 egg whites, beaten
1½ Tbsp. melted butter

Mix all together, adding egg whites last. Bake at 450° until light brown. Reduce heat to 350° and bake until done.

Grandma's Custard Pie

½ c. sugar
½ c. brown sugar
2 Tbsp. flour
2 eggs, separated
2½ c. milk

Mix sugars and flour. Add ½ c. milk and egg yolks. Heat 2 c. milk to boiling and add to mixture. Fold in stiffly beaten egg whites last. Pour into unbaked pie crust. Bake at 450° until lightly browned. Reduce heat to 350° and bake until done.

Custard Pie

1½ c. sugar
1½ c. brown sugar
2 Tbsp. flour
1 Tbsp. gelatin
2 cans evaporated milk
10 eggs, separated
6 c. milk
1½ tsp. vanilla

Mix together sugars and flour. Add egg yolks, evaporated milk and vanilla. Add gelatin, soaked in a little water, and milk, heated to boiling. Fold in 6 beaten egg whites last. Pour in 3 unbaked pie crusts. Bake at 450° till lightly browned. Reduce heat to 350° and bake until done.

Lizbet and Daughters—Country Cooking

Custard Pie

1 c. sugar
1 c. brown sugar
5 Tbsp. flour
dash of salt

6 eggs
7 c. milk, heated
1 c. half & half
2 tsp. vanilla

Mix sugars, flour and salt together. Separate eggs. Add yolks to dry ingredients and beat whites until stiff. Add half & half and vanilla to dry ingredients and yolks. Beat until smooth. Add heated milk then egg whites. Pour into pie shells. Bake at 400° for 10 minutes, then reduce heat to 350° for 30 minutes. Makes 3 pies.

Eggnog Pie

1 tsp. gelatin
1 Tbsp. cold water
1 c. milk
½ c. sugar
2 Tbsp. cornstarch

½ tsp. salt
3 egg yolks, beaten
1 Tbsp. butter
1 Tbsp. vanilla
2 c. whipped topping

Soak gelatin in cold water. Scald milk. Combine sugar, cornstarch and salt and mix well. Add to milk and cook until thick. Add eggs and cook a little longer. Add butter, gelatin and vanilla. Cool, then fold in whipped topping and pour in baked pie shell. This is good to fill pie shell halfway full then top with your favorite fruit pie filling. Good with fresh strawberry pie filling. Or add 2 Tbsp. cocoa to mixture for chocolate pie.

Take good care of yourself.
You'll find it hard to get a replacement.

Ground Cherry Pie

1¼ c. ground cherries
1 c. water
½ c. sugar
½ c. brown sugar

2 Tbsp. clear jel
¼ tsp. salt
1 Tbsp. butter
1 Tbsp. lemon juice

Put cherries in saucepan. Add water, salt and half of sugar. Bring to a boil and thicken with clear jel stirred in a little water. Reduce heat and boil for 2 minutes. Remove from heat and add rest of sugar, butter and lemon juice. Pour into pie shell and put crust on top. Bake at 450° until golden brown.

Sour Cream Cherry Pie

2½ c. cherries
1 c. sugar
1 c. sour cream

3 oz. cream cheese
2-3 Tbsp. flour

Crumbs-
1 c. flour
½ c. sugar

¼ c. butter

Combine sugar and flour. Add sour cream and cream cheese. Blend well. Put fruit in unbaked pie shell. Pour mixture over fruit. Top with crumb topping. Always have cream cheese and sour cream at room temperature. Bake at 425° for 15 minutes. Reduce heat to 350° and bake for 25 minutes. Also good with pineapples, blueberries, apples or raspberries. Makes 2 pies.

Any Fruit Flavor Chiffon Pie

1 can sweetened condensed milk
2 c. pie filling, thickened

12 oz. Cool Whip

Mix together and pour in baked crust.

Lizbet and Daughters—Country Cooking

Peach Custard Pie

1 unbaked pie shell
6 peaches, sliced
¼ c. flour
1 c. sugar

1 c. sweet cream
2 eggs, beaten
1 tsp. vanilla

Arrange peaches in pie shell. Mix rest of ingredients and pour over peaches. Bake at 425° for 10 minutes. Reduce heat to 350° and bake until custard is set (about 30 minutes).

Colorado Peach Cream Pie

6 peaches, sliced
1 unbaked pie shell
¼ c. flour
¾ c. sugar

1 c. sweet cream or sour cream
½ tsp. vanilla
1 egg, beaten

Topping-
⅓ c. flour
⅓ c. brown sugar

2 Tbsp. butter

Arrange peaches in pie shell. Mix flour, sugar and cream. Add vanilla and egg. Pour over peaches. Top with crumbs. Bake at 425° for 10 minutes. Reduce heat to 350° and bake until pie is set.

Coconut Cream Pie

5 c. milk
1⅓ c. white sugar
1 tsp. salt
5 Tbsp. cornstarch
2 Tbsp. flour

6 egg yolks
1 Tbsp. vanilla
2 Tbsp. butter
1½ c. coconut

Scald 4 c. milk in saucepan. Combine sugar, salt, cornstarch and flour. Stir in remaining milk and egg yolks. Stir into hot milk and cook until thickened. Remove from heat. Add butter, vanilla and coconut. Makes 2 (9") pies.

Chocolate Mocha Pie

1 Tbsp. unflavored gelatin
¼ c. cold water
2 Tbsp. cocoa
¾ c. sugar
⅛ tsp. salt
1 tsp. instant coffee
1¼ c. milk
1 c. whipping cream
 or 2 c. Cool Whip
1 tsp. vanilla

Soften gelatin in cold water. Combine cocoa, sugar, salt, coffee and milk in a saucepan. Bring to a boil, stirring constantly. Remove from heat. Add gelatin. Cool until slightly thickened. Beat heavy cream and vanilla. Fold into cooked mixture. Pour into a baked pastry shell. Top with nuts or chocolate curls.

Caramel Pie

18 caramels
1 c. milk
1 tsp. gelatin
8 oz. Cool Whip

Melt caramels in milk. Dissolve gelatin in water and add to melted caramels. Cool. Let thicken slightly. Add Cool Whip. Pour in pie crust and cover with whipped topping and drizzle with caramel ice cream topping. This pie is good with graham cracker crust.

If you need a facelift, try smiling.

Lizbet and Daughters—Country Cooking

Peanut Butter Cup Pie

Bottom Part–
1½ c. sugar
3 Tbsp. flour
3 Tbsp. cocoa

¾ c. milk
3 eggs, beaten

Top Part–
8 oz. cream cheese
½ c. peanut butter
1 c. powdered sugar

8 oz. whipped topping, whipped
1 tsp. vanilla

Bottom part: Combine ingredients and pour into 2 unbaked pie shells. Bake until set. Chill. Top part: Mix together and pour over bottom part. Put whipped topping on top and sprinkle with grated chocolate.

Peanut Butter Pie

8 oz. cream cheese
¾ c. powdered sugar
⅓ c. peanut butter
8 oz. Cool Whip

1 tsp. vanilla
2 tsp. milk
1 pie crust or graham cracker crust

Combine peanut butter, cream cheese, powdered sugar, milk and vanilla. Beat until smooth. Fold in Cool Whip. Pour into crust. Sprinkle graham cracker crumbs on top. Freeze two hours or until firm.

Peanut Butter Pie

3 pkg. instant vanilla pudding
4½ c. milk
16 oz. cream cheese, softened

16 oz. whipped topping
2 c. powdered sugar

Crumbs-
⅔ c. peanut butter

½ c. powdered sugar

Beat together milk and pudding. Add whipped topping. Mix cream cheese and powdered sugar. Add to pudding mixture. Put crumbs in bottom of baked pie crust. Pour in filling. Top with whipped cream and peanut butter crumbs. Makes 3 pies.

Creamy Vanilla Crumb Pie

2 (9") unbaked pie crusts
8 oz. cream cheese
½ c. sugar

1 egg, beaten
½ tsp. salt
1 tsp. vanilla

Filling-
2 c. water
1 c. sugar
1 Tbsp. flour

1 c. corn syrup
1 egg, beaten
1 tsp. vanilla

Crumb Topping-
2 c. flour
½ c. brown sugar
½ c. butter

1 tsp. soda
½ tsp. cream of tartar

Beat together cream cheese, sugar, egg, salt and vanilla. Spread into pie crusts. In a saucepan bring 2 c. water to a boil. Combine sugar, flour, corn syrup and egg. Stir into hot water. Bring to a boil. Let cool. Add vanilla. When cooled pour this over cream cheese layer. Mix the topping ingredients until crumbly. Spread over top of pie. Bake at 375° for 30-40 minutes.

Lizbet and Daughters—Country Cooking

Delicious Crumb Pie

1½ c. brown sugar
1 tsp. vanilla
3 c. water

2½ Tbsp. clear jel, heaping
½ c. butter
2 (8") unbaked pie shells

Crumb Topping-
2 c. flour
½ c. butter
¼ tsp. cream of tartar

½ c. sugar
¼ tsp. soda
½ tsp. salt

Cook sugar, clear jel, butter and water until thick. Cool. Add vanilla and pour into shells. For topping: Mix until crumbly and pour over pie mixture. Bake at 400° until crust is baked.

Lemon Pie

2½ c. water
1 c. sugar
juice and grated rind of 1 lemon

3 egg yolks
3 Tbsp. cornstarch
1 Tbsp. butter

Combine cornstarch, sugar and lemon juice. Beat egg yolks. Add to cornstarch mixture. Slowly add to boiling water. Stir and boil 3 minutes. Remove from heat and add butter. Put in baked pie crust. Top with meringue or whipped cream.

Pineapple Pie

1 (20 oz.) can crushed pineapples
1 lg. pkg. instant vanilla pudding
1 c. sour cream

8 oz. cream cheese
12 oz. Cool Whip

Mix instant pudding with pineapple. Stir in remaining ingredients. Put in baked pie crust. Makes 2 pies.

Pecan Praline Pie

1 baked pie crust
¼ c. butter

¼ c. brown sugar
1 c. pecans

Filling–
2 c. milk
½ c. sugar
2 Tbsp. flour
2 Tbsp. cornstarch

½ tsp. salt
2 egg yolks
1 Tbsp. butter
1 tsp. vanilla

Melt butter in saucepan and add brown sugar and nuts. Cook for 2 minutes. Cool and put in pie crust. Scald ½ c. milk in saucepan. Combine sugar, flour, cornstarch and salt. Stir in remaining milk and egg yolks. Stir flour mixture into hot milk and stir until thickened. Remove from heat. Add butter and vanilla. Let cool and pour on top of pecan mixture. Top with Cool Whip when ready to serve.

Cream Cheese Pecan Pie

8 oz. cream cheese
½ c. sugar
1 egg, beaten

½ tsp. salt
1 tsp. vanilla
1¼ c. chopped pecans

Topping–
6 eggs
2 c. light corn syrup

½ c. sugar

Cream together cream cheese, sugar, egg, salt and vanilla. Spread into 2 unbaked pie crusts. Sprinkle nuts on cheese mixture. Beat together topping ingredients and pour over nuts. Bake at 375° for 45 minutes.

Lizbet and Daughters—Country Cooking

Pecan Praline Pie

⅓ c. butter
⅓ c. brown sugar
½ c. chopped pecans

1 box instant vanilla pudding
1⅓ c. milk
2 c. Cool Whip

Cook together butter, sugar and pecans until bubbly. Pour into baked pie crust and cool. Stir together last 3 ingredients and put on top of pecan filling. Top with dabs of Cool Whip and pecans. Makes 1 pie.

Pecan Pie

½ c. sugar
1 c. light Karo syrup
2 eggs, beaten
2 Tbsp. melted butter

2 Tbsp. flour
½ c. water
1 c. pecans

Beat eggs, then add rest of ingredients. Pour in 8" unbaked pie crust. Bake at 375°. Do not overbake.

Dear Abby's Pecan Pie

9" unbaked pie shell
1 c. light Karo syrup
1 c. brown sugar, firmly packed
3 eggs, slightly beaten

⅓ c. butter, melted
⅓ tsp. salt
1 tsp. vanilla
1 c. pecan halves

In large bowl combine Karo syrup, sugar, eggs, butter, salt and vanilla. Mix well. Pour filling into unbaked pie shell. Sprinkle with pecan halves. Bake at 350° for 45-50 minutes or until center is set.

Butterscotch Pie

6 Tbsp. flour
1½ c. brown sugar
2 c. hot milk
½ c. butter

3 egg yolks
⅛ tsp. salt
1 tsp. vanilla

Mix flour, salt and sugar. Add hot milk slowly and cook until it thickens. Add butter and beaten egg yolks slowly, stirring constantly. Add vanilla and pour into 9" baked pie shell. Top with whipped topping before serving.

Old-Fashioned Butterscotch Pie

First Part–
½ c. brown sugar
3 Tbsp. boiling water
1 Tbsp. butter

½ tsp. salt
½ tsp. vanilla
⅛ tsp. soda

Second Part–
1 egg yolk
½ c. flour
½ c. sugar

1½ c. boiling water
1 baked pie crust

Combine brown sugar, boiling water, butter and salt. When mixture begins to boil, add soda. Boil until syrup forms a hard ball in cold water. Combine egg yolk, sugar and flour. Slowly add the hot water. Add second mixture to first and bring to a boil. Pour into baked pie crust. Top with meringue and bake at 325° till golden brown. Or use whipped cream on top.

Lizbet and Daughters—Country Cooking

Oreo Pie

3 pkg. instant vanilla pudding
4½ c. milk
16 oz. cream cheese, softened

16 oz. whipped topping
2 c. powdered sugar
Oreo cookies, crushed

Beat together milk and pudding. Add whipped topping. Mix cream cheese and powdered sugar. Add to pudding mixture. Add crushed Oreo cookies. Pour into baked pie shells. Makes 3 pies.

Oats 'n Honey Granola Pie

1 pie crust
½ c. butter
½ c. brown sugar
¾ c. corn syrup
⅛ tsp. salt
1 tsp. vanilla

3 eggs, lightly beaten
4 oats and honey granola bars, crushed
½ c. chopped walnuts
¼ c. quick oats
¼ c. chocolate chips

Heat oven to 350°. Place crust in 9" glass pan. Heat butter until melted. Stir in sugar and corn syrup. Beat in salt, vanilla and eggs. Stir in crushed granola bars and rest of ingredients. Pour into pie crust. Bake 40-50 minutes or until set. Cover crust with foil the last 15-20 minutes. Cool 30 minutes before serving.

Raisin Crumb Pie

¾ c. raisins
2 c. water
1 c. brown sugar

1 Tbsp. vinegar
dash of salt

Crumbs-
1 c. flour
¼ c. butter

½ c. brown sugar
½ tsp. salt

Cook raisins in as little water as possible until soft. Add rest of ingredients. Thicken with clear jel. Pour in unbaked pie shell and put crumbs on top. Bake at 350°.

Raisin Cream Pie

1 c. cooked raisins
½ c. brown sugar
½ c. sugar
2 egg yolks, beaten
4 Tbsp. flour
2 c. milk
1 Tbsp. butter
1 tsp. vanilla

Heat milk. Combine sugars, egg yolks and flour mixed with a little milk to make a paste. Add to milk and cook until thick. Add butter, vanilla and raisins last.

Raisin Cream Pie

1 c. raisins
2 Tbsp. brown sugar
8 oz. cream cheese
¼ c. powdered sugar
1 sm. pkg. instant vanilla pudding
¾ c. milk
¾ c. Rich's topping

Cook raisins, sugar and ½ c. water until soft. Cool. Mix cream cheese and powdered sugar. Mix pudding and milk together and add to cream cheese. Whip topping and add to rest of mixture. Add raisins.

Shoestring Apple Pie

2 c. sugar
2 Tbsp. flour
3 eggs
dash of salt
4 Tbsp. water
4 c. apples, chopped
cinnamon

Beat eggs. Add sugar, flour, salt and water. Add apples and mix. Put in crusts and sprinkle tops with cinnamon. Bake like custard pie. Makes 2 small pies.

Dutch Apple Pie

1 Tbsp. clear jel
1 c. water
1 c. brown sugar
1 tsp. ReaLemon

¾ tsp. cinnamon
1 Tbsp. butter
salt
¾ qt. fine apples

Crumbs-
½ c. flour
½ c. Bisquick
½ c. brown sugar

¼ c. butter
½ tsp. soda
½ tsp. cream of tartar

Cook together clear jel, water, brown sugar, and ReaLemon. Add cinnamon, butter and salt. Stir in apples. Put in pie shell. Mix crumb ingredients together and put on top. Bake at 350° until crumbs are browned. Makes 1 pie.

Dutch Apple Pie

2 c. sugar
6 Tbsp. clear jel
4 Tbsp. butter
8 apples, approximately

2 c. water
4 Tbsp. corn syrup
½ tsp. cinnamon

Topping-
1 c. flour
1 c. quick oats

1 c. brown sugar
½ c. butter

Boil water, sugar, clear jel and corn syrup until thick. Remove from heat and stir in butter and cinnamon. Peel and shred apples. Stir into cooked mixture. Put in unbaked pie shell. For topping: Mix into crumbs. Put crumbs on top and bake at 350°.

A happy home does not just happen.

Coconut Oatmeal Custard Pie

1 c. brown sugar
1 c. white sugar
1 c. maple flavored Karo
4 Tbsp. flour
5 Tbsp. butter, melted

6 eggs, separated
4 c. milk
1 c. oatmeal
1 c. coconut
pinch of salt

Beat egg whites and fold in last. Bake for 10 minutes at 400°. Reduce heat to 325° and bake until done. Makes 3 small pies.

Rhubarb Meringue Pie

3 c. chopped rhubarb
1 c. sugar
2 Tbsp. flour

dash of salt
3 egg yolks
1 c. heavy whipping cream

Meringue–
4 tsp. sugar
2 tsp. cornstarch
⅓ c. water

3 egg whites
⅛ tsp. cream of tartar
⅓ c. sugar

Place rhubarb in crust. Whisk together sugar, flour, salt, egg yolks and cream. Pour over the rhubarb. Bake at 350° for 50-60 minutes or until center is set. In a small saucepan combine 4 tsp. sugar, cornstarch and water. Bring to a boil, stirring constantly. Cool. Beat egg whites and cream of tartar until frothy. Add cornstarch mixture and beat until soft peaks form. Gradually beat in ⅓ c. sugar until stiff peaks form. Spread over hot filling, sealing edges to crust. Bake for 15 minutes or until meringue is golden brown.

Lizbet and Daughters—Country Cooking

French Rhubarb Pie

1 egg
1 c. sugar
1 tsp. vanilla

2 c. diced rhubarb
2 Tbsp. flour

Topping–
¾ c. flour
½ c. brown sugar

⅓ c. butter

Mix together egg, sugar, vanilla, rhubarb and flour. Put rhubarb mixture into an unbaked pie crust. Cover with topping. Bake at 400° for 10 minutes. Reduce to 350° and bake for 30 minutes or until done.

French Rhubarb Pie

4 Tbsp. flour
2 c. sugar
4 c. rhubarb, cut up

2 tsp. vanilla
4 eggs, beaten
1 c. half & half or milk

Crumbs–
1¾ c. flour
1 tsp. baking powder

¾ c. brown sugar
½ c. butter

Mix all together and pour in unbaked pie shell. Put crumbs on top. Bake at 425° for 12 minutes. Reduce heat to 350° and bake for 40 minutes. Makes 2 pies.

Blushing Rhubarb Pie

pastry for 2-crust pie
1½ c. sugar
⅓ c. flour

⅛ tsp. salt
4 c. rhubarb, cut up
2 Tbsp. butter

Fit crust into 9" pie pan. Mix dry ingredients. Combine with rhubarb. Fill crust and dot with butter. Place on top crust. Trim and crimp edges. Bake at 425° for 45 minutes or until crust is browned and rhubarb is tender.

White Christmas Pie

1 Tbsp. gelatin
¼ c. cold water
½ c. sugar
4 Tbsp. flour
½ tsp. salt
1½ c. milk
1½ tsp. vanilla
½ c. Rich's topping, whipped
3 egg whites
¼ tsp. cream of tartar
½ c. sugar
1 c. coconut

Dissolve gelatin in cold water. Cook sugar, flour, salt and milk over low heat until boiling, stirring constantly. Boil for 1 minute. Remove from heat and stir in gelatin mixture. Cool. When partly set beat until smooth. Blend in vanilla, whipped topping, egg whites beaten stiff, cream of tartar, sugar and coconut. Pile into baked pie crust. Sprinkle top with coconut and can also put a few Christmas sprinkles over top if desired.

Fry Pies

Dough-
9 c. cake flour
3 c. shortening
1 Tbsp. salt
2 Tbsp. sugar
1 pt. cold water

Glaze-
8 lb. powdered sugar
½ c. cornstarch
⅓ c. evaporated milk
1 tsp. vanilla
2½ c. hot water

Mix dough ingredients with hands like pie dough. Roll out thin and fill with pie filling. Fry at deep fry temperature until golden brown. We use same kind of shortening to fry them that we use in dough. I usually don't put in quite as much water. This is enough glaze for 4 batches of fry pies. Mix all together and glaze. Makes approximately 30 pies.

Strawberry Danish Dessert Filling

1¼ c. clear jel
2 c. sugar
2 pkg. strawberry Kool-Aid

Combine and mix well. Store dry mix until ready to use. To each ¾ c. mix, add 2 c. water. Cook until thickened. Add fresh sliced strawberries when cool. Use as pie filling or dessert topping. Variation: 3 oz. strawberry Jell-O may be added to dry mixture for more flavor.

Streusel Topping for Apple Pie

1 c. quick oats
⅓ c. brown sugar
⅓ c. chopped nuts
½ tsp. cinnamon
⅓ c. melted butter

Mix together.

Fresh Fruit Pie Filling

1½ c. granulated sugar
4 c. water
⅔ c. clear jel
1 sm. pkg. unsweetened Kool-Aid

Cook until clear and shiny. Cool and add fresh fruit. Enough for 2 pies.

Meringues

3 egg whites
¼ tsp. cream of tartar
dash of salt
1 tsp. vanilla
1 c. sugar

Beat egg whites, cream of tartar, salt and vanilla till it forms a peak. Very slowly add 1 c. sugar. Beat in till stiff, but not dry. Use glass or steel bowl.

Topping for Pineapple Pie

¼ c. brown sugar
2 Tbsp. butter
1 Tbsp. corn syrup
½ c. chopped pecans

Cook brown sugar, butter and corn syrup over low heat and stir until sugar is dissolved. Add pecans. Spread over hot baked pie and put in broiler until bubbly.

Blueberry Sour Cream Pie

1 c. sour cream
2 Tbsp. flour
¾ c. sugar
1 tsp. vanilla
¼ tsp. salt
1 egg, beaten
2½ c. fresh blueberries

Crumbs–
3 Tbsp. flour
1½ Tbsp. butter

chopped nuts

Combine first six ingredients and beat until smooth. Fold in blueberries and pour in pie shell. Bake at 400° for 25 minutes. Remove from oven and sprinkle with crumbs. Bake 10 minutes more.

Filling for Fruit Pies

4 oz. cream cheese, softened
½ c. sour cream
2 Tbsp. sugar
1 tsp. vanilla

Mix together. Put in baked pie crust and fill with your favorite fruit filling.

Lizbet and Daughters—Country Cooking

Double Layer Pumpkin Pie

Part 1–
4 oz. cream cheese
1 Tbsp. milk
1 Tbsp. sugar
1½ c. Cool Whip

Part 2–
1¼ c. milk
2 pkgs. instant vanilla pudding
1 c. pumpkin
1 tsp. pumpkin pie spice
1 c. Cool Whip

Part 1: Combine ingredients. Mix well and spread in bottom of baked crust. Part 2: Mix ingredients well and spread over cream cheese layer. Garnish with whipped topping.

Marshmallow Pie

32 large marshmallows
 or 3 c. mini marshmallows
¾ c. milk
¼ tsp. salt
1 c. whipping cream or Rich's topping
1 tsp. vanilla
2 (1 oz.) sq. chocolate, grated

Combine marshmallows, milk and salt in saucepan. Cook over low heat, stirring constantly, until marshmallows are melted. Chill until partially set. Beat topping until stiff, then stir in marshmallow mixture. Add vanilla and grated chocolate. Spread in pie shell. Chill until set.

Half Moon Pies

1 qt. dried apple snitz
1½ c. water
1 qt. applesauce

1½ c. brown sugar
1 Tbsp. cinnamon
½ tsp. salt

Boil snitz in water until soft and no water remains. Put through sieve and add applesauce, brown sugar, cinnamon and salt. Make pie dough, then shape dough to the size of a large egg. Roll out this as pie dough. Fold over to make a crease through center. Fold back and make 2 holes in top part of the dough. On the other half place ½ cup of the filling. Wet edges and fold over. Press edges together. Cut off remaining dough with pie crimper. Brush top with buttermilk or beaten egg. Bake at 450° until brown.

Caramel Raisin Pie

3 c. raisins
2 c. brown sugar
3 c. water
1 can evaporated milk
2 Tbsp. butter

2 c. water
½ c. water
4½ heaping Tbsp. clear jel
1½ c. rich milk
dash of salt

Boil raisins and 3 c. water. In another pan boil brown sugar and ½ c. water. Boil each for 7-10 minutes. Add sugar and water mixture to raisins and an additional 2 c. water. Bring to a boil again and add clear jel. Immediately add evaporated milk and milk. Boil a few minutes. Add butter and salt. More sugar may be used to suit taste. May be used for two crust pies or for baked crusts. Makes 3 pies.

Sweet and Sour Cherry Pies

1 pt. canned dark cherries, drained
1 can pie filling
3 c. water, including cherry juice
3 Tbsp. clear jel

sugar to taste
almond flavoring
1 (3 oz.) box cherry Jell-O

Thicken cherry juice and water with the clear jel to the right thickening. Add cherries and the pie filling, Jell-O, flavoring and sugar to taste. Enough filling for 2 pies.

Lizbet and Daughters—Country Cooking

Better Bought Pie Filling

3 cans cherry pie filling
4 c. water

2 c. sugar
clear jel

Bring water and sugar to a boil. Thicken with clear jel. Add cherry pie filling. Makes 3 pies.

Coconut Oatmeal Pie

3 eggs, beaten
⅔ c. sugar
½ c. brown sugar
2 Tbsp. butter, melted
⅔ c. quick oats

⅔ c. coconut
1 c. milk
1 tsp. vanilla
1 Tbsp. flour
⅓ c. Karo

Mix together. Bake at 400° for 8 minutes. Reduce heat to 350° and bake until done.

Snitz Pie Filling

1 gal. dried apples
3 c. sugar
1 Tbsp. salt

1 Tbsp. cinnamon
3 Tbsp. ReaLemon

Soak apples overnight, then using the same water, cook over low heat for 3-4 hours. Put through sieve. If there's too much water left over, let set to evaporate. Add remaining ingredients. Put in jars and cold pack for 15 minutes.

You can't expect a person to see eye to eye with you when you are looking down on them.

Candies & Snacks

Wan die family zomma komma dut
Uff Oschder, Danksaagdaag,
Grischdaag un all so daage,
Mir schwetza, mir singa, mir lacha,
Schpiele games un hen fun!
Awver mir gleicha aw so gutte-e
Sacha essa deby!

When the family gets together
On Easter, Thanksgiving Day,
Christmas and all such days,
We talk, we sing, we laugh,
Play games and have fun!
But we also like to have
Good stuff to eat.

Notes

Peanut Butter Reese's Cups

3 pkg. graham crackers
3 lb. powdered sugar
3 c. butter, softened
4½ c. peanut butter

Crush graham crackers, not fine, and add powdered sugar. Mix together butter and peanut butter. Slowly add graham cracker mixture. Roll in balls the size of a nickel. Dip in chocolate coating.

Fut Nudge

2 buttlespoons of tabler
2 c. shanulated grugar
3 cuppers qt. of crin theam
2 chaws of squair kolet
2 sabel tunes of sorn keerup
1 nup of kelled shuts
1 vittle lanilla

Shook the grugar, the chilk, the mawkolet and the sorn keerup until the mawkolet chelts. Still without burring to 325 deheeze of gret, then dairfully crop a little of the mott mixture into a wawt of cold cupper. If a little bawft sawl forms in the cottum of the bupp… the didge is fun. Remove the hann from the peat, bad the utter, let canned until stool and fladd the aivoring. Speat with a boon until quik and thooey. Nop in the druts; empty into a battered punn and swark in mairs. You may marsh admallows if you have a particulary tweet sooth. This serves a gruzzen daonups or two bean aged toys. Enjoy.

Honey Party Mix

½ c. honey
½ c. butter
2 c. pretzels
2 c. Crispix
1 c. pecans
1 c. cashews

Cook honey and butter for 5 minutes. Pour over mixture and bake for 1 hour at 250°. Cool. Store in a tight container.

Lizbet and Daughters—Country Cooking

Caramel Pretzels

1 pkg. pretzel rods
1 pkg. caramels
1 can sweetened condensed milk
2 c. chopped peanuts or walnuts

Melt caramels and condensed milk. Dip pretzels in caramel mixture, then roll in nuts.

Yummy Chex Snacks

1 box Rice Chex
1 lb. nuts, cashews or mixed pretzels, optional
1 c. butter
1 c. brown sugar

Melt together sugar and butter and boil for 3 minutes. Mix well and pour over Chex and nuts. Put in roaster and cover. Put in oven for 6 minutes at 350°. Mix once; put back in oven for another 6 minutes. Cool. Delicious.

Ranch Party Mix

1 box Quaker Oat squares
1 bag oyster crackers
1 bag goldfish crackers
1 bag butter pretzels
1 pkg. Ranch mix
1 c. vegetable oil

Put first 4 ingredients in large bowl. Mix Ranch mix and oil. Pour over party mix and mix well. Put in oven for 1 hour at 200°. Stir often.

The best way for a stay-at-home mom to get a few minutes to herself at the end of the day is to start doing the dishes.

Party Mix

1 c. butter
1 tsp. onion salt
1 tsp. garlic salt
1 tsp. celery salt
½ tsp. Tabasco sauce
1 tsp. Worcestershire sauce
shoestring potatoes

2 c. Cheerios
2 c. Rice Chex
2 c. Wheat Chex
2 c. Corn Chex
1 bag pretzels
2 c. nuts

Melt butter and add salts and sauces. Pour over mixed cereals, pretzels and nuts and toss together. Bake at 200° for 1½ hours, stirring every 30 minutes. Add M&M's after it is cooled.

Baked Peanut Butter Popcorn

3 qt. popped corn
1 c. sugar
⅔ c. light Karo syrup

⅔ c. peanut butter
1 tsp. vanilla
½ tsp. baking soda

In heavy 1½ qt. saucepan, stir together sugar and corn syrup. Stirring constantly, cook over medium heat until mixture boils. Stir in peanut butter. Continue cooking for 5 minutes. Do not stir. Remove from heat; stir in vanilla and baking soda. Pour over popcorn. Stir to coat. Bake ¾ hour at 250°. Spread out and cool. Store in a tight container.

Munchies

1¼ lb. white coating
3 c. Rice Chex
3 c. Corn Chex

3 c. Cheerios
2 c. pretzels
1 lb. M&M's

Melt coating in oven at 200°. When melted mix with Rice Chex, Corn Chex, Cheerios and pretzels. Add M&M's last.

Lizbet and Daughters—Country Cooking

Ranch Snack Crackers

16 oz. oyster crackers or mini snack crackers
1 pkg. dry Ranch dressing mix
¾ tsp. dill weed
¼ tsp. garlic powder
¾ c. vegetable oil

Combine dressing mix, dill weed, garlic powder and oil. Pour over crackers and mix well until all crackers are coated. Spread on cookie sheet and bake at 200° for 15-20 minutes, stirring once or twice. Cool, then store in airtight container. This is also good using pretzels and Ritz crackers.

Caramel Corn

7 qt. popped corn
2 c. brown sugar
½ c. light Karo
1 c. butter
½ tsp. salt
1 tsp. soda
1 tsp. vanilla

Boil butter, sugar, Karo and salt together for 5 minutes. Remove from stove; add vanilla and soda. Pour over popped corn and mix well. Bake at 250° for 1 hour, stirring every 15 minutes. Spread out on countertop until cool. Store in tight container.

Caramel Rice Krispie Treats

2¼ sticks butter
8 c. marshmallows
8 c. Rice Krispies
48 milk caramels
1 can sweetened condensed milk

First layer: Melt half of marshmallows and ½ stick butter. Do not boil. Add half of Rice Krispies. Put in greased 9" x 13" pan. Second layer: Melt caramels and 1¼ sticks butter and milk in saucepan over medium heat, stirring constantly. Double boiler can also be used. Third layer: Repeat directions of first layer. Cool between each layer. Cool and cut into bars.

Macaroons

⅔ c. sweetened condensed milk 1 tsp. vanilla
3 c. shredded coconut

Mix condensed milk and coconut. Add vanilla. Drop by spoonful on greased baking sheet about 1" apart. Bake in 350° oven for 10 minutes or until a delicate brown. Remove from pan immediately. Yield: 30.

Snowy Fudge

1½ c. peanut butter   1 c. marshmallow créme
2 c. sugar   1 tsp. vanilla
⅔ c. milk

Cook sugar and milk to 234° or until syrup forms a soft ball which flattens when removed from water. Add other ingredients. Mix well. Pour into a buttered 8" x 6" x 2" pan.

Cheerio Bars

1 c. sugar   1 c. light Karo
1 c. peanut butter   6 c. Cheerios

Mix sugar and Karo and boil for 30 seconds. Add peanut butter and beat until smooth. Pour over cereal and place in buttered pan.

Cashew Brittle

1 c. raw cashews   1 rounded c. sugar
1 c. butter

Put all together and boil until cashews are light brown, stirring constantly. Pour in cookie sheet and break in pieces when cool.

Lizbet and Daughters—Country Cooking

Twix Bars

Club crackers
1½ c. brown sugar
1 c. sugar
1 c. butter

2 c. graham cracker crumbs
⅔ c. milk
2 c. chocolate chips
½ c. peanut butter

Layer bottom of cookie sheet with Club crackers. Melt butter and add milk, sugars and graham cracker crumbs. Cook. Pour over Club crackers. Top with another layer of Club crackers. Melt chocolate chips and peanut butter. Put on top of crackers. Chill.

Rice Krispie Bars

¼ c. butter
4 c. mini marshmallows

6 c. Rice Krispies

Melt butter and marshmallows together on low heat. Stir in Rice Krispies. Press into pan. Cut in desired sizes.

Caramel Cups

1 c. sweetened condensed milk   chocolate

Cook condensed milk for three and a half hours in saucepan, covered with water. Put melted chocolate in little paper cups. While chocolate is still warm drop one teaspoon caramel in chocolate. Then top with chocolate again.

Children's Treat

1 lb. caramels
¼ c. butter
½ can sweetened condensed milk

large marshmallows
Rice Krispies

Melt caramels, butter and condensed milk. Dip marshmallows in mixture, then roll in Rice Krispies.

Scotcharoos

1 c. sugar
1 c. light Karo
1 c. peanut butter
6 c. Rice Krispies
1 c. chocolate chips
1 c. butterscotch chips

Bring Karo and sugar to a slight boil. Add peanut butter and stir until smooth. Pour mixture over Rice Krispies and mix well. Pour into 9" x 13" pan. Melt chips over very low heat. Spread over Rice Krispy bars. When cool, cut into bars.

English Toffee

½ c. butter
½ c. sugar
3 Tbsp. brown sugar
¼ tsp. soda
1 tsp. vanilla
1 Tbsp. water
1 Tbsp. light corn syrup

Melt butter and add sugars, syrup and water. Bring to a boil, stirring constantly, and cook until 290°. Remove from heat; stir in soda and vanilla. Pour into buttered pan. Allow to set for 3 minutes. Pour melted chocolate over top.

Peanut Clusters

1 can sweetened condensed milk
8 oz. cream cheese
1 tsp. maple flavoring
powdered sugar

Mix together condensed milk, cream cheese and maple flavoring. Add powdered sugar to thicken. Shape into small balls; slightly flatten. Cool in refrigerator. Dip bottom in melted chocolate, then spoon mixture of crushed peanuts and melted chocolate on top.

Lizbet and Daughters—Country Cooking

Buckeye Bars

1 c. peanut butter
1 c. butter
2 c. graham cracker crumbs
2½ c. powdered sugar
10 oz. milk chocolate chips
6 Tbsp. cooking oil

Soften butter and peanut butter. Stir in cracker crumbs and powdered sugar. Mix well. Pat in 9" x 13" pan. On low heat melt chocolate chips and stir in oil. Pour over crust and cool for several hours. Cut into bars and enjoy.

Caramel Candy Apples

12 medium red apples
1 lb. light colored caramels
¼ c. light cream

Wash and dry apples. Stick skewers in stem end. Put caramels and cream in top of double boiler. Cook, stirring occasionally, until caramels are melted. Dip apples into syrup; twirl once or twice to cover evenly. Place on tray and cover with wax paper or foil. Put in refrigerator for 2 hours. Yield: 12.

Ritzy Delights

1 box Ritz crackers
1 c. chopped dates
1 can sweetened condensed milk
1 c. chopped nuts

Heat milk and dates until thick, stirring constantly. Add nuts. Spread 1 teaspoon mixture on each cracker. Bake at 250° for 5 minutes.

In our health conscious society, some families count calories more than blessings.

Cane Molasses Cracker Jack

1 c. brown sugar
½ c. cane molasses
½ c. water
2 Tbsp. vinegar
2 Tbsp. butter
½ tsp. soda
12 c. warm popcorn

Cook together brown sugar, molasses, water, vinegar and butter until it threads. Add soda. Mix well. Pour over popcorn. Mix. Place in oven and bake at 300° for 30 minutes, stirring every few minutes. Spread out on countertop and let cool. Store in tight container.

Hopscotch Candy

6 oz. butterscotch chips
½ c. peanut butter
2 c. chow mein noodles

Melt chips in double boiler, then add peanut butter. Add the noodles.

Rice Krispy Roll-Ups

¼ c. butter
4 c. marshmallows
4 c. Rice Krispies
1 c. Rice Krispy Fruit Pebbles

Filling–
1 c. white chocolate chips
½ c. peanut butter chips
½ c. chocolate chips
½ c. peanut butter

Melt butter and marshmallows. Add cereal. Press in lightly greased cookie sheet. For filling: In double boiler melt chips and add peanut butter. Spread filling on top of cereal and roll up into a log. Let set for a half hour before slicing.

Candies and Snacks

Lizbet and Daughters—Country Cooking

Chocolate Caramel Candy

1 c. milk chocolate chips
¼ c. butterscotch chips

Filling-
¼ c. butter
1 c. sugar
¼ c. evaporated milk
1½ c. marshmallow créme

Caramel Layer-
14 oz. caramels

Icing-
1 c. milk chocolate chips
¼ c. butterscotch chips

¼ c. creamy peanut butter

¼ c. creamy peanut butter
1 tsp. vanilla
1½ c. chopped salted peanuts

¼ c. cream

¼ c. creamy peanut butter

Combine first three ingredients in saucepan. Stir over low heat until melted and smooth. Spread onto bottom of greased 9" x 13" pan. Refrigerate until set. For filling: Melt butter in saucepan. Add sugar and milk. Bring to a boil and stir for 5 minutes. Remove from heat. Stir in marshmallow créme, peanut butter, vanilla and peanuts. Spread over first layer. Refrigerate until set. Combine caramels and cream in saucepan. Stir over low heat until caramels are melted. Spread over filling. Refrigerate until set. In another saucepan combine chips and peanut butter. Stir over low heat until melted. Pour over caramel layer. Refrigerate at least 1 hour.

Easy Turtles

Cook sweetened condensed milk for 3½ hours. Cool unopened can in refrigerator for 24 hours. When ready to use put a teaspoon of caramel on 2 pecan halves. Dip in chocolate. Makes approximately 24 turtles per can. Since these are hard to dip, I just spoon chocolate over them and let it harden, then I turn them around and put a little chocolate on the bottom of them.

Chocolate Drops

2 c. sugar
1 c. light cream

¼ tsp. cream of tartar

Boil until it forms a hard ball in water. Remove from stove to a cool place, but do not stir until it is so cool you can place your hand at bottom of saucepan. Add flavoring and stir until it turns white or isn't glossy. Let cool. Form into balls and cool again. Dip in coating chocolate.

Oh Henry Bars

First Part-
2½ c. sugar
⅓ c. light Karo syrup
⅔ c. milk

1 Tbsp. butter
⅓ c. peanut butter

Second Part-
½ c. brown sugar

1 c. white Karo syrup

Cook sugar, Karo syrup, milk and butter to a soft ball. Remove from heat and add peanut butter. Beat real well and set aside to cool. When cold, shape in rolling pieces and set where they get really cold. Cook brown sugar and Karo syrup until it forms a hard ball in cold water. This has to be kept hot so you can dip your centers, as it is cooked pretty heavy. Best to set pan in hot water while dipping. When center is dipped, roll in crushed peanuts. Last dip in chocolate. Tastes just like real Oh Henry bars.

Oh Henry Bars

4 c. oatmeal
1 c. brown sugar
¾ tsp. salt
1 c. butter

½ c. sugar
1 tsp. vanilla
12 oz. chocolate chips
¾ c. peanut butter

Mix together first six ingredients and press into 10" x 16" pan. Bake 15 minutes at 325°; cool slightly. Melt chocolate chips, add peanut butter and spread over bars.

Lizbet and Daughters—Country Cooking

Caramels

1 lb. brown sugar
14 oz. sweetened condensed milk
1 c. butter
1 c. light Karo

Melt butter, then add rest of ingredients. Boil for 12 minutes. Pour into greased pan. When cooled, cut and wrap in waxed paper.

Indoor S'mores

⅔ c. light Karo
2 T. butter
12 oz. chocolate chips
1 tsp. vanilla
3 c. mini marshmallows
8 c. broken graham crackers
   or 12 oz. Golden Grahams cereal

Heat Karo, butter and chocolate chips to boiling, stirring constantly. Remove from heat and add vanilla. Pour over crackers in a large bowl, tossing quickly until completely covered. Fold in marshmallows. Press mixture evenly in 9" x 13" pan with back of buttered spoon. Cut into bars when cool.

Mounds Bars

1½ c. graham cracker crumbs
⅓ c. butter, melted
⅓ c. granulated sugar
2 c. coconut
14 oz. sweetened condensed milk
1 c. chocolate chips
2 Tbsp. peanut butter

Combine first three ingredients. Press into bottom of 10" x 11" pan. Blend together coconut and milk. Spread over crust. Bake at 350° for 15 minutes. Melt together chocolate chips and peanut butter. Spread over warm crust. Cool. Cut into bars.

Farmers' Hats

Ritz crackers
large marshmallows
peanut butter

Spread Ritz crackers with peanut butter. Put a marshmallow on top. Put in 350° oven until marshmallows are brown.

Molasses Taffy

3 c. molasses
1½ c. brown sugar
1½ Tbsp. vinegar
1½ Tbsp. butter
⅓ tsp. soda

Boil ingredients together until brittle when dropped in cold water. Pour into greased pans. When cool enough to handle, wet hands in cold water or grease them with butter. Stretch and pull until light colored. Cut in small pieces. This is something to do with the children on cold winter evenings. It's fun and makes memories.

Chocolate Fudge

12 oz. semisweet chocolate chips
14 oz. sweetened condensed milk
1¼ c. walnuts, chopped
1 tsp. vanilla

Combine chocolate chips and milk. Stir over low heat until chocolate chips are melted. Add nuts and vanilla. Pour in an 8" pan. Chill until firm (about 2 hours).

Lizbet and Daughters—Country Cooking

Puppy Chow

¼ c. butter
1 c. chocolate chips
¾ c. peanut butter
8 c. Crispix cereal
2 c. powdered sugar

Melt first 3 ingredients. Pour over cereal; stir well. Pour powdered sugar in a brown grocery bag. Add cereal and shake well to coat evenly. Spread on cookie sheet until set.

Creamy Mints

6 oz. cream cheese
1½ lb. powdered sugar
¼ tsp. oil of peppermint
food coloring, optional
granulated sugar

Combine first four ingredients in a large bowl and mix until smooth and creamy. Knead with hands. Roll in balls then in granulated sugar. Press in desired molds, then release. Store in covered containers.

Glazed Pecans

1 egg white
1 tsp. cold water
4 c. pecan halves
½ c. sugar
¼ tsp. salt
½ tsp. cinnamon

Lightly beat egg white; add water; beat until frothy, but not stiff. Add pecans; stir until well coated. Combine sugar, salt and cinnamon. Sprinkle over pecans; toss to mix. Spread in 10" x 15" baking sheet. Bake at 250° for 45 minutes, stirring often. Cool, then store in airtight container.

In labors of love,

every day is payday.

Large Quantity Recipes

"…Teach the young women to be sober…
discreet, chaste, keepers at home…" Titus 2:4,5.

A "keeper at home" I have promised to be,
How many the duties now waiting for me.
I'm mistress of dust rags, mops and brooms,
A sweeper of spiders in corners of rooms.
I'm a shaker of rugs, a duster of chairs;
I'm a cooker of meats, of breads and pies
And other good things that bring joy to the eyes.
The planner of meals and the cleaner up too,
For dishes need to be washed when cooking is through.
A tender of gardens, a planter of seeds,
A gath'rer of bounties, a hoer of weeds.
My duties are many and all the day through
One task or another I hasten to do,
And when I am tempted to scold or to frown,
My mind goes to those who must work in town.
I would not trade places with any who roam—
Thank you, Lord, for letting me be a "keeper at home."

– L.B.

Notes

Potluck Potatoes

1 c. butter, melted
1 Tbsp. chopped onion
1 pt. sour cream
1 can cream of mushroom soup
2 cans cream of chicken soup
½ tsp. pepper
1 Tbsp. seasoned salt

1 Tbsp. onion salt
½ c. sour cream and onion powder
5 c. milk
½ c. flour
1½ lb. Velveeta cheese
6-7 lb. frozen, shredded hash browns

Heat the milk and flour together to make a paste. Add cut up Velveeta and stir until melted. Add to other ingredients. Enough to fill a Lifetime roaster.

Dressing

12 eggs
3½ qt. milk
3 c. chicken broth
2 Tbsp. chicken base
1 Tbsp. onion flakes
2 Tbsp. seasoned salt
1 Tbsp. celery salt

1 Tbsp. salt
1 tsp. pepper
4 c. potatoes, diced
3 c. carrots, diced
3 c. celery, diced
5 c. deboned chicken
7 qt. toasted wheat bread

Cook carrots and potatoes until tender. Beat eggs, milk, broth and seasonings in a 13-qt. mixing bowl. Add vegetables and chicken. Add bread cubes last. Fry with butter in skillet until well done. We use this recipe for weddings in our family.

Lizbet and Daughters — Country Cooking

Ham and Potato Soup

6 qt. shredded potatoes, cooked
2 Tbsp. onion flakes
8 lb. shredded ham
1½ c. butter
5 Tbsp. flour, heaping

1½ gal. milk
2 lbs. Velveeta cheese
salt to taste
pepper to taste

Cook potatoes; do not drain. Add onion flakes while cooking. Add ham. In 6 qt. kettle melt butter until lightly browned. Add flour and milk and let thicken, then pour over potatoes and ham in canner. Add Velveeta cheese, salt and pepper. Makes 1 canner full.

Gravy

6 qt. chicken broth
6 egg yolks
2½ c. all-purpose flour
1 c. cornstarch

1 qt. water
chicken seasoning to taste
salt to taste

Stir eggs with flour, cornstarch and water in large mixing bowl. Pour boiling broth over flour mixture, while stirring with a whisk. Add seasonings. Do not put back on burner. Keep in a warm place until ready to serve.

Noodles – Large Batch

2 (48 oz.) cans chicken broth
2 (50 oz.) cans cream of chicken soup
1¼ lb. butter

¾ jar chicken base
6 cans hot water
5 lb. noodles

Brown butter in 21 qt. stainless steel canner. Add chicken soup. When hot, add chicken base, stirring until well melted. Add chicken broth and hot water; cover and bring to a boil, stirring occasionally because it will stick to bottom! When boiling, add noodles. Stir and bring to a boil again. When it starts to boil, turn off heat and do not stir. Do not add extra salt. Let stand 1 hour before serving. Serves around 80-100 people.

Large Quantity Recipes

Breakfast Haystack – for 90 people

100 biscuits
2-8 qt. kettles sausage gravy
1 Lifetime roaster homefries
10 dozen eggs, scrambled
2 (8 qt.) kettles cheese sauce
25 lb. bacon, fried and crumbled

I fried the bacon the day before and heated in oven the next day. Serve with 4 fruit pizzas and 2 large pans cinnamon rolls.

Dinner – for 50 people

2 turkeys
1 (8 qt.) + 1 (6 qt.) mashed potatoes
1 large batch dressing
4 qt. gravy
5 qt. corn
1 Fix-n-Mix bowl tossed salad
1 Fix-n-Mix bowl date pudding
2 cakes
2 (5 qt.) pails mixed fruit

Ham and Cheese Sandwiches

36 sandwich buns
3½ lb. chipped ham
cheese slices

Place approximately 4 slices ham on each sandwich bun. Add cheese slices. Wrap in foil and put in 350° oven for 10 minutes or until hot.

Enough for 100 People

4 Lifetime roasters chicken
2 smaller roasters dressing
2 (6 qt.) kettles mixed vegetables
4 (6 qt.) kettles mashed potatoes
6 qt. gravy
2 Fix-n-Mix bowls tossed salad
5 Cold Cut Keepers pudding
4 cakes
3 (5 qt.) pails mixed fruit

Lizbet and Daughters — Country Cooking

Serves 100 People

- 30-36 lb. hamburger
- 24 lb. meatloaf
- 6 gal. milk
- 40 lb. ham
- 40 lb. beef
- 25 lb. wieners
- 40 lb. pork roast
- 150 dinner rolls
- 10 loaves bread
- 3 lb. butter
- 35 lb. potatoes
- 5 gal. baked beans
- 3 lb. coffee
- 20 heads lettuce
- 12 qts. potato salad
- 5 gal. scalloped potatoes
- 5 gal. soup
- 2 qt. pickles
- 40 lb. vegetables
- 18 pies
- 8 cakes
- 3 lb. cheese
- 12 qt. fruit salad
- 4 gal. ice cream

Dinner — for 34 people

- 1 Lifetime roaster Tater Tot casserole
- 1 (6 qt.) kettle noodles (1½ lb.)
- 1 lg. and 1 sm. pan ribbon salad
- 2 cakes
- 4 pies
- 2 freezers homemade ice cream

Cooking for Company

- Noodles – 20 people per 1 lb. noodles
- Potatoes – 1 normal size for each person and a couple extra
- Meatloaf – 1 lb. hamburger feeds 4 people
- 1 cake – 24 pieces

Chicken Barbecue – for 50 people

25 chicken halves
50 chicken leg quarters
3 lb. noodles
1 Lifetime roaster baked beans

2 medium bowls potato salad
2 cakes
3 Cold Cut Keepers frozen cheesecake
3 bowls snack

Communion Church Recipe

25 lb. cheese
15 lb. meat
18 pies
6 containers cookies
30 loaves bread

2 canners ¾ full of soup
1 pail peanut butter spread
5 qt. pickles
8 lb. crackers

This will feed 100 people for dinner and supper.

Underground Ham

First Layer–
6 Tbsp. butter
1 large onion, chopped

2 Tbsp. Worcestershire sauce
10 c. cubed ham

Second Layer–
3 c. Velveeta cheese
3 cans cream of mushroom soup

2 c. milk

Third Layer–
6 qt. mashed potatoes
1 pt. sour cream
1 c. milk

salt to taste
1 lb. bacon, fried and crumbled

Fry onions, butter, Worcestershire sauce and ham and put in bottom of Lifetime roaster. Add second layer. Cook potatoes until soft, then mash and add sour cream and milk. Add salt to taste. Put on second layer and top with bacon. Bake at 350° for 2 hours.

Lizbet and Daughters — Country Cooking

Meal — for 100 people

- 2 Lifetime roasters poor man's steak (20 lb. hamburger)
- 2 Lifetime and 1 smaller roaster potluck potatoes
- 2 (6 qt.) kettles vegetables — baby carrots and peas
- 2 Fix-n-Mix bowls tossed salad
- 4 sheet cakes
- 3 (5 qt.) pails mixed fruit
- 3 pails ice cream

Dinner — for 70 people

- 20 lb. ham
- 85 pieces chicken
- 2 Lifetime roasters dressing
- 3 (6 qt.) kettles mashed potatoes
- 1 (8 qt.) kettle gravy
- 2 (4 qt.) kettles mixed vegetables
- 3 Fix-n-Mix bowls taco salad
- 3 Fix-n-Mix bowls date pudding
- 2 (5 qt.) pails mixed fruit
- 4 cakes

Haystack — for 125 people

- 24 lb. hamburger
- 18 c. minute rice
- 2 (8 qt.) kettles cheese sauce
- 7 heads lettuce
- 4 boxes crackers
- 3 qt. tomatoes
- 5 bags chips

Barbecue Ham Sandwiches

50 lb. chipped ham
6 onions, chopped
20 c. ketchup
2½ c. vinegar
7½ c. brown sugar

Combine onions, ketchup, vinegar and brown sugar. Pour over ham. Alternate layers. Bake uncovered in roasters at 300°. Stir a few times.

Wieners for Church

Use 2 roasters for 12 pkg. wieners or more. Melt ½ c. butter in each one. Put wieners in on end. Have temperature of oven at 275° unless you see they don't get ready. Shake every half hour with lid on. If they want to burst open shake more often. Leave lid off for roasting. Start as soon as church has started.

Corn Made in Oven

7 qt. frozen corn
7 tsp. salt
1 lb. butter

Put ½ lb. of butter in roaster and add corn. Top with salt and rest of butter. Cover and bake at 300° for 3 hours.

Middle age is when the narrow waist and the broad mind begin to exchange places.

Lizbet and Daughters—Country Cooking

Scalloped Potatoes — for 25-30 people

10 lb. potatoes
2 qt. milk
1⅓ c. flour
3 Tbsp. salt
½ tsp. pepper

1¼ c. butter
1 lb. Velveeta cheese
1 tsp. Worcestershire sauce
5 lb. cubed ham, optional
16 oz. sour cream

Peel potatoes, then put through coarse Salad Master. Cook potatoes, but not soft. Drain well; put in roaster. Melt butter in saucepan, then add flour and stir well. Add milk, cheese, salt, pepper and Worcestershire sauce. Heat until cheese is melted. Mix cheese sauce with ham and potatoes and bake for one hour.

Cheese Sauce — for 8 qt. kettle

1 c. butter
2 c. Calla Lily flour
1¼ gal. milk

2 cans cheddar or nacho soup
¾ box Velveeta cheese

Melt butter and stir in flour. Add milk. Heat until thick. Add soup and cheese. Do not boil after cheese is added.

Sausage Gravy

4 lb. fresh sausage
3 c. flour
butter, optional

2 Tbsp. salt
½ Tbsp. pepper
18 c. milk

Fry sausage. Add flour and brown. If sausage is too dry, you may need to add some butter when adding flour. Add salt and pepper. Stir well and add milk. Heat to boiling point; reduce heat and simmer for a few minutes. Makes approximately 5 qt. gravy.

Fry Pies –400

30 lb. Velvet cake flour
20 lb. Creamtex
15 lb. Super Fry

20 lb. powdered sugar
1½ lb. cornstarch
1 can Carnation milk

Dough–
9 c. flour
3 c. Creamtex

1 Tbsp. salt

Glaze–
8 lb. powdered sugar
½ c. cornstarch
½ c. Carnation milk

2¼ c. water
vanilla

Mix dough ingredients like pie dough. Add 2 c. water with 2 Tbsp. sugar (in water). Roll out thin and fill with pie filling. Fry at deep fry temperature until golden brown. Mix glaze together and glaze fry pies.

Practice makes perfect, so be careful what you practice.

Lizbet and Daughters—Country Cooking

Canning & Freezing

I read today of Africa,
Where drought and famine are,
Where many millions suffer want,
They wander near and far
In search of insects, mice and leaves
To eat to stay alive.

I think today of all we have,
Abundant food to spare.
We canned and harvested so much,
We eat without a care.
My mother-heart can't comprehend
How hopeless it must be
To have no food to give a child,
What dreadful grief to see!

I cannot feed the multitudes
That starve away each day;
The gift of money we may give
A little loss will stay.
But we can teach our children how
To truly thankful be,
And serve up meals with gratitude
And with simplicity.

—*Thankful*

Notes

Bread and Butter Pickles

- 1 gal. unpeeled cucumbers, sliced thin
- 8 sm. onions, sliced thin
- ½ c. salt
- 5 c. sugar
- 1½ tsp. turmeric
- 2 tsp. mustard seed
- 2 c. vinegar
- 2 c. hot water

Mix cucumbers, onions and salt together. Cover with water. Let stand for three hours: Drain well and add rest of ingredients. Bring to boil and can.

Bread and Butter Pickles

- 1 gal. thinly sliced cucumbers (do not peel)
- 8 small onions, sliced
- 2 green peppers, chopped fine
- 5 c. sugar
- ½ c. salt
- 1½ tsp. turmeric
- 2 Tbsp. mustard seed
- 3 c. vinegar
- 1 c. water

Mix cucumbers, onions and peppers, then mix in salt and put in water. Let stand for 3 hours. Drain well and add sugar, turmeric, mustard seed, vinegar and water. Bring to a boil and can.

Sweet Dill Pickles

- 1 qt. vinegar
- 1 pt. water
- ¼ c. salt
- 4 c. sugar
- 4 onions, cut up
- 2 tsp. dill seed (to each qt.)
- 1 tsp. garlic salt (to each qt.)

Slice cucumbers. Pack pickles, dill seed and garlic salt in jars. Bring liquid to rolling boil and pour over pickles. Set jars in boiling water long enough so they will seal. Makes 4 quarts.

Lizbet and Daughters—Country Cooking

Refrigerator Pickles

6 c. cucumbers, sliced thin
1 c. dark vinegar
1 tsp. salt

1 c. onion, sliced thin
2 c. sugar
1 tsp. celery seed

Combine cucumbers and onions in bowl. Combine sugar, vinegar, salt and celery seed. Do not cook syrup. Pour over cucumbers and put in jars. Refrigerate for 5 days before using. These will keep in refrigerator for 1 year.

Bean Pickle

2 qt. green beans
2 qt. yellow beans
1 can kidney beans, drained
3 c. granulated sugar
½ pt. vinegar

2½ pt. water
1 tsp. dry mustard
1 tsp. celery seed
2 tsp. turmeric

Cut beans in 1 inch pieces. Cook in salt water till tender, not too soft. Combine sugar, vinegar and spices. Cook together. Add beans. Bring to a boil. Pack in jars and seal.

Red Beets

1 gal. beets, cooked
2 tsp. salt
1¼ c. brown sugar

1¼ c. white sugar
1 c. vinegar
2½ c. water (in which beets were cooked)

Cook beets until tender; skin. Cut in size you want. Mix sugars, salt, vinegar and water. Heat to boiling. Pour over beets and bring to boil. Put in jars and seal.

Mixed Pickle

2 qt. lima beans
1 qt. celery
6 red peppers
6 green peppers
1 qt. carrots
2 heads cauliflower

1 qt. string beans
2 qt. small cucumbers
1 qt. kidney beans
1 qt. wheel macaroni
1 qt. small onions

Brine-
10 c. sugar
8 c. water
4 c. vinegar

2 tsp. turmeric
1 tsp. cinnamon
4 tsp. celery seed

Cook all separately in salt water except cucumbers. Do not cook too soft. Mix all together. Bring brine to a boil. Pour over the vegetables. Put in jars and cold pack for 30 minutes.

Canned Peppers

peppers, cut up
½ Tbsp. cooking oil
1 clove garlic
dash of alum

½ gal. water
1 c. vinegar
½ c. salt

Place peppers in pint jars; add cooking oil, garlic and alum to each one. Mix together water, vinegar and salt and bring to a boil. Pour over peppers and seal.

Banana Pepper Relish

10 green peppers
20 banana peppers
1 qt. mustard
1 qt. vinegar

1 Tbsp. salt
5 c. sugar
1½ c. flour
2 c. water

Grind the peppers real fine. Mix the sugar, flour and salt together, then add water, vinegar and mustard. Add to peppers and cook till thickened. Put in jars and seal.

Lizbet and Daughters—Country Cooking

Mom Miller's Sandwich Spread

- 1 bunch celery
- 2 c. green tomatoes
- 3 c. pickles
- 2 c. onions
- 1 red and green pepper
- 4 c. white sugar
- 2 c. vinegar
- 1 sm. jar French's mustard
- 1 Tbsp. salt
- 1 c. flour
- 1 c. sugar
- 1 c. vinegar
- 2 Tbsp. turmeric

Grind together celery, tomatoes, pickles, onions and peppers. Add sugar, vinegar, mustard and salt. Boil all together for 15 minutes. Make a sauce of flour, sugar, vinegar and turmeric. Add to relish mixture and boil 15 minutes. Put in jars and seal. Great on egg and meat sandwiches. For tartar sauce for fish sandwiches, mix a couple tablespoons sandwich spread to a cup of salad dressing.

Canned Sweet Corn

Cut corn off cob. Fill quart jars with corn. To each jar add ¾ tsp. salt and ½ Tbsp. vinegar or place 1 small slice tomato on top. Seal and pressure cook at 10 lb. pressure for 15 minutes. It tastes just like fresh corn.

Cold Pack Sausage

- 1 gal. water
- 1 c. brown sugar
- ½ c. salt
- 1 Tbsp. black pepper

Cut stuffed sausage to equal lengths. Put in jars raw, packing sausage loosely. Pour this brine over sausage. Cold pack for 2 hours.

A smart husband buys his wife fine china so she won't trust him to wash it.

Ham

ham slices   brown sugar

Slice and cut ham to fit in canning jars. Make a syrup of ½ c. brown sugar to 2 qt. water. Pour over ham in jars. Pressure cook for 90 minutes at 10 lb. pressure.

Steak

1 c. brown sugar   1 gal. water
1 c. salt, scant

Mix together and bring to a boil. Cool. Divide this liquid in 14 quart jars. Add sliced steak, one piece at a time. Do not pack the steak in the jar solidly as the brine should come up to cover the meat. Cold pack for 3 hours or pressure can for 90 minutes at 10 lb. pressure.

Canned Meatloaf

15 lb. hamburger   ½ c. salt, scant
4 eggs   1 c. rolled oats
7 slices bread   pepper to taste
36 white crackers   3 c. water

Mix together and put in tapered jars. Cold pack for 3 hours or 1 hour in pressure cooker. When ready to use, slice and roll in flour. Fry in butter or Crisco. I like to use venison burger for this.

Chunk Meat

Combine equal amounts of brown sugar and salt. Add some black pepper. Layer chunk meat into containers. (I use ice cream pails.) Sprinkle with salt mixture. Continue until container is full. Refrigerate up to 4 days. Put chunks in jars; do not add water. Cold pack for 3 hours or 90 minutes at 10 lb. pressure in pressure cooker. This makes a very tender chunk.

Lizbet and Daughters—Country Cooking

Homemade Bologna

25 lb. fresh hamburger
¾ lb. Tenderquick
1 qt. water
1 Tbsp. pepper

¼ c. seasoned salt
1 tsp. garlic salt
2 tsp. liquid smoke
1 qt. warm water

Mix together hamburger, Tenderquick and water and let stand overnight. Next morning add pepper, seasoned salt, garlic salt, liquid smoke and water. Mix all together thoroughly and press into wide-mouth jars and pressure can at 10 lb. pressure for 70 minutes.

Pizza Sauce

2½ gal. tomato juice
4 green peppers
8-10 onions
1 pt. oil
2 Tbsp. basil
1 c. sugar
2 Tbsp. oregano

6 bay leaves, crushed
2 Tbsp. red pepper, crushed
3 Tbsp. pizza seasoning
1 Tbsp. Italian seasoning
½ gal. tomato paste
1 tsp. garlic powder
½ c. salt

Cook together juice, peppers and onions for 1 hour. Strain through Victorio strainer. Return to kettle and add the rest of ingredients. Cook for 1 hour, then add ½ gal. or 13 (6 oz.) cans tomato paste and mix well. Ladle into jars and process in hot water bath for 10 minutes. Yield: about 25 pints. This tastes very much like Pizza Hut's sauce.

Many a woman who goes on a diet finds out that she is a poor loser.

Pizza Sauce

- 1 bushel tomatoes
- 10 onions
- 8 large peppers
- 2 garlic bulbs
- 1 tsp. red pepper
- 2 tsp. black pepper
- 1 Tbsp. seasoned salt
- 1 Tbsp. chili powder
- 1 Tbsp. paprika
- 1 Tbsp. taco seasoning
- 4 Tbsp. oregano
- 1 Tbsp. garlic salt
- 1 c. salt
- 3 c. sugar
- 3 c. clear jel
- 2 c. vegetable oil

Cook together tomatoes, onions, peppers and garlic bulbs and put through strainer. Add rest of ingredients except clear jel and cook for 3 hours before adding thickener. Mix clear jel mixed with juice or add some tomato paste, then not as much clear jel. Fill stainless steel canner ¾ full of juice, add spices and thicken. We love this sauce!

Spaghetti Sauce

- 6-10 lb. hamburger, browned
- 1½ Tbsp. pepper
- 3 Tbsp. garlic salt
- 6 Tbsp. parsley flakes
- 6 Tbsp. butter
- 2 c. sugar
- 3 onions, chopped
- 3 peppers, chopped
- 3 sm. cans mushrooms, chopped
- ½ c. cooking oil
- 3 (12 oz.) cans tomato paste
- 2 jars Ragu spaghetti sauce
- 3 (12 oz.) cans water
- 6 qt. tomato juice
- 3 Tbsp. salt

Combine and cook for 1 hour. Put in jars and cold pack 2 hours. Yield: 13 quarts.

Lizbet and Daughters—Country Cooking

Pork and Beans

8 lb. navy beans
⅓ c. salt
4 qt. tomato juice
½ tsp. pepper
1 tsp. cinnamon
1 large onion

1½ lb. bacon
3 c. sugar
4 c. brown sugar
1 tsp. mustard
1 (26 oz.) ketchup
4 Tbsp. cornstarch

Soak beans overnight and cook until soft. Mix the rest of ingredients and cook a few minutes. Add to beans and mix well. Put in jars, seal and cold pack for 1½ hours.

Pork and Beans

8 lb. navy beans
⅓ c. salt
4 lb. bacon
96 oz. ketchup

1 tsp. mustard
3 c. sugar
5 c. brown sugar
½ tsp. pepper

Soak navy beans overnight. Drain. Cook beans with water and salt until soft. Fry bacon (cut in pieces) and mix with ketchup, mustard, sugars and pepper. Heat on medium heat, stirring occasionally, until it cooks. Add this to beans and reheat until it cooks again. Put in quart jars. Pressure cook at 10 lbs. pressure for 35 minutes. Pints: 20 minutes. Yield: 14 quarts.

Heinz Ketchup

8 qt. cut up tomatoes
3 large onions
green and hot peppers, optional
12 oz. tomato paste
4 c. sugar

3 tsp. salt
1 pt. vinegar
½ tsp. cloves
½ tsp. cinnamon, very scant
½ tsp. dry mustard

Boil tomatoes, onions and peppers until soft, then put through Victorio strainer. Drain in bag for 2 hours. Add remaining ingredients to pulp. Boil 10 minutes. Pour into jars and cold pack 10 minutes. Double recipe—9 pints.

Sandwich Spread

6 green and red peppers
6 green tomatoes
1 onion
½ c. mustard
½ c. vinegar

1½ c. sugar
½ Tbsp. celery seed
½ c. flour
1 pt. salad dressing

Grind together peppers, tomatoes and onion. Drain. Add mustard, vinegar, sugar and celery seed. Boil for 10 minutes. Add flour. Bring to a boil, remove from heat and add salad dressing. Put in jars and seal.

Dark Sweet Cherries

5 lb. cherries, pitted
3 c. sugar

3 oz. black cherry Jell-O
3 c. hot water

Make syrup as for canning, using sugar and water. When hot, add Jell-O and stir until dissolved. Cool. Put cherries in containers and freeze.

Peaches and Glaze

4 c. water
3 c. pineapple juice
7 c. sugar

⅓ c. peach or apricot Jell-O
1¾ c. clear jel or Therma-Flo
5½-6 qts. peaches

Mix first four ingredients and thicken with clear jel. Add peaches. Cold pack 20 minutes.

Lizbet and Daughters—Country Cooking

Freezing Peaches

1 sm. can orange juice concentrate, frozen
4 c. sugar
3 c. water

Mix together thoroughly and slice peaches into juice. Ladle into boxes to freeze. Continue to slice peaches into juice until all used up. Hint: Save your yogurt dishes with lids to freeze your peaches. Those are just the right size for lunch buckets. If you put those frozen in your buckets in the morning, they are just right to eat by lunchtime. Our children's favorite!

Peach Pie Filling

5½ c. water
2½ c. sugar
1 c. Fridgex
⅓ c. Karo
¾ c. Jell-O
peaches

Cook together water, sugar, Fridgex, Karo and Jell-O for 4 minutes. Cool. Add peaches and freeze.

Peach Slush

1 peck peaches, sliced
6 (20 oz.) cans pineapples
3 (12 oz.) cans frozen orange juice concentrate
8½ lb. bananas
9 c. sugar
10 c. water
1 liter 7-Up

Dissolve sugar in hot water; add orange juice and prepared fruits. Add 7-Up last. Mix in 21 quart canner.

Apple Pie Filling

28 c. apples, shoestring
7 c. water
3 c. fresh cider
4½ c. sugar
1 tsp. salt
2 tsp. cinnamon
1 c. clear jel
3 Tbsp. lemon juice

Bring water, cider and sugar to a boil. Dissolve clear jel in 1 c. cold water. Mix cinnamon and salt; add to boiling syrup. Stir until clear and thick. Add lemon juice and apples. Remove from heat; cover for 10 minutes. Put in jars and cold pack 20 minutes. Yield: 7 quarts.

Apple Pie Filling

7 c. hot water
7 c. sugar
1 c. clear jel
½ c. butter
¼ c. lemon juice
3 tsp. salt
3 tsp. cinnamon
4 qt. shredded apples, heaping

Heat water, sugar and clear jel to boiling. Add butter, lemon juice, salt and cinnamon. Add shredded apples. Put in jars and cold pack 20 minutes. 1 batch—7 quarts. 1 bushel—5 batches.

Apple Pie Filling

18 c. apples, shredded
3 Tbsp. lemon juice
4½ c. sugar
1 c. Perma-Flo
2 tsp. cinnamon
1 tsp. salt
¼ tsp. nutmeg
10 c. water

In a large bowl toss apples with lemon juice. Set aside. Combine sugar, Perma-Flo, cinnamon, salt and nutmeg. Add water and bring to a boil. Boil for 2 minutes. Add apples. Put in jars and cold pack 10 minutes. Yield: Approximately 6 quarts.

Lizbet and Daughters—Country Cooking

Corncob Syrup

12 cobs of field corn
4 qt. water
1½ c. brown sugar

2½ c. sugar
maple flavoring

Break up the cobs and boil in water for 30 minutes. Drain and strain liquid. Add sugars and bring to a boil. Simmer until syrup consistency. Add maple flavoring. Use as a substitute for maple syrup.

Grape Sunshine

1 qt. whole grapes
1 qt. sugar

2 Tbsp. water

Cook for 20 minutes, then put through sieve. Bring to boiling point again and pour in jars and seal. This is also good to freeze.

Red Beet Jelly

6 c. juice from cooked beets
2 pkg. Sure-Jell
½ c. lemon juice

8 c. sugar
2 (6 oz.) pkg. red raspberry Jell-O

Heat beet juice, Sure-Jell and lemon juice to a boil. Add sugar and Jell-O. Bring to a boil for 5 minutes. Fill jars and seal.

Hot Pepper Jelly

2½ c. ground peppers
apple juice or cider

5 c. sugar
1 box Sure-Jell

Add enough apple juice or cider to peppers to make 4 cups. Boil for a few minutes, then add sugar and Sure-Jell. Cook according to directions on Sure-Jell box. Put in jars and seal. Good on sandwiches. Best to wear rubber gloves while cutting and grinding the hot peppers. Use 2 cups green bell peppers and only ½ c. hot peppers or jelly will get too hot.

Hot Pepper Jelly

12 hot peppers
12 lg. red peppers
1 Tbsp. salt
2 c. vinegar
3 c. white sugar

Chop peppers. Add salt and let set for 3½ hours. Drain in colander. Heat peppers, vinegar and sugar and cook for 1 hour. Add clear jel if needed. Note: Soften 8 oz. cream cheese, add 1 pt. hot pepper jelly and mix well. Serve on snack crackers.

Green Tomato Raspberry Jelly

5 c. ground green tomatoes
4 c. sugar
1 (6 oz.) red raspberry Jell-O

Bring tomatoes and sugar to rolling boil, and boil for 20 minutes. Keep stirring. Remove from heat and add Jell-O. Stir until dissolved. Put in jars and let seal. Delicious—tastes like the real thing.

Very Good Apple Butter

1½ gal. applesauce
(made from tart apples)
8 lb. granulated sugar
½ gal. light Karo
½ gal. dark Karo

Mix all together and pour in roasting pan. Let cook at 350° for three hours, stirring every 15 minutes, or until thick. Put in hot jars and seal.

Brine to Keep Bologna

1 c. brown sugar
½ c. salt
1 gal. water

Make a liquid with ingredients. Put in crock and keep where it is cold. Put something on top to keep bologna under brine.

Lizbet and Daughters—Country Cooking

Brine for Turkey

1½ c. Morton's sugar cure 1½ gal. water

Mix in five gallon pail. Put turkey in and keep in cold place 5-6 days. Drain and bake in oven until tender. If you don't have Morton's sugar cure you can use following recipe.

1 c. Tenderquick ¼ c. liquid smoke
½ c. brown sugar 1½ gal. water

Mix in five gallon pail. Put turkey in and keep in cold place 5-6 days. Drain and bake in oven until tender.

Grape Juice

3 qt. grapes 2 c. sugar

Put grapes in 8 quart kettle. Add sugar and fill kettle with water up to 2" from top. Bring to boiling and simmer 5 minutes. Strain and put in jars and seal.

Grape Wine

6 c. sugar 2 qt. unwashed grapes

Combine grapes and sugar. Squeeze and mash with hands, then use potato masher to mash with. Let stand for one week. Stir once a day to make sure sugar is dissolved. Add 1 gallon lukewarm water and drain through organdy or cloth. Add 4 c. sugar to a gallon of juice or wine. Put in jugs. Do not put cap on tight for at least two weeks, then turn on tight.

Frozen Strawberries

4 c. sugar
2 c. mashed strawberries
10 c. sliced or mashed strawberries
1 pkg. Sure-Jell
¾ c. water

Add sugar to the 2 cups mashed berries. Cook Sure-Jell and water for 1 minute. Add to the sugar mixture. Stir until sugar is dissolved. Add the remaining strawberries. Freeze. Yield: 4 quarts.

Barbecue Sauce

15 c. tomato juice
4 c. chopped onions
¾ c. ReaLemon
⅔ c. sugar
2 bottles Worcestershire sauce
3 c. vinegar
8 c. brown sugar
¾ c. mustard
⅓ c. paprika
⅔ c. liquid smoke
⅔ c. salt
1¾ c. Perma-Flo

Cold pack 10 minutes.

Canning Potatoes

Don't let the newly dug small potatoes go to waste. Scrape them, pack them into a jar, and add 1 tsp. salt and fill with water. Cold pack for three hours. To use, drain off water and fry in butter. To make it easy to wash small potatoes, put them in the wash machine with an old towel and let them wash themselves. P.S. Don't forget to start the wash machine!

Amish Flu—First you get a little buggy, then you get a little hoarse.

Lizbet and Daughters—Country Cooking

Thick and Chunky Salsa

14 lb. tomatoes, scalded, peeled and cut up
5 c. chopped onions
10 green peppers, chopped
1 c. vinegar
½ c. brown sugar
¼ c. salt
1 tsp. garlic powder
2 tsp. oregano flakes
3 tsp. cumin
3 tsp. chili powder
1 pkg. Mrs. Wage's salsa mix
10 Tbsp. clear jel

Mix all the above ingredients except clear jel. Boil 45 minutes. Thicken with clear jel. Stir clear jel in water until smooth before adding to the rest of ingredients. Cold pack 20 minutes. Yield: 16 pints.

Miscellaneous

We look up to our Father
To give us daily bread,
With His provisions for us
Our little ones are fed.
These ample loaves of plenty
Are given from God's hand;
With butter, cheese and honey
In this productive land.
He loves to give unsparing,
Our bread and more besides:
Today, these needs our Father
Abundantly provides.
Let's not allow this plenty
To draw our hearts away,
Forgetting God, who gives us
So liberally today.
As we receive His bounty
May we His bounties share,
And humbly plead His mercy,
Lest we forget His care.

Notes

Mucka Slapper Bubbles

6 c. water
¾ c. Karo

2 c. dishwashing soap

Peanut Butter –for church

4 c. brown sugar
2 c. boiling water
¼ c. light Karo
2 tsp. maple flavoring
2½ lb. peanut butter
1 qt. marshmallow créme

Bring first four ingredients to a boil. Cool, then add peanut butter and marshmallow créme. If this recipe is doubled plus a half it will almost fill an eight quart bowl. A little pancake syrup may be added for a different taste.

White Church Molasses

3½ lb. granulated sugar
2 c. brown sugar
2 qt. light Karo
¼ c. water
5 egg whites, beaten
maple flavoring

Take 2 cups sugar out of bag. Heat first 4 ingredients to a boil and remove from heat. Cool and pour over egg whites. Add maple flavoring. Beat until fluffy.

Homemade Eagle Brand Milk

1 c. instant powdered milk
⅔ c. sugar
½ c. boiling water
3 Tbsp. butter
2 Tbsp. light corn syrup

Put in bowl and mix until smooth. Makes same amount as 1 can Eagle Brand milk.

Honey Butter

1 c. butter, softened
¼ c. honey
1 Tbsp. brown sugar

Mix everything together. Good on muffins and bread.

Lizbet and Daughters—Country Cooking

Cinnamon Butter

1 c. butter
¼ c. powdered sugar

1 Tbsp. honey
2 tsp. cinnamon

Mix all together.

Homemade Noodles

3 doz. egg yolks
½ c. water

1 tsp. salt
all-purpose flour

Beat egg yolks with the salt, then add the water and beat until foamy. Mix in the flour with a fork. Last work in the flour until you can shape into a ball. Let stand for 30 minutes, then knead a bit and make into noodles.

How to Dry Corn

Cook corn for 10 minutes. Cut from cob. To each gallon corn add ¾ c. sweet cream, ½ c. white sugar and some salt to taste. Pour into flat pans and place in 200° oven to dry. Stir often so the corn will dry evenly. Store dried corn in pint jars. When ready to make a meal, add a little water and cook until ready.

Flu Tonic

1 c. Gatorade
1 c. water

1 tsp. sugar
dash of salt

Mix together and drink.

On Mother's Day, after a big dinner, when Mother started cleaning up, one of the girls said to her, "Don't bother with these dishes. Today is Mother's Day. You can always do them tomorrow."

Diet Soup

½ head cabbage
1 onion
4-5 stalks celery
1 green pepper

3 pt. tomato juice
1 pt. water
1 pkg. beef onion soup mix

Chop vegetables and simmer until done. Delicious! The more you eat the more you lose, because it takes more calories to digest the soup than there are in it.

Grape Juice Diet

Eat no solid food in the forenoon, but early in the morning begin slowly sipping 24 oz. of unsweetened Concord grape juice or you can use your own pure grape juice. Have finished drinking juice by 10:00. Wait until noon to eat lunch. Eat no pork at any time. Eat supper as usual. Continue with the grape juice diet for 6 weeks. If your stomach can't tolerate the pure juice of the grape, repeat the juice diet, using smaller amounts of juice diluted with the same amount of water. Gradually increase the amount of juice and soon stomach will be able to take juice at full strength. A very good blood cleanser.

Jogging in a Jug

1 qt. apple juice, unsweetened
1 qt. grape juice, unsweetened

1 c. vinegar

Drink 2 oz. a day to keep your cholesterol in check. Also makes you feel good.

Consideration for others can mean taking a wing instead of a drumstick.

Lizbet and Daughters—Country Cooking

Birthday Gift Idea

On a large piece of cardboard, print this birthday message, using candy bars to complete the message. Mr./Mrs. *Whatchamacallit*, We were going to give you *100 Grand*, but the money slipped through our *Butterfingers* and we couldn't wait until *PayDay*, so we looked on *Fifth Avenue* and found a trip to *Mars* and the *Milky Way*, but neither seemed appropriate. We wish you *Mounds* of *Almond Joy* as you *Crunch* through another year. Sincerely, *Mr. Goodbar*, the *Three Musketeers* and *Baby Ruth*. P.S. We promise not to *Snicker* at your age.

Cookie Mix in a Jar

Ingredients to layer in wide-mouth jar–

¼ c. granulated sugar
⅝ c. oatmeal
¼ tsp. salt
¼ c. brown sugar
⅞ c. flour

1 c. chocolate chips
⅝ c. oatmeal
¼ c. brown sugar
⅓ c. walnuts, M&M's, coconut

Ingredient list to attach to jar–

½ c. butter, softened
1 egg
½ tsp. baking soda

1 Tbsp. milk
1 Tbsp. vanilla

Add mix from jar. Mix well. Drop by teaspoon on cookie sheet. Bake at 375° for 10 minutes.

Drying Parsley

Preheat oven to 350° until hot then turn off. Cut stems off parsley and dry just tops. Put on cookie sheets. Leave in oven several hours or until dry. Stays nice and green.

Gooey Slime

⅛ c. borax laundry detergent
1½ c. hot water

1 c. white Elmer's glue
1 c. hot water

Mix borax with 1½ c. water. Stir until dissolved. Mix glue and 1 c. water. Put ½ c. plus 2 Tbsp. glue mixture in a medium Ziploc bag and add 2 drops food coloring. Add ¼ c. borax mixture. Squish the bag to mix the ingredients well. Soon you'll have slime. Put in small containers overnight. Children have fun playing with it and it's not messy.

Play Dough

2 c. flour
½ c. cornstarch
1 Tbsp. powdered alum

2 c. water
1 c. salt
1 Tbsp. salad oil

Place all ingredients in saucepan. Stir constantly over low heat until mixture thickens. Remove from heat and let cool until it can be handled. Knead like bread dough until smooth. Add food coloring. Store in airtight container. Keeps for a month. This gives children something to do on winter days.

Bird Muffins

1 c. cornmeal
1 c. flour
1 c. bread crumbs
½ tsp. soda

¾ c. raisins
1 Tbsp. finely chopped eggshells
½ c. bacon drippings or lard, melted
1 c. water

Mix in order given. Stir well. Spoon into muffin cups. Bake at 350° for 15 minutes.

Lizbet and Daughters—Country Cooking

Bird Suet

1 c. lard
2 c. quick oats
1 c. flour

1 c. crunchy peanut butter
2 c. cornmeal
⅓ c. sugar

Melt lard and peanut butter. Stir in remaining ingredients. Birds love it.

Pantry Plant Food

1 tsp. baking powder
1 tsp. Epsom salt

1 tsp. saltpeter
½ tsp. ammonia

Mix with 1 gallon lukewarm water. Give this to plants every 4-6 weeks. This works very good to perk up houseplants. I also use when transplanting vegetables and flower plants in spring.

How to Care for Roses

Do your roses bloom nice in the spring then leaves get black spots, turn yellow and fall off? After that, all that is left is stems and roses. Even after spraying for black spots, the leaves that are left are not nice. Try this: In the spring start fertilizing every two weeks with Miracle Gro. Then take a gallon of warm water; add 1 tsp. of dish soap (not antibacterial) and 1 tsp. of Listerine mouthwash. Pour 1 cup boiling water over some dried hot pepper or ground hot pepper, whatever you can get. Last resort—use ½ tsp. Tabasco. Now strain peppers out of liquid and add to your gallon of mixture. Spray on roses before last frost in spring when daytime temperatures are over 50°. Spray again every two weeks. Don't spray around blooms. In Sept. start fertilizing again every two weeks until frost. Enjoy and smell the roses.

If the shoe fits, wear it.

Crumbly Soap

10 c. water
9 c. melted lard
½ c. ammonia
3 Tbsp. borax
1 can lye

Mix in order given in a large granite container. Sprinkle the lye over last. Let stand 5-10 minutes. Stir frequently the first hour, then every hour throughout the day. Let set in container a few days, then put in tight containers.

Soft Soap

1 can lye
7 c. melted lard
1 c. ammonia
2 c. borax
3 c. Wisk

Use 5 gallon bucket or crock and fill half full of soft water. Add lye and melted lard. Add ammonia, borax and Wisk. Mix all together and fill container with water to make 5 gallons. Stir a few times a day for a week. This is great for washing clothes or dishes or getting grease off a mechanic's dirty hands.

Stainless Steel Cleaner

1 can lye
1 c. Tide
1 c. bleach
2 qt. cold water

Put lye in cold water, then fill granite pan or stainless steel canner half full with hot water. Add Tide and bleach. Good to dip silverware, pie pans, Tupperware or Corelle. Makes it shine again and takes off stains. Be sure to lay heavy layer of newspaper over countertop and take all handles and knobs off cookware before dipping. Wash in hot soapy water. A job to be careful with. Wear rubber gloves.

Lizbet and Daughters—Country Cooking

Baby Wipes

You will need a 10 cup Rubbermaid container with lid, 1 big roll of Bounty paper towels, 1¾ c. water, 2 Tbsp. baby oil and 1 Tbsp. baby shampoo. In container put water, baby oil and shampoo and stir. Cut roll of paper towels in half. Place half of roll in container (smooth side down). Let sit one minute. Turn over and let sit a few minutes. Cardboard center should lift out after a few minutes. Pull wipes from center.

Coal Flowers

several pieces of coal	6 Tbsp. bluing
6 Tbsp. water	2 Tbsp. ammonia
6 Tbsp. salt	red, green and blue food coloring

Put pieces of coal in a deep glass bowl or dish. Combine water, salt, bluing and ammonia. Pour around, but not over coal. Dot coal with drops of food coloring. Do not move dish. Coral-like crystals will soon appear on the coal and will grow to a height of ½-1" and will have a sponge-like appearance.

For a Clogged Kitchen Drain

Pour 1 cup baking soda and 1 cup vinegar in drain and let set a couple of seconds. Last pour 1 quart hot water down drain.

Hair Thickener

1 env. unflavored gelatin	1 c. boiling water
¼ c. lemon juice	

Soften gelatin in lemon juice, then quickly add boiling water. Mix well and allow to cool. Comb through clean hair and set or dry as usual. Your hair will have a healthy body and be easy to manage. Pour in jar and can be used over and over by dipping comb in it.

Equivalents

3 tsp.–1 Tbsp.
4 Tbsp.–¼ cup
8 Tbsp.–½ cup
12 Tbsp.–¾ cup
16 Tbsp.–1 cup
2 cups–1 pint
2 pints–1 quart
4 cups–1 quart
4 quarts–1 gallon
8 quarts–1 peck
4 pecks–1 bushel
8 oz.–1 cup
32 oz.–1 quart
1 oz.–2 Tbsp.

1 lb. cheese–4 cups grated
1 pt. cream–4 cups whipped
1 lb. cake flour–5 cups sifted
1 lb. all-purpose flour–4 cups plus 2 tsp. sifted
6 oz. evaporated milk–¾ cup
14 oz. condensed milk–1¼ cups
1 lb. rice–7½ cups cooked
1 lb. brown sugar–3 cups firmly packed
1 lb. granulated sugar–2⅓ cups
1 lb. powdered sugar–3⅓ cups
1 lb. ground coffee–40 cups
1 c. macaroni–2¼ cups cooked
1 pkg. plain gelatin–1 Tbsp. gelatin
1 pkg. active dry yeast–1 Tbsp. yeast
1 lb. butter–2 cups
1 square chocolate–3 Tbsp. cocoa
1 cup buttermilk–1-2 Tbsp. vinegar with sweet milk to fill 1 cup. (Let set for 5 minutes.)

Lizbet and Daughters—Country Cooking

Substitutes for Missing Ingredients

1 Tbsp. cornstarch–2 Tbsp. flour
1 tsp. baking powder–¼ tsp. soda and ½ tsp. cream of tartar
1 Tbsp. clear jel–1 Tbsp. cornstarch
1 c. sifted all-purpose flour–1 cup plus 2 Tbsp. sifted cake flour
1 whole egg–2 egg yolks (in custards)
1 whole egg–2 egg yolks and 1 Tbsp. water (in cookies, etc.)
1 cup sour milk or 1 cup buttermilk–1 Tbsp. lemon juice or vinegar and sweet milk to make one cup. Let sit for 5 minutes.
1 square unsweetened chocolate–3 Tbsp. cocoa plus 1 Tbsp. veg. oil
¼ cup raw onion–1 Tbsp. dried onion
1 cup milk–½ cup evaporated milk plus ½ cup water
1 cup honey–1¼ cups sugar plus 1 cup liquid

Cooking Hints

- A cold Lifetime roaster takes three hours to heat.
- Add a little lemon juice to scrambled eggs and they will not turn dark.
- One pound of boneless chicken or ham will feed three people.
- If the rubber ring inside pressure canner doesn't seal, try rubbing cooking oil over it.
- To beat eggs quickly, add a pinch of salt.
- Before heating milk in a saucepan, rinse the pan with cold water. It will not scorch as easily.
- A pinch of soda added to any boiled syrup will keep it from crystallizing.
- To keep icing soft, add a pinch of soda to egg whites before beating them, then beat the usual way and pour the hot syrup over beaten eggs. Frosting stays soft and creamy.
- When making custard pies, always heat milk to boiling before adding to beaten eggs. This keeps the crust crisp.
- To brown and glaze pies, brush tops with beaten egg white.
- Measure shortening before molasses in baking and it will not stick to cup.
- A cloth saturated with vinegar every day and spread over raw ham will keep it from molding for weeks.
- Whenever I cook cabbage, I put a piece of celery in as well. It mutes the cabbage odor.

Kitchen Hints

- Store cottage cheese upside down in refrigerator. It will keep twice as long.
- To keep strawberries fresh longer, place them in a Tupperware bowl and cover with a paper towel, then put lid on.
- When using fresh farm milk for instant puddings, bring milk to a boil and cool before adding it to the instant pudding mix. If you don't heat it first, the pudding will taste soapy.
- To keep fruit pies from boiling over when baking, always have pie filling cold and wet the edge of bottom crust. Press bottom and top crust together and bake in hot oven.
- To save mess in making bread, cracker or cornflake crumbs, place in a plastic bag and roll with rolling pin.
- When frosting cookies with brown sugar icing the frosting will have a glossy look if cookies are frosted while still warm.
- To clean a scorched saucepan, fill pan halfway with water and add ¼ c. baking soda. Boil awhile until the burned portions loosen and float to the top.
- For sour milk, add 1 Tbsp. vinegar to 1 c. sweet milk. To prevent onions from burning your eyes, hold under water while peeling.
- Instead of baking a whole recipe of cookies at one time, arrange some of them on a cookie sheet and freeze them overnight. The next morning, they can be put in a plastic bag and put in freezer. Anytime you want fresh cookies, put on cookie sheet, let thaw for about 1 hour, then bake.
- To get sparkling clean meat jars: After taking meat out of jars, put 2 tsp. ammonia and ¼ c. water in jar. Swish around a few times while washing dishes, then wash jar. No need to soak until next dishwashing.
- How to keep corn on the cob garden fresh for up to a week: Immediately husk corn and remove silk. Place cobs in zip top plastic bags in between layers of paper towels that have been soaked in cold water. Refrigerate. When ready to cook, remove as many cobs you need.
- Clean up trick works while you sleep! Lay barbecue or oven racks in lawn overnight, and the dew will combine the enzymes in the grass to loosen burned on grease.

Lizbet and Daughters — Country Cooking

Household Hints

- Onion odor may be removed from hands by rubbing them with dry salt.
- Dip a cloth in diluted peroxide and rub scorched spot. The stain will disappear when ironed.
- A black spot on your covering left by a fly can be removed with a Q-tip dipped in bleach or peroxide.
- Hair spray removes ink from clothes.
- Add vinegar to your water when cold packing meat to keep jars free from grease.
- Rub vinegar or rubbing alcohol on hands just before hanging out laundry in cold weather. Dry hands thoroughly before going out. Hands will not get as cold.
- Cut flowers will last longer in a vase if ¼ tsp. or 20 drops of bleach is added to each quart of water.
- To clean gardener's hands, rub them clean with vinegar. Let dry and apply hand lotion.

Garden Hints

- Lay black plastic for peppers, pickles, melons and sweet potatoes. Results: No weeds and double yields.
- Rabbits will not eat lettuce, beets, etc. if dusted with talcum powder.
- Prune tomato plants by cutting off the long, wild shooting vines. You will have nicer and larger tomatoes.
- Put wood ashes on the ground where you planted radishes to keep away worms.
- Wood ashes and lime is also good for dusting cabbage.
- Plant marigolds by the squash plants to keep bugs away.
- To get rid of flies at windows, like attics and upstairs, set a small tin of kerosene on windowsill. Watch them tumble in!
- Raspberry plant food: Mix 1 gal. wood ashes, 1 gal. lime and a handful of sulfur. Put a handful to each plant once a month in February, March and April and again when they have small berries. Add again once in the fall.
- In the fall, throw a handful blood meal and bonemeal over strawberry plants.
- Handmade bug killer can be made in a plastic milk jug by mixing 1 c. sugar, 1 c. vinegar and a banana peel. Hang open jug under grape vines or place in garden. Really works!

Index

Prayer by Our Kitchen Sink

Thank God for dirty dishes,

They have a tale to tell.

While others are going hungry,

We are eating well.

With home and health and happiness

We shouldn't want to fuss,

For by this stack of evidence,

God is very good to us.

. . . . .

Hunger is die beste koch.

Es geht besser fa kocha

For abber mit un guter appedit!

Hunger is the best cook.

It goes better to cook

For someone with a good appetite!

Index

Appetizers, Beverages and Dips

Appetizer Roll-Ups	11
Apple Punch	3
Bacon Dip	9
Cappuccino	6
Caramel Dip for Apples	12
Cheese Ball	13
Cheese Ball	13
Cheesy Chicken Dip	8
Cheesy Dip	9
Cheesy Hamburger Chip Dip	8
Cheez Whiz	12
Chocolate Chip Cheese Ball	13
Chocolate Syrup	6
Community Dip	10
Cream Cheese and Salsa Dip	7
Cream Cheese Salsa Dip	7
Dill Vegetable Dip	10
Eagle Brand Finger Jell-O	15
Eggnog	5
Finger Jell-O	14
Finger Jell-O	15
Fresh Salsa	7
Fruit Dip	11
Fruit Dip	12
Fruit Dip	12
Fudgesicles	14
Golden Punch	4
Hot Chocolate Mix	6
Ice Slush	3
Kraft Cheese	7
Layered Taco Delight	9
Maple Hot Chocolate	6
Orange Slush Drink	3
Patty Shells	15
Pineapple Cheese Ball	13
Pinwheel Finger Jell-O	14
Popsicles	14
Purple Cow	4

Lizbet and Daughters — Country Cooking

Quick and Easy Tortilla Roll-Ups 10
Quick Root Beer 5
Rhubarb Punch 5
Sausage Dip 8
Sherbet Punch 3
Slushy Drink 4
Tea Concentrate 5
Tortilla Pinwheels 11
Warm Taco Dip 8
Wedding Punch 4

Breads, Rolls, Muffins and Cereals

Apple Fritters 34
Biscuits Supreme 29
Blueberry Sour Cream Streusel Muffins 32
Bread 20
Bread 20
Bread 20
Bread Sticks 21
Butterhorns 27
Cappuccino Muffins with Espresso Spread 33
Cheddar Garlic Biscuits 28
Cheesy Onion Burger Buns 22
Chocolate Chip Granola Cereal 35
Cinnamon Apple Muffins 33
Cinnamon Rolls 26
Cinnamon Rolls in a Snap 23
Corn Bread or Muffins 31
Doughnuts from Mix 29
Doughnuts from Scratch 25
Easy Cake Mix Rolls 25
Family Reunion Buns 22
Garlic Toast 29
Grandma Miller's Cinnamon Rolls 23
Grapenuts 34
Honey Bread 19
Lollipops 34
Mini Garlic Bread 30
Pluckets 27
Pumpkin Bread 30
Pumpkin Cream Cheese Muffins 31
Recipe for Life 19
Refrigerated Crescent Rolls 26
Refrigerator Rolls 24
Soft Pretzels 30
Sour Cream Rolls 24
Southern Biscuits 28
Sweet Potato Butterhorns 28
Sweet Rolls 25
Tips for Breadmaking 19

Zucchini Muffins	32
Zucchini Pizza Bread	21

Breakfast

Bacon Roll-Ups	41
Baked Oatmeal	42
Barbecue Smokies	48
Blueberry French Toast	44
Breakfast Pizza	42
Breakfast Pizza	42
Breakfast Pockets	39
Campfire Breakfast	41
Caramel Breakfast Ring	46
Caramelized French Toast	44
Cheese Flitzes	46
Cranberry Meatballs and Sausage	40
Easy Caramel Rolls	47
Egg in a Hole	48
Favorite Pancakes	45
French Toast	43
Frozen Fruit Slush	48
Ham and Cheese Oven Omelet	39
Mice	47
Nutty Baked French Toast	43
Pancake Syrup	45
Quick Rolls	47
Sausage Gravy	41
Smokies in a Blanket	40
Sunrise Burritos	40
Waffles	45

Soups, Salads and Salad Dressings

7-Layer Salad	63
Amish Bean Soup	57
Apple Salad Dressing	74
Applesauce Salad	70
Apricot Salad	73
Baked Potato Soup	51
Bean with Bacon Soup	53
Broccoli Cheese Soup with Noodles	55
Broccoli Salad	62
Broccoli Salad	62
Broccoli Soup	59
Cheeseburger Soup	57
Cheesy Bacon Potato Soup	56
Cheesy Ham Chowder	56
Chicken Chowder	51
Chicken Noodle Soup	54
Chili Corn Bread Salad	59
Chili Soup	52
Chili Soup	53
Chunky Vegetable Soup	54
Coated Grapes	75

Lizbet and Daughters—Country Cooking

Coffee Soup	56
Coleslaw	64
Coleslaw Dressing	64
Cooked Salad Dressing	66
Cool Whip – Cottage Cheese Salad	71
Cottage Cheese Salad	74
Cranberry Salad	68
Creamy Grape Salad	68
Cucumber Salad	64
Geauga Soup	58
Grape Cottage Cheese Salad	71
Jell-O Pudding	69
Just-Like-Campbell's Tomato Soup	52
Like Hartville Sweet and Sour	65
Lime Cottage Cheese Salad	66
Lime Crust Salad	67
Lime Salad	73
Loaded Baked Potato Salad	61
Orange Ring Salad	69
Pasta Salad	60
Pineapple Salad	72
Potato Salad	62
Quick and Delicious Jell-O Dessert	67
Rainbow Jell-O Salad	70
Ramen Noodle Salad	60
Ranch Dressing	65
Ribbon Salad	73
Rivel Soup	58
Russian Dressing	66
Slim Soup Mix	51
Sparkling Summer Salad	67
Split Pea Soup	57
Spring Salad	72
Strawberry Jell-O Salad	71
Summer Surprise	74
Sweet and Sour Dressing	64
Sweet and Sour Dressing	65
Taco Salad	61
Taco Seasoning Mix	63
Taco Soup	58
Tasty Tomatoes	66
Thousand Island Dressing	65
Topping for Jell-O Salads	74
Vegetable Pizza	63
Vegetable Soup	55

Meats and Main Dishes

Baked Ham and Swiss Sandwiches	118
Barbecue Chuck Roast	113
Barbecued Beef Sandwiches	119
Barbecue on a Budget	113

Index

Barbecue Sauce 81
Barbecue Sauce 116
Basic White Sauce 79
Batter for Deep Frying 81
Beef and Potato Loaf 95
Beef or Deer Jerky 115
Beef Stew 104
Big Mac Sauce 117
Bubble Up Pizza 107
Cheddar Parmesan Potatoes 93
Cheesy Chicken and Rice
  Casserole 85
Chicken and Dumplings 84
Chicken and Rice Casserole 85
Chicken Barbecue Sauce 116
Chicken Breading 80
Chicken Casserole 85
Chicken Enchiladas 87
Chicken Flour 79
Chicken Gumbo 83
Chicken Nuggets 88
Chicken or Ham Roll 87
Chicken Rice Casserole 86
Chicken Salad Sandwiches 119
Cornmeal Mush 120
Cornmeal Mush 121
Corny Dogs 117
Country Chicken and Biscuits 84
Creamed Eggs and Toast 122
Crunchy Baked Chicken 82
Dandelion Gravy 80
Deep Fried Fish 81
Delicious Baked Beans 98
Easy Chicken Potpie 84
Egg Dutch 122
El Paso Casserole 100
Enchiladas 104
Escalloped Cabbage 97
Favorite Barbecued Burgers .. 118
Frankfurter Bake 106
German Pizza 96
Green Beans 96
Green Bean Supreme 97
Grilled Thighs and Drumsticks 82
Ground Beef Grand Style 106
Ham and Noodles 101
Ham Loaf 115
Haystack 102
Hearty Twice Baked Potatoes ..93
Juicy Roast 114
Kabobs 121
Lasagna 109
Make-Ahead Potatoes 92
Marinade for Chicken 81
Mashed Potato Casserole 89
Meatballs 110

Lizbet and Daughters—Country Cooking

Meatball Stew 105	Salisbury Steak 112
Meatloaf 111	Saucy Meatballs 111
Mexican Chicken Roll-Ups 86	Shipwreck 100
Mexican Lasagna 109	Sloppy Joes 120
Mock Turkey 104	Smoky Ribs 114
Mushroom Pizza 107	Southern Chicken Pie 83
No-Fuss Lasagna 110	Spam Burgers 120
Norwegian Parsley Potatoes 90	Spanish Rice 103
Onion Patties 99	Squash Patties 100
Parmesan Potatoes 93	Steak Marinade 115
Penny Saver Casserole 95	String Bean Patties 97
Pickled Tongue and Heart 117	Stromboli 108
Pineapple Sauce for Ham 116	Stuffed Green Peppers 98
Pizza 107	Taco Bake 103
Pizza Burgers 119	Taco Shells 108
Pizza Cups 108	Taco Skillet Meal 102
Poor Man's Steak 112	Tasty California Blend
Porcupine Meatballs 106	Vegetables 96
Pork Chop Supreme 114	Tasty Potato Casserole 91
Potato Pancakes 95	Tater Tot Casserole 105
Potato Roll Meatloaf 94	Tomato Gravy 80
Potato Stack Casserole 90	Turkey or Chicken Supreme 87
Potato Stacks 94	Underground Ham Casserole . 88
Potluck Potatoes 89	Vegetable and Rice Dish 86
Quiche 121	Venison Roast 113
Quick Baked Beans 98	Wigglers 101
Quick Scalloped Potatoes 92	Yummasetti 101
Ranch Potato Casserole 91	Yummy Summer Sausage 112

Zucchini Casserole 99
Zucchini Patties 99

Cookies and Bars

1-2-3- Coffee Bars 149
Betty Crocker Bars 152
Brownie Cheesecake Bars 148
Buttermilk Cookies 137
Butterscotch Cookies 134
Butterscotch Cookies 135
Butterscotch Crunch Sandwich
   Cookies 134
Butterscotch Delights 135
Butter Sugar Cookies 136
Can't Leave Alone Bars 157
Candy Bar Cookies 160
Chocolate Chip Oatmeal
   Cookies 128
Chocolate Chip Pudding
   Cookies 128
Chocolate Crinkles 130
Chocolate Marshmallow Bars 151
Chocolate Twinkies 160
Cocoa Sandwich Cookies 131
Coffee Bars 151
Cream Cheese Brownies 149
Cream Wafer Cookies 139

Dad's Chocolate Chip
   Cookies 127
Date or Raisin Filled Cookies 141
Date Pinwheel Cookies 140
Delicious Molasses Cookies .. 133
Disappearing Molasses
   Cookies 133
Double Chocolate Bars 152
Double Chocolate Jumbo
   Crisps 130
Double Deck Brownies 155
Double Treat Cookies 126
Dutch Sugar Cookies 137
Easy Filled Drop Cookies 141
Fruit Bars 145
Fruit Swirl Bars 152
Fudge Brownies 154
Fudge Nut Bars 159
Granola Bars 145
Honey Cookies 143
Hot Water Cookies 136
Just Right Chocolate Chip
   Cookies 129
Lemon Bars 149
Maple Leaf Cookies 138
Molasses Cookies 132
Monster Cookie Bars 144
Monster Cookies 127

Lizbet and Daughters—Country Cooking

Monster Cookies 127
Mud Hen Bars 158
No Bake Cookies 162
One Bowl Brownies 155
Orange Cookies 143
Oreo Cookies 131
Peanut Blossom Cookies 126
Peanut Butter Cookies 125
Peanut Butter Dream Bars 144
Peanut Butter Honey Cookies 126
Peanut Butter Temptations.... 125
Pecan Pie Bars 156
Pecan Tarts 140
Pumpkin Bars 148
Pumpkin Cookies 139
Raisin Bars 154
Reese's Pieces Bars 153
Rhubarb Custard Bars............. 159
Rhubarb Dream Bars 157
Russian Tea Balls 162
Sandwich Molasses Cookies . 133
Seven Layer Bars......................157
Sinfully Delicious Brownies .. 156
Snickerdoodles.........................137
Soft Batch Sandwich Cookies 129
Soft Chocolate Chip Cookies 128
Sour Cream Raisin Bars.......... 146
Spellbinders 138
Sunny Graham Chewies 153
The Best Cookies Ever............ 130
Thumbprint Cookies 142
Toffee Topped Bars 146
Toll House Marble Squares.... 158
Trail Mix Bars..........................161
Tri-Level Brownies 150
Trilbies...................................... 142
Triple Layer Cookie Bars 147
Triple Treat Cookies 125
Twinkies....................................161
Vanilla Cream Wafers.............. 139
Whole Wheat Chip and Coffee
 Bars 150
Whoopie Pies........................... 132
Zucchini Brownies 147

Cakes and Frostings

Alaska Sheet Cake.................... 178
Amish Cake 174
Angel Food Cake...................... 180
Banana Cake.............................181
Blueberry Coffee Cake............. 169
Brown Sugar Frosting 190
Bunny Cake 165
Butter Cream Frosting.............191
Butter Pecan Dessert Cake 186
Butterscotch Cake.................... 175

Index

Caramel Frosting 190
Carrot Cake 172
Cherry Crumb Cake 171
Chocolate Cake 179
Chocolate Frosting 193
Chocolate Jelly Roll 188
Chocolate Mocha Torte 184
Christmas Fruitcake 185
Cocoa Crumb Cake 172
Coconut Pecan Frosting 192
Coffee Cake 167
Cookies and Cream Cake 187
Cream Cheese Frosting 192
Cream Filled Coffee Cake 166
Diabetic Cake 166
Dutch Apple Cake 176
Earthquake Cake 184
Finnish Coffee Cake 168
Flowerpot Cupcakes 165
Fluffy Frosting 191
Fluffy Lemon Cake 185
Frosting for Coffee Cakes 192
Gingerbread 170
Graham Streusel Cake 180
Granny Cake 173
Heath Bar Cake 173
"Herman" Cake 194
"Herman" Cinnamon Rolls 194

"Herman" Cookies 195
Ho-Ho Cake 183
Honey Chocolate Cake 174
Jell-O Cake 182
Jelly Roll 188
Jelly Roll 189
Lazy Cake 171
Lemon Streusel Cake 175
Magic Cupcakes 165
Maple Nut Twist Coffee Cake 169
Marshmallow Frosting 189
Mayonnaise Cake 178
Oatmeal Cake Supreme 176
Our Favorite Frosting 190
Pineapple Sheet Cake 183
Pistachio Cake 186
Pumpkin Pecan Cake 177
Pumpkin Pudding Cake 177
Pumpkin Roll 187
Quick Banana Cake 182
Quick Chocolate Frosting 189
Raspberry Cream Coffee
    Cake 168
Smooth and Creamy Frosting 191
Sour Cream Caramel Frosting 193
Spice Cake 177
Starter "Herman" 193
Strawberry Shortcake 170

Lizbet and Daughters—Country Cooking

Texas Sheet Cake 181
Turtle Cake 185
Walnut Wonder Coffee Cake . 167
Whoopie Pie Filling 192
Yellow Sponge Cake 179
Zucchini Cake 182

Desserts

Angel Delight 207
Angel Food Cake Dessert 224
Apple Crisp 203
Apple Dumplings 202
Apple Pudding 203
Baked Chocolate Fudge
    Pudding 208
Butterfinger Pudding 224
Butterscotch Tapioca 219
Butterscotch Topping 230
Butterscotch Topping 230
Cake Dessert 210
Caramel Apple Slices 204
Caramel Tapioca 220
Cheesecake Dessert 222
Cherry Berry on a Cloud 205
Cherry Chiffon Dessert 208
Cherry Delight 207
Chocolate Angel Dessert 207
Chocolate Eclairs 212

Chocolate Peanut Log 227
Cinnamon Pudding 212
Cornstarch Pudding 205
Creamy Tapioca 220
Crepes 221
Custard 210
Date Pudding 206
Date Pudding 206
Date Pudding Sauce 206
Delicious Custard 220
Delicious Pudding 204
Eclair Pudding 200
Fluff Pudding 218
Frosty Strawberry Dessert 226
Frozen Cheesecake 225
Frozen Oreo Cookie Dessert 226
Fruit Pizza 215
Fruit Pizza 216
Fruit Pizza Crust 216
Grandma's Graham Cracker
    Pudding 213
Homemade Applesauce 203
Homemade Ice Cream 227
Hot Chocolate Fudge 229
Hot Chocolate Sauce 230
Hot Fudge Brownie Sundae .. 222
Hot Fudge Cake 222
Hot Fudge Sauce 229

Hot Fudge Sauce	229	Rhubarb Torte	217
Ice Cream	228	Russian Creme	219
Ice Cream	228	Simple Fruit Pizza Crust	216
Ice Cream Dessert	227	Soft Custard Ice Cream	228
Ice Cream Pudding	225	Strawberry Cheesecake Trifle	223
Ice Cream Sandwich Pudding	225	Tapioca	221
Ice Cream Topping	229	Triple Orange Dessert	199
Lemon Cheesecake	223	Tropical Fruit Dessert	217
Lemon Fluff	199	Yogurt	221
Lowfat Cheesecake	214		
Maple Sponge Pudding	201	## Pies	
Mini Cheesecakes	214	Any Fruit Flavor Chiffon Pie	239
Minute Tapioca Pudding	218	Basic Cream Pie	235
Oreo Pudding	199	Better Bought Pie Filling	258
Overnight Salad	209	Blueberry Sour Cream Pie	255
Peaches -n- Cream Cheesecake	209	Blushing Rhubarb Pie	252
		Bob Andy Pie	237
Peanut Delight Dessert	215	Butterscotch Pie	247
Pineapple Rings	211	Caramel Pie	241
Pine Scotch Pudding	200	Caramel Raisin Pie	257
Pumpkin Festival Dessert	201	Chocolate Cream Cheese Pie	235
Pumpkin Pecan Smash Dessert – diabetic	213	Chocolate Fudge Pie	235
		Chocolate Mocha Pie	241
Pumpkin Torte	202	Coconut Cream Pie	240
Quick Butterscotch Apples	204	Coconut Oatmeal Custard Pie	251
Raspberry Cream Torte	211	Coconut Oatmeal Pie	258
Red Hot Cinnamon Apples	210	Colorado Peach Cream Pie	240
Rhubarb Crunch	218	Cream Cheese Pecan Pie	245

Lizbet and Daughters—Country Cooking

Creamy Vanilla Crumb Pie ... 243	Peach Custard Pie 240
Custard Pie 237	Peanut Butter Cup Pie 242
Custard Pie 238	Peanut Butter Pie 242
Dear Abby's Pecan Pie 246	Peanut Butter Pie 243
Delicious Crumb Pie 244	Pecan Pie 246
Double Layer Pumpkin Pie ... 256	Pecan Praline Pie 245
Dutch Apple Pie 250	Pecan Praline Pie 246
Dutch Apple Pie 250	Pie Crust 233
Dutch Chocolate Pie 236	Pie Crust Mix 233
Eggnog Pie 238	Pie Crust Mix 233
Filling for Fruit Pies 255	Pineapple Pie 244
French Rhubarb Pie 252	Pumpkin Pie 236
French Rhubarb Pie 252	Pumpkin Pie 236
Fresh Fruit Pie Filling 254	Raisin Cream Pie 249
Fry Pies 253	Raisin Cream Pie 249
Fudge Sundae Pie 234	Raisin Crumb Pie 248
Graham Cracker Pie Crust 234	Rhubarb Meringue Pie 251
Grandma's Custard Pie 237	Rice Krispie Pie 234
Ground Cherry Pie 239	Shoestring Apple Pie 249
Half Moon Pies 257	Snitz Pie Filling 258
Lemon Pie 244	Sour Cream Cherry Pie 239
Marshmallow Pie 256	Strawberry Danish Dessert Filling 254
Meringues 254	Streusel Topping for Apple Pie 254
Oatmeal Pie Crust 233	Sweet and Sour Cherry Pies ... 257
Oats 'n Honey Granola Pie 248	Topping for Pineapple Pie 255
Old-Fashioned Butterscotch Pie 247	White Christmas Pie 253
Oreo Pie 248	

Candies and Snacks

Baked Peanut Butter Popcorn 263
Buckeye Bars 268
Cane Molasses Cracker Jack .. 269
Caramel Candy Apples 268
Caramel Corn 264
Caramel Cups 266
Caramel Pretzels 262
Caramel Rice Krispie Treats .. 264
Caramels 272
Cashew Brittle 265
Cheerio Bars 265
Children's Treat 266
Chocolate Caramel Candy 270
Chocolate Drops 271
Chocolate Fudge 273
Creamy Mints 274
Easy Turtles 270
English Toffee 267
Farmers' Hats 273
Fut Nudge 261
Glazed Pecans 274
Honey Party Mix 261
Hopscotch Candy 269
Indoor S'mores 272
Macaroons 265
Molasses Taffy 273
Mounds Bars 272
Munchies 263
Oh Henry Bars 271
Oh Henry Bars 271
Party Mix 263
Peanut Butter Reese's Cups 261
Peanut Clusters 267
Puppy Chow 274
Ranch Party Mix 262
Ranch Snack Crackers 264
Rice Krispie Bars 266
Rice Krispy Roll-Ups 269
Ritzy Delights 268
Scotcharoos 267
Snowy Fudge 265
Twix Bars 266
Yummy Chex Snacks 262

Large Quantity Recipes

Barbecue Ham Sandwiches ... 283
Breakfast Haystack –for 90 people 279
Cheese Sauce –for 8 qt. kettle 284
Chicken Barbecue –for 50 people 281
Communion Church Recipe .. 281
Cooking for Company 280
Corn Made in Oven 283
Dinner –for 34 people 280

Lizbet and Daughters—Country Cooking

Dinner –for 50 people............ 279
Dinner –for 70 people............ 282
Dressing...................................... 277
Enough for 100 People........... 279
Fry Pies –400............................ 285
Gravy.. 278
Ham and Cheese Sandwiches 279
Ham and Potato Soup 278
Haystack –for 125 people 282
Meal –for 100 people 282
Noodles –Large Batch............ 278
Potluck Potatoes 277
Sausage Gravy 284
Scalloped Potatoes –for 25-30
   people...................................... 284
Serves 100 People 280
Underground Ham.................. 281
Wieners for Church................. 283

Canning and Freezing

Apple Pie Filling...................... 301
Apple Pie Filling...................... 301
Apple Pie Filling...................... 301
Banana Pepper Relish 293
Barbecue Sauce 305
Bean Pickle 292
Best Ever Sweet Pickles........... 290
Best Sweet Pickles.................... 290
Bread and Butter Pickles......... 291
Bread and Butter Pickles......... 291
Brine for Turkey....................... 304
Brine to Keep Bologna............ 303
Canned Meatloaf 295
Canned Peppers....................... 293
Canned Sweet Corn 294
Canning Potatoes..................... 305
Chunk Meat.............................. 295
Cold Pack Sausage 294
Corncob Syrup......................... 302
Dark Sweet Cherries 299
Freezing Peaches...................... 300
Frozen Strawberries 305
Grape Juice 304
Grape Sunshine........................ 302
Grape Wine 304
Green Tomato Raspberry
   Jelly 303
Ham.. 295
Heinz Ketchup 298
Homemade Bologna 296
Hot Pepper Jelly 302
Hot Pepper Jelly 303
Mixed Pickle............................. 293
Mom Miller's Sandwich
   Spread..................................... 294
Peaches and Glaze 299

Peach Pie Filling 300	Cooking Hints....................... 318
Peach Slush 300	Crumbly Soap 315
Pickles for Church 289	Diet Soup 311
Pizza Sauce 296	Drying Parsley 312
Pizza Sauce 297	Equivalents 317
Pork and Beans 298	Flu Tonic 310
Pork and Beans 298	For a Clogged Kitchen Drain 316
Pressure Canning 289	Garden Hints......................... 320
Red Beet Jelly 302	Gooey Slime 313
Red Beets 292	Grape Juice Diet....................311
Refrigerator Pickles 292	Hair Thickener 316
Sandwich Spread 299	Homemade Eagle Brand Milk 309
Spaghetti Sauce 297	Homemade Noodles 310
Steak 295	Honey Butter......................... 309
Sweet Dill Pickles 291	Household Hints.................... 320
Thick and Chunky Salsa......... 306	How to Care for Roses 314
Time Tables to Can................ 289	How to Dry Corn 310
Very Good Apple Butter 303	Jogging in a Jug 311
	Kitchen Hints 319

Miscellaneous

Baby Wipes............................ 316	Mucka Slapper Bubbles.......... 308
Bird Muffins 313	Pantry Plant Food.................. 314
Bird Suet 314	Peanut Butter –for church 309
Birthday Gift Idea.................. 312	Play Dough 313
Cinnamon Butter................... 310	Soft Soap 315
Coal Flowers.......................... 316	Stainless Steel Cleaner............ 315
Cookie Mix in a Jar 312	Substitutes for Missing Ingredients........................... 318
	White Church Molasses......... 309

337

Favorites